CSS3
FOR
DUMMIES
A Wiley Brand

by John Paul Mueller

FOR
DUMMIES
A Wiley Brand

CSS3 For Dummies®

Published by: **John Wiley & Sons, Inc.,** 111 River Street, Hoboken, NJ 07030-5774, www.wiley.com

Copyright © 2014 by John Wiley & Sons, Inc., Hoboken, New Jersey

Published simultaneously in Canada

For general information on our other products and services, please contact our Customer Care Department within the U.S. at 877-762-2974, outside the U.S. at 317-572-3993, or fax 317-572-4002. For technical support, please visit www.wiley.com/techsupport.

Wiley publishes in a variety of print and electronic formats and by print-on-demand. Some material included with standard print versions of this book may not be included in e-books or in print-on-demand. If this book refers to media such as a CD or DVD that is not included in the version you purchased, you may download this material at http://booksupport.wiley.com. For more information about Wiley products, visit www.wiley.com.

Library of Congress Control Number: 2013948027

ISBN 978-1-118-44142-8 (pbk); ISBN 978-1-118-46210-2 (ebk); ISBN 978-1-118-61240-8 (ebk); ISBN 978-1-118-61261-3 (ebk)

Manufactured in the United States of America

10 9 8 7 6 5 4 3 2 1

Contents at a Glance

Table of Contents

Introduction

Cascading Style Sheets (CSS) help you define a website's presentation and special effects. Because of this capability, most books about CSS on the market are written for designers. They get into the artistic elements of CSS and make you create everything from scratch. *CSS3 for Dummies* is different. It was written with the developer in mind. It may not seem as if a developer necessarily would need to know about presentation and design-related issues, but users want applications that are pleasant to use, so developers need to know about both topics. This book assumes that you're a developer, and that you're busy — that you really need to get a great-looking application out yesterday because the boss is breathing down your neck. You don't need to be an artist to produce spectacular sites — you just need a helping hand. Most of the artwork's already done for you — you just need to know where to find it.

About This Book

Your time is valuable. This book helps you understand quickly how to use tools to create great-looking applications that provide all the right user prompts in a fraction of the time it would take you to write the application from scratch. In fact, once you know the secrets in this book, you may wonder why other people think working with CSS3 is hard. By the time you complete this book, you'll be able to dazzle the user and make your boss think you spent days working on the page that only took a few hours to write this morning. Even though complete applications will take longer, you can create usable mockups of what your application will look like in an incredibly short time.

However, this book isn't all about tools. When necessary, you see how things work at a much lower level so that you can maintain the code you create with the same ease that you experienced when putting it together. Instead of covering absolutely every nuance of CSS3 development, though, *CSS3 For Dummies* concentrates on the CSS3 features you use most often and examines them in a real-world functional environment.

No, this book won't turn you into a designer, but that's the point. You'll become a developer who can compete with the best designers out there, on your own terms, by using tools that designers generally don't rely upon. The difference is that your sites won't be unique one-offs — they'll rely on the huge base of predefined templates and tools that already exist for everyone to use. Even so, everyone will think your offerings are unique because of the way you can use these various tools together to create results that look unique.

The chapters were written for everyday developers, but note that a portion of most chapters contains advanced material, mostly in sidebars, that will interest only some readers. When you see one of these specialized topics, feel free to skip it.

You can also skip any material marked with a Technical Stuff icon. This material is helpful, but you don't have to know it to work with CSS3, HTML, or JavaScript. I include this material because I find it helpful in my programming efforts and believe that you will, too.

This book uses special typefaces to emphasize some information. For example, entries that you need to type appear in **bold**. All code, website URLs, and onscreen messages appear in `monofont type`. When I define a new word, you see that word in *italics*.

Because you use multiple applications when you're working with CSS3, I always point out when to move from one application to the next. Note, however, that the testers for this book tried out the code with the Internet Explorer, Firefox, and Chrome browsers on the Macintosh, Linux, and Windows platforms. One tester also checked at least some of the code using a Windows 8 phone. In most cases, you shouldn't experience any problem working with your application unless specifically noted in the application description. Please let me know (at `John@JohnMuellerBooks.com`) if you ever experience a problem with one of the examples.

Foolish Assumptions

You might find it difficult to believe that I've assumed anything about you — after all, I haven't even met you yet! Although most assumptions are indeed foolish, I made these assumptions to provide a starting point for the book.

It's important that you're familiar with the platform and browser you want to use because the book doesn't provide any handholding in this regard. To focus on CSS3 (and HTML5 and JavaScript when needed) as fully as possible, the book covers browsers marginally and platform requirements not at all. You really do need to know how to install applications, use the browser, and generally work with your chosen platform before you begin working with this book.

Knowing a little about both HTML5 and JavaScript is helpful but not essential. Any experience you have with programming will be helpful as well. The book doesn't assume you have any knowledge of CSS3.

Icons Used in This Book

As you read this book, you'll see icons in the margins that indicate material of interest (or not, as the case may be).This section briefly describes each icon in this book.

Tips are nice because they help you save time or perform some task without a lot of extra work. The tips in this book are timesaving techniques or pointers to resources that you should try to get the maximum benefit from CSS3 (or HTML5 or JavaScript in some cases).

I don't want to sound like an angry parent or some kind of maniac, but you should avoid doing anything marked with a Warning icon. Otherwise you could find that your program only serves to confuse users who will then refuse to work with it.

Whenever you see this icon, think *advanced* tip or technique. You might find these tidbits of useful information just too boring for words, or they could contain the solution you need to get a program running. Skip these bits of information whenever you like.

If you don't get anything else out of a particular chapter or section, remember the material marked by this icon. This text usually contains an essential process or a bit of information that you must know to write CSS3 programs successfully.

Beyond the Book

A lot of extra content that you won't find in this book is available at www. dummies.com. Go online to find the following:

✔ **Source code for the examples in this book at**

```
www.dummies.com/extras/css3
```

This book contains a lot of code, and you might not want to type it. In fact, it's probably better if you don't type this code manually. Fortunately, you can find the source code for this book on the Dummies. com website at www.dummies.com/extras/css3. The source code is organized by chapter, and I always tell you about the example files in the text. The best way to work with a chapter is to download all the source code for it at one time.

  ✔ **Online articles covering additional topics at**

    www.dummies.com/extras/css3

  Here you'll find out how to access multiple Google API libraries and use them in a single app, how to use Komodo Edit to create CSS files, and how to create table-like effects using CSS3 and HTML5 tags, among other details to aid you in your CSS3 journey.

  ✔ **The Cheat Sheet for this book is at**

    www.dummies.com/cheatsheet/css3

  Here you'll find a roadmap to common CSS3 properties and selectors.

  ✔ **Updates to this book, if we have any, are also available at**

    www.dummies.com/extras/css3

Where to Go from Here

It's time to start your CSS3 adventure! If you're a complete CSS3 novice, start with Chapter 1 and progress through the book at a pace that allows you to absorb as much of the material as possible. If you're in an absolute rush to get going with CSS3 as quickly as possible, you could possibly skip to Chapter 2 with the understanding that you may find some topics a bit confusing later.

Advanced readers, those who already have a basic understanding of CSS3, can save time by moving directly to Chapter 6. You can always go back to earlier chapters as necessary when you have questions. However, it's important that you understand how each example works before moving to the next one. Every example has important lessons for you, and you could miss vital content if you start skipping too much information.

Part I
Getting Started with CSS3

getting started
with
CSS3

In this part . . .

- ✔ Discover why CSS3 is such an important technology
- ✔ Create simple pages that rely on CSS for formatting
- ✔ Use fonts and colors to add pizzazz to your site
- ✔ Add graphics to make your site more appealing and to convey nonverbal information
- ✔ Understand the shortcuts you can use to make working with CSS3 easier

Chapter 1

Understanding CSS3

There was a time when even websites painstakingly formatted with arcane tags still ended up boring or unattractive because the tags simply didn't provide much flexibility in presenting content. In addition, the tags were supported in different ways by each of the browsers that were popular at the time, so that your beautifully rendered page ended up looking terrible on another user's system. The improper use of tags (such as those used to define tables) also caused problems for people with special needs when their software failed to work with the tags. In short, developers needed something better than tags to create nicely formatted presentations — that something better is Cascading Style Sheets (CSS).

The stated purpose of *CSS* is to provide a human-readable method of separating the content on a page from the presentation of that content. Separating content from presentation allows users to substitute style sheets that present information in a manner that works better for them (such as the substitution of larger fonts or specific color combinations for sight-impaired users). Separating presentation from content also means that you can define a presentation once and use it on a variety of pages and formats. When you decide you need to change a presentation, all you need to do is change the CSS, rather than edit the specific tags on every page of your site.

However, CSS has gone well beyond simple presentation on HTML pages. CSS also works with a wide variety of other content types such as XML. In addition, CSS makes it possible to create special effects on your page, so that you get the appearance of programming without actually writing any code to do it. The term *special effect* covers a lot of ground. It includes everything from mouseover effects (a change that occurs when you hover the mouse over a page element) to the use of transparency to fool the eye into seeing both foreground and background elements in specific ways. You can also use special effects to perform tasks such as giving a page a three-dimensional (3D) look.

Even through CSS is standardized through various organizations such as the Internet Engineering Task Force (IETF) as Request for Comment (RFC) 2318 (see `www.faqs.org/rfcs/rfc2318.html`) and the World Wide Web Consortium (W3C) as specific version-level specifications (see `www.w3.org/TR/CSS21/` for the version 2.1 specification), there are differences in the way browsers work with CSS. For the most part, you'll find that every browser supports the basic CSS formatting functionality without any problem. It's when you get into the special effects that you may notice some differences, so this chapter has a special section that discusses some of the differences you need to consider. The differences between browsers is one reason that this book focuses on third-party tools that address these differences for you so that you can focus on creating great-looking pages.

The chapter ends with some simple examples of working with CSS to create some simple effects. You'll also discover how various units of measure affect the manner of presentation on a page.

Defining the CSS3 standard

The CSS3 standard is a combination of a number of existing and new W3C standards. The base standard is the CSS2.1 standard found at `www.w3.org/TR/CSS21/`. Added to this standard are the following standards:

✔ CSS Style Attributes (`www.w3.org/TR/css-style-attr/`)

✔ Media Queries Level 3 (`www.w3.org/TR/css3-mediaqueries/`)

✔ CSS Namespaces (`www.w3.org/TR/css3-namespace/`)

✔ Selectors Level 3 (`www.w3.org/TR/css3-selectors/`)

✔ CSS Color Level 3 (`www.w3.org/TR/css3-color/`)

At some point, the W3C will combine all of these independent pieces into a single standard. For now, you can find the pieces documented at `www.w3.org/TR/CSS/#css3`. Although looking at the standards can be interesting, you don't actually need to know anything about them when using this book. You'll find that this book does all of the heavy lifting for you so that you can focus on creating great content, rather than on trying to figure out the arcane wording used by standards organizations to create a precise definition of a technology.

Defining Why You Need CSS3

The introduction to this chapter discusses some of the reasons you need CSS. The most important reason is that you need some means of separating content from presentation so that it's easier to maintain a site, and so that people with special needs can still access your site by using a different style sheet from the one used by everyone else. There have actually been a lot of style sheet standards in the past, but CSS has special functionality that makes it unique. The defining functionality is the ability to combine several style sheets together to create an overall appearance for a page. These style sheets *cascade* — that is, one flows into another — so that every style sheet is represented in the output. The standard provides rules for resolving conflicts between style sheets so that you always know how the output will appear.

The early versions of CSS provided a wealth of functionality. Even if you were still limited to the features provided by these early versions, you'd still have good reasons to use CSS in your next project. You'll find that just about every browser on the planet supports these basic features, which include

- Font characteristics such as typeface and emphasis
- Text element characteristics such as letter spacing, word spacing, and spacing between lines
- Color characteristics of all elements including fonts and backgrounds
- Alignment of various elements including text, images, controls, and tables
- Positioning and size of spacing elements such as borders, padding, and margins
- Identification and classification of groups of attributes

Two groups commonly use CSS because of the functionality it provides:

- *Developers* use CSS to create robust applications that are less likely to encounter browser-specific tag issues.
- *Designers* use CSS to provide specific presentation characteristics or to make it easy to present the same content in a number of ways.

This book favors developers who need to create great looking pages quickly, even when it might mean creating a page that lacks that certain pizzazz that designers favor. With this in mind, you also need to consider that later versions of CSS provide these additional features:

✔ Absolute, relative, and fixed positioning of elements so that you can create a precise alignment of application elements on screen

✔ The use of a z-index to control the stacking of elements on screen so that one element can hide another as part of an application's functionality

✔ Support for various media types so that a developer need not be an artist to create dramatic looking pages

✔ Support for aural style sheets where content is read instead of merely being presented in print form for these uses:

- To help those with special visual needs

- To help teach people to read

- Creating an environment in which users who can speak another language but can't read it can still interact with the page

- Developing home entertainment systems

- Interacting with web content in a car

- Presenting content that has no written counterpart

✔ Rendering bi-directional text (text that can flow either left to right or right to left)

✔ Adding new font effects, such as shadows

CSS3 makes things even better! When working with CSS3, you use a new concept called modules. A *module* is an individual CSS feature that has its own specification (a written description of how the feature should work that is provided by a standards group). As a result of using modules, you no longer need to wade through a single huge CSS document looking for the CSS feature you want to interact with. Instead, you can locate precisely what you need in a much smaller document that's easier to search. (For more on modules, see the section, "Obtaining an Overview of the CSS Modules," later in this chapter.) There are actually fifty different specifications that are either completed or under consideration now. You can see them at www.w3.org/Style/CSS/specs. This book addresses the main specifications — the ones you use most often.

The point to this section is that CSS3 can help you perform a huge number of tasks in a manner that will likely work with a large number of browsers on many different platforms. By following the standard, you create an environment in which any vendor who also follows the standards can run your application unimpeded, and your users will gain access to an application that works anywhere at any time on any platform and using any browser. Given the Bring Your Own Device (BYOD) craze that's sweeping industry right now (read about BYOD at www.zdnet.com/topic-byod-and-the-consumerization-of-it/), using CSS is your best bet for writing applications that users will actually enjoy using.

Understanding How Browser Support Affects You

CSS3 is a complex specification and it will require time to implement fully in every browser out there. The support your browser provides might vary from other browsers. In fact, it's almost guaranteed that the support levels will vary unless you have an incredibly strict policy about browser usage in your organization.

There are many different techniques you can use to ensure that your application will work as intended when working with CSS3. However, some techniques work significantly better than others. Smart developers usually focus on the three specific strategies that work best:

✔ Use a third-party library that uses special coding techniques to work around the browser compatibility issues.

✔ Avoid using CSS3 features that don't work with the browsers you plan to target with your application.

✔ Verify in advance that the user's browser provides the required support, and if not, suggest that the user perform an update (including a link to the update on your site if at all possible).

Most of this book focuses on the first technique. It's fast, easy, reliable, and most importantly, requires the least amount of work. Using well-designed third-party solutions makes your work considerably easier. Starting with Part II of this book, you use third-party libraries and tools to perform all sorts of tasks in a manner that makes your workload light, while producing reliable code that works as it should.

Sometimes a third-party solution can't work around a particular issue because no workaround exists. For example, even though CSS3 currently supports bookmarks, no browsers currently implement this support. No third-party solution can get around this problem. Consequently, you can add bookmark functionality to your application, but no existing browser will put that feature into effect (at least, until a browser implements the required functionality). Use the chart at `www.w3schools.com/cssref/css3_browsersupport.asp` to determine whether the browsers you're targeting provide the required support. Using this chart, you can determine that a user requires Internet Explorer 10, Firefox 16, or Opera 12.1 to have support for animations. Safari and Chrome both require special coding to provide animation support (which is where a third-party library comes in handy).

The reason I'm not including this compatibility chart in the book is that the level of support provided by browsers changes constantly. When creating browser-based applications, you want to be sure that the online resources you use are updated frequently to ensure you have the best information possible. The `www.w3schools.com/cssref/css3_browsersupport.asp` site provides such support, but there are many other sites that also provide great support.

In some cases, the user is trying to work with your application using an ancient browser — say, the version of Internet Explorer the dinosaurs used. No third-party heavy lifting can help you here. Your best bet is to detect really old browsers and do anything you can to get their users to upgrade. Chapter 6 shows you how to perform this technique using jQuery — a third-party library that makes the task simple and painless.

Obtaining an Overview of the CSS Modules

Previous versions of CSS relied on a single specification document to detail all of the features it provided. CSS3 takes a different approach — it relies on the concept of modules to provide the specification. Each module appears in a separate document and details a particular CSS3 feature. This approach provides several benefits:

- ✔ You don't have to sift through a huge document to locate the one little piece of information you need.

- ✔ Each module can be released independently, which means that the standard will be available (in part) sooner.

- ✔ Specialized groups can work on each module to ensure that it contains the best possible features.

- ✔ Because modules are smaller, it's easier to obtain agreement on a standard than to obtain the same agreement for CSS3 as a whole.

At this time of writing, there are fifty modules that could appear as part of a CSS3 standard, but only some of these modules are currently approved — and you really require only a subset of them to create most applications. The following table displays the essential modules you need to know about in order to work with CSS3 successfully (along with their documentation sites and the locations they're discussed in the book):

Module	Documentation online at	Discussed in this book in
CSS Values and Units Module Level 3	`www.w3.org/TR/css3-values/`	Chapter 1
Selectors Level 3	`www.w3.org/TR/css3-selectors/`	Chapter 2
CSS Basic Box Model	`www.w3.org/TR/css3-box/`	Chapter 2
CSS Fonts Module Level 3	`www.w3.org/TR/css3-fonts/`	Chapter 3

Module	*Documentation online at*	*Discussed in this book in*
CSS Text Module Level 3	www.w3.org/TR/css3-text/	Chapter 3
CSS Color Module Level 3	www.w3.org/TR/css3-color/	Chapter 3
CSS Speech	www.w3.org/TR/css3-speech/	Chapter 3 (replaces the older CSS Aural Style Sheets specification)
CSS Backgrounds and Borders Level 3	www.w3.org/TR/css3-background/	Chapter 4
CSS Transforms	www.w3.org/TR/css3-transforms/	Chapter 4
CSS Multi-column Layout Module	www.w3.org/TR/css3-multi col/	Chapter 5
CSS Basic User Interface Module Level 3	www.w3.org/TR/css3-ui/	Chapters 2 through 5
CSS Animations	www.w3.org/TR/css3-animations/	Explored as part of third party library support in various chapters

Using this set of twelve modules will provide most of the functionality you need for every application. Some of the other fifty modules aren't even implemented yet (and may never be). For example, the CSS Extended Box Model hasn't been started yet, but it should provide some exciting new functionality when someone puts it together.

A few of the fifty modules that don't appear in this table are used for something other than standard applications. The CSS Marquee module is implemented and available, but you normally use it with smartphones. The groups working on these standards have also combined a few of the modules to make them easier to work with. The CSS 2D Transformations Module and the CSS 3D Transformations Module have been combined into a single CSS Transforms module. So, even though there are three entries in the list, there's only one implemented module to think about.

Understanding Styles

You could look at styles created by other people and quickly become lost in all the arcane ways they're used. The best way to start with styles is to view them simply as a means of formatting information onscreen. Because most of the information you'll work with is text, it's easiest to start with text as the basis for understanding styles. Let's start with this basic HTML5 formatted page:

```
<!DOCTYPE html>

<html>
<head>
    <title>A Simple Page</title>
</head>

<body>
    <h1>A Simple Heading</h1>
    <p>Simple text to go with the heading.</p>
</body>
</html>
```

There's nothing complex about this page. It simply displays a heading and a paragraph of text. Figure 1-1 shows how this page looks. (Your page may look a little different from the information shown here due to differences in platform and browser configuration.)

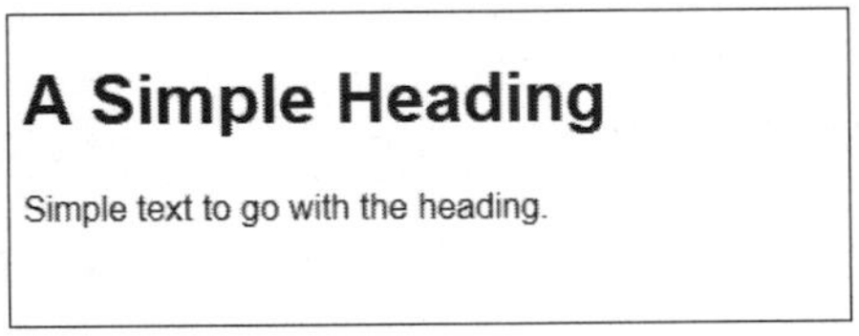

Figure 1-1:
A simple
HTML5 doc-
ument used
for testing
purposes.

A Simple Heading

Simple text to go with the heading.

At the moment, the heading and the paragraph are rather plain. The text will appear in whatever default font you've chosen for your browser. Typically, the text is black on a white background unless you or your browser vendor have chosen a different color combination.

At this point, you can begin playing with the page a little to see how to format it differently. The following procedure helps you modify the basic page so it looks a little more interesting. You can use any text editor you like, so long as it doesn't add any formatting. However, using a product such as Komodo Edit (www.activestate.com/komodo-edit) will make the task considerably easier by providing you with help in writing your code. (Dedicated editors will display tooltips on what to write or what options are available; and they also provide advanced features such as debuggers.).

1. **Create a new HTML5 file with your text editor.**

   Your editor may not support HTML5 files. Any text file will do. Using a specific file type usually means that the editor inserts some of the code for you automatically, which will save you typing time.

2. **Type the code for the HTML page.**

   Make sure you type the code precisely as it appears earlier in this section.

3. **Insert the following code immediately after the** `<title>` **tag.**

```
<style type="text/css">

</style>
```

The `<style>` tag defines the beginning of a style. When you place the `<style>` tag directly in the page like this, it's called an *internal style*. You can also create *external style sheets*. External style sheets reside in `.css` files.

The type attribute tells the browser the `<style>` tag contains CSS information in text format.

4. **Within the** `<style>` **tag, (between the** `<style>` **and** `</style>` **entries, type the following code.**

```
p
{
    font-family: cursive;
    font-size: large;
    color: #0000ff;
    background-color: #ffff00;
}
```

This looks complicated, but it really isn't. The p stands for the `<p>` (paragraph) tag. Everything in this entry will affect the `<p>` tags in your document.

The curly braces ({}) tell the browser that all of the formatting instructions between them apply to the `<p>` tags in the document. You always include the curly braces as part of the style definition.

Within the curly braces, you see attribute name and value pairs. For example, `font-family` is the name of a CSS attribute that defines which font to use. In this case, the attribute specifies the default cursive font for the platform and browser. Using the CSS generic names ensures that your application will produce generically compatible results on all platforms, using any browser.

The `font-size` attribute defines a relative size. In this case, `large` specifies you want to make the font large compared to its default size. You aren't specifying a specific font size, which means that each platform and browser can render the font larger than normal for that individual environment.

The `color` attribute specifies a red, green, blue value to use for the font's color. The value is preceded by a hash (#) followed by hexadecimal color values from 0 to `ff`. In this case, the font will be the brightest blue supported by the platform. Likewise, the `background-color` attribute specifies the background for the text, which will be yellow in this case.

5. Save the page and load it in your browser.

You see the effects of the style change as shown in Figure 1-2. Your page may look different from the one in the book because your platform or browser may use different values for the font family or font size. If the book were able to present color, you'd see that the colors on your display would be close to those shown in the example.

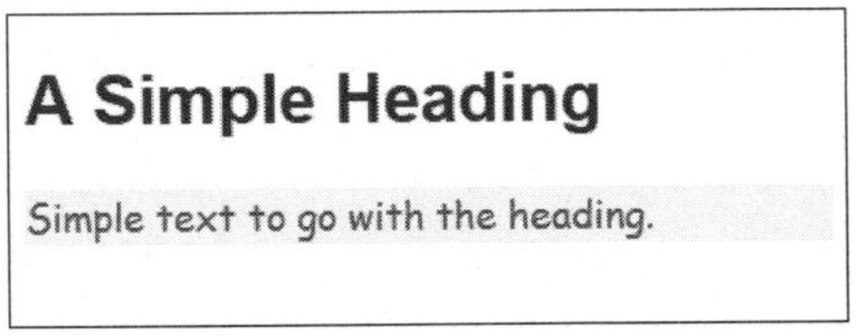

Figure 1-2:
The para-
graph text
has changed
to match the
style specifi-
cations.

A Simple Heading

Simple text to go with the heading.

6. Type the following code after the p style within the `<style>` **tag.**

```
h1
{
    font-family: "Times New Roman",Georgia,serif;
    font-size: 40px;
    text-align: center;
    text-decoration: underline;
    color: #ff0000;
    background-color: #00ffff;
}
```

This style affects the `<h1>` tag entries and it has many of the entries used for the `<p>` tag style. However, notice that this time the `font-family` attribute contains three entries: The Times New Roman value is the most specific, followed by Georgia, followed by the least specific — serif (you don't need to know the specifics of how this works now — Chapter 3 discusses the topic in detail). When working with a value that contains spaces, you must enclose the value in quotes as shown.

Using the three-entry approach gives you more control over the appearance of the output, but still makes it possible for browsers that don't support a specific font to render the content correctly. When supplying a specific font, make sure you also supply less specific fonts for browsers that don't have access to your specified font.

The `font-size` attribute is also different. This time the style uses a specific size of 40 pixels. Even though a specific value can make it possible to create special effects onscreen, using a specific value also creates problems. A 40px entry will work just fine on the desktop or laptop, but might cause problems with a tablet, and will definitely make the content impossible to display on a smartphone.

This style also includes some entries that change the appearance of the text. The `text-align` attribute determines where the text is placed on screen, while the `text-decoration` attribute determines any special font features. In this case, the font is displayed centered onscreen with an underline.

6. **Save the page and load it in your browser.**

    You see the effects of the style change as shown in Figure 1-3. The heading appears in red text on a pale blue background, and the paragraph is shown as blue text on a yellow background.

Figure 1-3:
The heading text has changed to match the style specifications.

Creating External Styles

The preceding "Understanding Styles" section of this chapter describes styles in general and then shows you an example of a simple internal style. Internal styles can be useful on pages — especially when the page has some type of specialized requirement not found on other pages on the site — but they are less common than the external kind. Most developers use external styles to reduce the amount of work required to maintain a site. A single .CSS file contains all of the styles for the site, which means that changing a style site-wide is as simple as changing that one file (rather than each individual page). Because the change occurs in just one place, there isn't any chance of missing one or more changes on individual pages.

Creating and using an external style sheet isn't much different from using an internal style sheet. The following example uses the techniques found in the preceding section to create an external style sheet:

1. **Create a new HTML5 file with your text editor.**

2. **Type the code for the HTML page found in the "Understanding Styles" section of this chapter.**

    Make sure you type the code precisely as you would to start the previous example. What you should end up with is the same plain page — one without any styles.

3. **Type the following code immediately after the** `<title>` **tag.**

```
<link rel="stylesheet" href="ExternalCSS.CSS" />
```

The `<link>` tag tells the browser to look for an external resource. In this case, the `rel` attribute says that it should look for a style sheet and the `href` attribute provides the name of that style sheet.

4. **Save the HTML5 file to disk.**

5. **Create a new** `.css` **file with your text editor.**

Your editor may not support `.css` files. Any text file will do.

6. **Type the following code in the** `.css` **file.**

```
p
{
    font-family: cursive;
    font-size: large;
    color: #0000ff;
    background-color: #ffff00;
}

h1
{
    font-family: "Times New Roman",Georgia,serif;
    font-size: 40px;
    text-align: center;
    text-decoration: underline;
    color: #ff0000;
    background-color: #00ffff;
}
```

Yes, this is the same code that you used before. The only difference is that it now resides in an external file.

7. **Save the CSS file to disk as** `ExternalCSS.CSS`.

It's absolutely essential that the name of the file precisely match the name found in the `href` attribute. Some platforms are case sensitive, so you must use the same case for the filename. For example, `externalcss.css` might be viewed as a different file from `ExternalCSS.CSS`.

8. **Load the page in your browser.**

You see the effects of the style change as shown in Figure 1-3.

Defining the CSS Units of Measure

There are many ways to specify a value when working with CSS. For example, you can simply say that the browser should use a large font (where medium is the default size). You can also tell the browser to compute a size based on the browser's configuration. Relative measurements make it possible for the browser to adjust the content presentation to match the size of the device displaying it, but using relative measurements also means that the user may not see the content as you originally wanted to present it. In rare cases, using relative measurements can actually make the content unusable because the browser doesn't know how to use the relative measurements to present the content correctly.

Absolute measurements have the advantage of allowing precise placement of content onscreen and making that content a specific size or giving the content a precise appearance. However, use absolute measurements only when you're certain about the user's configuration. For example, you could use absolute measurements when creating an application that's for internal use within your organization and the organization has mandated device configurations.

When creating absolute measurements, and some relative measurements, you need to use a unit of measure that the browser will understand. Table 1-1 shows the standardized units of measure that every browser will understand, along with a description of that measurement. You see many of these units of measure used in the examples in this book.

Table 1-1		Standard CSS Units of Measure	
Symbol	*Measure-ment*	*Type*	*Description*
%	Percent	Relative	A percentage of a particular element. For example, a table column can consume a percentage of the space allocated for the entire table's width.
in	Inch	Absolute	The number of screen or printed inches to use to display an element. The number of pixels in an inch varies according to device and device configuration.
cm	Centimeter	Absolute	The number of screen or printed centimeters to use to display an element. The number of pixels in an centimeter varies according to device and device configuration.
mm	Millimeter	Absolute	The number of screen or printed millimeters to use to display an element. The number of pixels in an millimeter varies according to device and device configuration.
em	Em	Relative	An em is computed based on the current font size. The default size for most desktop browsers is 16 px = 1 em. However, some-one might configure the browser to use a smaller or larger default font. See the side-bar, "Understanding Ems" for more details.

(continued)

Table 1-1 *(continued)*

Symbol	Measurement	Type	Description
ex	Ex	Relative	A counterpart to the em, the ex is the computed x-height of a font, rather than the full height of the font. Otherwise exs work the same as ems.
pt	Point	Absolute	Each point is approximately 1/72-inch.
pc	Pica	Absolute	Each pica is equal to twelve points.
px	Pixel	Relative	Specifies an individual dot on the screen. This is a relative measurement because it takes into account the variable number of pixels used by each device over a specific measurement (normally an inch or centimeter). Many developers use pixels when good presentation control is needed, but some flexibility in adapting to a particular platform is desired.

Understanding ems

Most web developers rely on the em as their basic unit of measure because ems automatically adapt to whatever the user relies upon. If a user has a special visual need, an em might be much larger than the default size of 16 px. On the other hand, someone using a smartphone might see an em as being only 10 px due to the small size of the screen. The point is that you can use a consistent measure for your pages that's then automatically translated to whatever the user needs. Here are the default sizes for an em when compared to pixels for various kinds of text:

- Headline 1 (<h1>) = 20px
- Headline 2 (<h2>) = 18px
- Headline 3 (<h3>) = 16px
- Main text (<p>) = 14px
- Sub text = 12px
- Footnotes (usually <footer>) = 10px

The feature that makes ems different from pixels or other relative measures is the concept of an inherited default font size. If you create an element that has a default font size different from the default size displayed by the browser, and then place another element within it, the child element will use the default size of the parent, and not that of the browser. For example, if you place a footnote inside a paragraph tag, the footnote will appear at 8.75 px instead of 10 px (the default font size). The way to calculate this value is (14 px <p> tag size / 16 px default text size) * 10 px footnote size. Likewise, placing a footnote inside an <h1> tag will display the footnote at 12.5 px.

Chapter 2

Performing Basic Tasks

*C*hapter 1 rushed you through a few examples that demonstrated how Cascading Style Sheets (CSS) work at a basic level. Of course, there's a lot more to CSS and this chapter helps you take the next step on the journey. There are a few essential tasks that you'll perform whenever you work with CSS simply because there isn't any way to avoid them.

One of these tasks is selecting objects to work with, as discussed in Chapter 1. Creating a p or h1 style involves selecting <p> and <h1> tags (objects) within the document. After these objects are selected, you can perform tasks with them. Note, however, that simple tags aren't the only objects, as you discover in this chapter.

You also need to know how layout works at a basic level. In this chapter you discover how CSS interacts with the drawing area onscreen. For example, you need to know the starting point for drawing new information onscreen and how the underlying platform deals with packaging objects for display. This is the same sort of information that developers need in order to create desktop applications, but it's CSS3-specific.

Finally, on websites, white backgrounds are boring. Adding a simple picture makes the background a lot more interesting and it doesn't require a lot of effort. Of course, you can add the background directly to the pages of your site, but using a style to add the background is better. If you decide to update the background, you can update all pages at once without difficulty. The whole idea behind using styles is to create an environment where you can perform tasks easily and reliably.

Working with Selectors

When you want to change something in your environment, you select the object associated with that factor and modify it in some way. For example, you select the remote control, point it at the television, and change the channel as needed to view your favorite show. If you're hungry, you open the refrigerator, select the food that's appealing at the moment, and then eat it. The objects in a web page work the same way. To change an object to look the way you want, first you select the object and then you make changes to it.

When creating a style sheet, HTML documents can be a problem. They can be long and so complex you can't tell what they contain. As a consequence, you need methods for selecting objects without knowing what those objects are in advance. For example, you know that you want all <p> tags to appear in a certain way, even though you don't know where they're placed on a page or whether the page even has any <p> tags at all. Consequently, CSS provides a number of techniques that allow you to find the objects you want to select without a problem.

Because the topic is relatively complex, it's important to find an easy way to determine which selector to use and when to use it. This chapter breaks selectors down into types so you can ease into them a little at a time, without the shock of seeing a huge, somewhat disorganized list of them displayed on a site. The following sections discuss the various ways in which you can use selectors to interact with objects on pages.

An overview of selectors

There's no reason that selectors should be complicated. All you're really trying to do is select an object on the current page so you can interact with it in some way. The idea is quite simple. It's the implementation that makes things complicated. However, you can reduce the complexity by viewing selectors in specific ways.

Most selectors fall into particular categories. Note, however, that a special selector, * (asterisk), selects every object in the document without regard for type or location. You use this selector when you want to format every object in the document in a certain way.

This chapter tells you about every selector you'll ever use (and probably a few you won't). To reduce the complexity of selectors, the chapter breaks them into functional categories like this (the standard doesn't categorize the selectors in this way — this breakdown is merely for your convenience):

✔ **Tag:** HTML tags form the basis of most documents. You can interact directly with any tag, such as <p> and <h1> on the page. CSS also makes it possible to be discriminating in your choices. For example, you could choose to interact only with <p> tags found within a <div>. A number of selector types work with tags in various ways.

✔ **Attribute:** HTML tags contain attributes. The most commonly used attributes with CSS are class and id. However, there are methods of working with tags containing any attribute. For example, you might want to interact in a specific way with tags that contain a target attribute and CSS provides the means to do that.

✔ **Pattern:** There are cases when you want to format content based on a pattern. For example, you might want to format every other list item <li> in a specific way to make the list items stand out — so the user can easily see each list item as a specific entity. If the page were to suddenly have another item in the list, the CSS would automatically reformat the items to match the pattern you created — all without any special changes on your part.

✔ **Event:** Some pages you visit look like someone has performed fancy programming to obtain the special effects that you see. In reality, many of these sites trap an event, such as a mouseover, and create CSS to interact with it. The object is formatted one way normally and then another way when the mouse passes over it. Depending on the complexity of the CSS you create, the effects can be truly amazing (and all without programming).

✔ **State:** Objects on a page have a specific state. For example, links are active, visited, or unvisited. You can choose to format these objects in special ways that depend solely on their state at any given time. A link that someone has visited might appear with a check mark next to it, while the link that's currently active might appear highlighted in some way. Just how you interact with the state information depends on the sort of effect you want to achieve.

The topic of selectors really is quite complicated. Don't even think about viewing the standards without a bottle of aspirin by your side. Fortunately, there are a few sites that you can reference that provide a list in a somewhat organized manner. For example, the W3C Schools site (www.w3schools.com/cssref/css_selectors.asp) provides a simple chart that tells you about the majority of the selectors in a straightforward manner. Short lists of selectors, such as the one at http://net.tutsplus.com/tutorials/html-css-techniques/the-30-css-selectors-you-must-memorize/, are also helpful. This particular site provides straightforward information about browser compatibility when working with selectors as well. If you really want to find out about browser compatibility, though, have your browser take the CSS Selectors Test at www.css3.info/selectors-test/.

Working with tag selectors

Tag (or element) selectors are character sequences you use to choose tags such as <h1> and <p>. In fact, you can select any HTML tag this way; Chapter 1 shows simple examples of a tag selector at work. A tag selector always relies on the tag name, such as p or h1. However, there are some interesting tag selector combinations you should know about. The following list tells you about tag selectors that you can use in addition to the simple tag selector shown in Chapter 1.

- ✔ ***Tag,Tag:*** Separating two tags with a comma means selecting both tags, regardless of where they appear in the document. For example, using p, div would select all <p> and <div> tags within the document.

- ✔ ***Tag>Tag:*** Separating two tags with a greater-than sign (>) tells the browser to select a tag that has another tag as a parent. For example, if you have <div><p /></div> and use div>p, the browser will select the <p> tag.

- ✔ ***Tag Tag:*** Separating two tags by a space tells the browser to select a tag that appears within another tag. This selector differs from using a greater than sign in that the first tag need not directly appear immediately before the second tag. For example, if you have <div><p /></div> and use div>p, the browser won't select anything. However, if you use div p instead, the browser will select the <p> tag.

- ✔ ***Tag+Tag:*** Separating two tags with a plus sign (+) tells the browser to select a tag that appears immediately after another tag. For example, if you have <div /><p /> and use div+p, the browser will select the <p> tag. Notice that the <p> tag doesn't appear within the <div> tag, it appears after the <div> tag.

- ✔ ***Tag~Tag:*** Separating two tags with a tilde (~) tells the browser to select every tag that appears after another tag. For example, if you have <div /><p /><p /> and use div~p, the browser will select both <p> tags. This differs from div+p, which tells the browser to select only the first <p> tag that follows the <div> tag.

- ✔ **:root:** Selects the root element of the document. The root element depends on the document type. This selector is normally used with XML documents, but you could potentially use it with any document type.

Even with this short list of tag selectors, you can see that CSS is quite flexible when working with tags. Seeing the selectors in action will help you understand them a bit better. The following procedure shows how to use the various tags:

1. **Copy the** ExternalCSS.HTML **and** ExternalCSS.CSS **files (created in Chapter 1) to a new folder.**

A number of examples in the book build on previous examples to save time and effort on your part. Make sure you create a *copy* of the existing example and use the copy for your work in this chapter.

2. **Open ExternalCSS.HTML.**

3. **Type the following code after the existing** `<p>` **tag in the file and save the changes to disk.**

```
<div>
    <p>Text within a DIV.</p>
    <span>
        <p>Text with a DIV parent.</p>
    </span>
</div>
<p>Text after a DIV.</p>
<p>More text after a DIV.</p>
```

This code simply adds tags in specific arrangements so that you can test the various selectors. If you open the resulting file now, you see that each of the `<p>` tags has been automatically formatted like the original `<p>` tag, as shown in Figure 2-1.

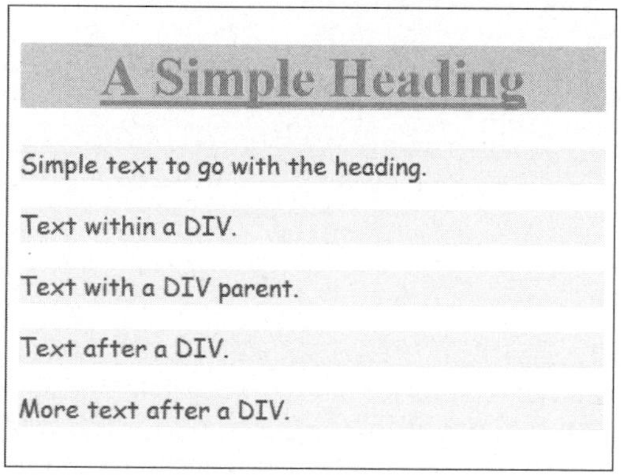

A Simple Heading

Simple text to go with the heading.

Text within a DIV.

Text with a DIV parent.

Text after a DIV.

More text after a DIV.

Figure 2-1:
CSS auto-matically formats any `<p>` tags you add.

Using the :not(*Selector*) Selector

Some of the selectors in this chapter are pretty specific. In some cases, it's easier to select objects according to characteristics that they *don't* have — that is, to select objects that *aren't* of a specific type. For example, you might want to change the formatting of every object that isn't within a `<p>` tag. In this case, you could create a list of tags using the comma selector and hope that your list is complete, or you could just use the `:not()` selector. For example, `:not(p)` selects every object that isn't a `<p>` tag. You also can create complex selections using the `:not()` selector: A selector of `:not(div>p)`, for instance, selects every `<p>` tag that doesn't have a `<div>` tag as a parent.

3. **Open ExternalCSS.CSS.**

4. **Type the following code after the existing styles and save the changes to disk.**

```
div>p
{
    text-align: right;
}
```

5. **Reload the test page.**

   The effect of making the style change is shown in Figure 2-2. Notice that the only <p> tag that's been affected is the one that has the <div> tag as a direct parent. In addition, notice that the previous formatting cascades into the current formatting. You haven't overridden any of the existing formatting, so the text appears as before — it simply uses right-justification instead of the default left-justification.

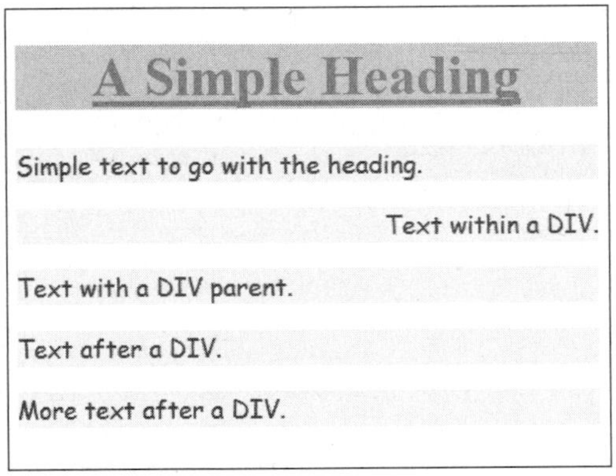

Figure 2-2:
Only the
<p> tag
with a <div>
as a direct
parent is
affected.

> **A Simple Heading**
>
> Simple text to go with the heading.
>
>   Text within a DIV.
>
> Text with a DIV parent.
>
> Text after a DIV.
>
> More text after a DIV.

6. **Type the following code after the existing styles and save the changes to disk.**

```
div p
{
    text-decoration: line-through;
    background-color: #ff7f7f;
}
```

7. **Reload the test page.**

   The effect of these style changes appears in Figure 2-3. Notice that two lines are affected this time. In addition, the background-color style has been changed, so these two lines use the new color — it takes precedence over the original color. When you think about the cascading part of CSS, think about a stream where changes downstream take precedence over the original state of the water.

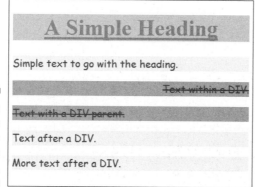

Figure 2-3:
All <p> tags
within <div>
tags are
affected.

8. **Type the following code after the existing styles and save the changes to disk.**

```
div+p
{
    font-family: monospace;
    font-style: italic;
}
```

9. **Reload the test page.**

The effect of these style changes appears in Figure 2-4. Only the line that appears directly after the <div> is affected: The font has changed to a monospace font (normally reserved for code) and is italicized.

Figure 2-4:
Only the <p>
tag directly
after the
<div> tag is
affected.

10. Type the following code after the existing styles and save the changes to disk.

```
div~p
{
    font-weight: bolder;
    font-size: 30px;
    margin: 0px;
    color: #7f007f;
}
```

11. Reload the test page.

You see the effects of this style change in Figure 2-5. Notice that both <p> tags that appear after the <div> tag are affected. The font now appears bold and is larger. The font color has also changed. Especially important in this part of the example is that setting the margin to 0px gets rid of the white space between lines.

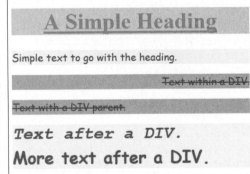

Figure 2-5: All <p> tags after <div> tags are affected.

Working with attribute selectors

Within many tags are attributes that describe tag properties. Two common attributes are the tag identifier (id) and CSS classification (class). However, CSS makes it possible to select objects by any attribute desired. The following list tells you about attribute selectors that you commonly use when creating styles.

- ✔ **.ClassName:** Selects any objects that have a class attribute value with the given name. For example, .StdPara would select every object that has a class="StdPara" attribute without regard for object type.

- ✔ **#Id:** Selects any objects that have an id attribute value with the given name. For example, #ThirdHeader would select every object that has an id="ThirdHeader" attribute without regard for object type.

✔ **:lang(*Language Identifier*):** Selects any object with the specified language value. For example, `:lang(en)` would select any object that uses English as its language. You can find a list of common language identifiers at `www.w3schools.com/tags/ref_language_codes.asp`.

✔ **[*Attribute*]:** Selects all objects that use a particular attribute regardless of the attribute's value. For example, `[lang]` would select all objects that use the `lang` attribute.

✔ **[*Attribute=Value*]:** Selects all objects that have an attribute with a particular value. The value must match precisely. For example, `[lang="en-us"]` would select every object that has a language attribute with a value of English.

✔ **[*Attribute~=Value*]:** Selects all objects that have an attribute that contains a particular value. The search value need only appear somewhere within the value as a whole. For example, `[title~="Secondary"]` selects all objects with title attributes that contain the word `Secondary` as a discrete word. This selector works with whole words.

It's possible to further restrict many of these attribute selectors by combining them with tag selectors. For example, `p[title~="Secondary"]` selects only the `<p>` tag objects with title attributes that contain the word `Secondary` as a discrete word. It's often possible to combine selectors in unique ways to create precisely the effect you want.

✔ **[*Attribute|=Value*]:** Selects all objects that have an attribute that begins with a particular value. The search value needs to appear at the beginning of the value as a whole, but need not be the entire value. For example, `[title|="Sub"]` selects all objects with title attributes that start with the word `Sub`. This selector works with hyphenated terms.

✔ **[*Attribute^=Value*]:** Selects all objects that have an attribute that begins with a particular value. For example, `[title|="Sub"]` selects all objects with title attributes that start with the word `Sub`. This form of the selector differs from the `[Attribute|=Value]` attribute in that it's less restrictive. Using this form will select `title="SubHeader"`, `title="Sub Header"`, or `title="Sub-Header"` with equal reliability.

✔ **[*Attribute$=Value*]:** Selects all objects that have an attribute that ends with a particular value. For example, `[title$="Secondary"]` selects all objects with title attributes that end with the word `Secondary`. This form of the attribute is nonrestrictive — it requires no special formatting.

✔ **[*Attribute*=Value*]:** Selects all objects that have an attribute that contains a particular value. For example, `[title$="Secondary"]` selects all objects with title attributes that contain the word `Secondary`. This form of the selector is less restrictive than the `[Attribute~=Value]` attribute. Using this form will select `title="SecondaryParagraph"`, `title="Secondary Paragraph"`, or `title="Secondary-Paragraph"` with equal reliability.

Now that you have some idea of how attribute selectors work, it's time to see them in action. The following procedure helps you understand what attribute selectors do and how you can use them to choose specific objects within a document for formatting.

1. **Copy the** `ExternalCSS.HTML` **and** `ExternalCSS.CSS` **files you created in Chapter 1 to a new folder.**

2. **Open** `ExternalCSS.HTML`.

3. **Type the following code after the existing** `<p>` **tag in the file and save the changes to disk.**

```
<h1 id="SecondHeader" class="SubHead"
    title="Sub-Header">
    Another Heading
</h1>
<p id="SecondaryPara" class="StdPara"
    title="Secondary-Paragraph">
    More Text
</p>
<h1 id="ThirdHeader" class="SubHead"
    title="Sub-Header Secondary">
    Another Heading Still
</h1>
<p id="SecondaryPara" class="StdPara"
    title="Secondary Sub-Paragraph">
    Still More Text
</p>
<p id="SecondaryPara" class="SubPara"
    title="Sub-Paragraph" lang="en-us">
    Even More Text
</p>
```

This code simply adds tags in specific arrangements so that you can test the various selectors. If you open the resulting file now, you see that each of the `<h1>` and `<p>` tags has been automatically formatted like the original `<h1>` and `<p>` tags; the result is similar to Figure 2-1.

3. **Open ExternalCSS.CSS.**

4. **Type the following code after the existing styles and save the changes to disk.**

```
.SubHead
{
    border: double;
    border-width: thick;
    border-color: Green;
}
```

5. **Reload the test page.**

   You see the effect of making the style change (as shown in Figure 2-6).
   Each object that has a `class` value of `SubHead` now has a thick double
   border colored green.

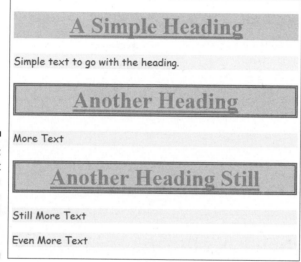

Figure 2-6:
Every object
that has a
class value
of SubHead
now has a
border.

There are many ways to define the colors you want to use. Many developers use the hexadecimal format shown so far because it's precise and
flexible. However, `#008000` is a little hard to read. Using the color name,
`Green`, is a lot easier. Of course, this means you need to know the name
of the color. Fortunately, you can find a list of names that browsers
understand at `www.w3schools.com/cssref/css_colornames.asp`.

6. **Type the following code after the existing styles and save the changes
   to disk.**

```
#ThirdHeader
{
    text-decoration: line-through;
}
```

7. **Reload the test page.**

   You see the effect of making the style change as shown in Figure 2-7.
   Each object that has an `id` value of `ThirdHeader` now has a `text-
   decoration` value of `line-through`, rather than `underline`. Notice
   that the new value overwrites the old value. If you want to preserve the
   original value, you must specify it again.

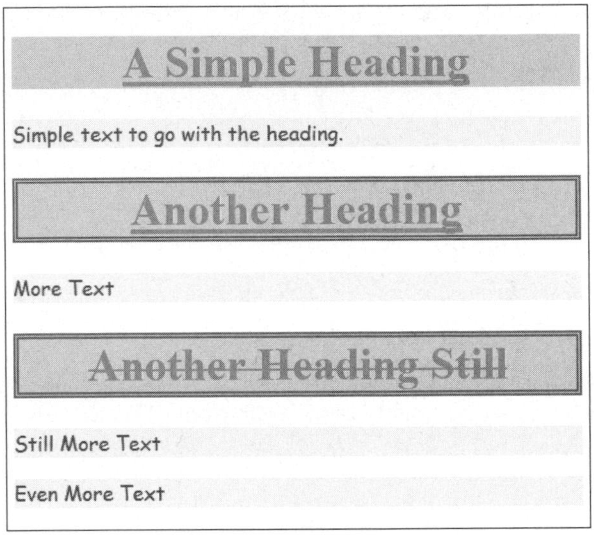

A Simple Heading

Simple text to go with the heading.

Another Heading

More Text

Another Heading Still

Still More Text

Even More Text

Figure 2-7: Every object that has an id value of ThirdHeader now has a line through its text.

The oddities of attribute selectors

Using the attribute selectors can be tricky at times. If you don't test your assumptions about them, using a simple test case with all of the browsers you want to work, your results could be surprising. For instance, the `[Attribute~=Value]` attribute works only with whole words. A selector of `[title~="Secondary"]`, then, matches `title="Secondary Paragraph"` and `title="Sub-Header Secondary"`. However, it won't match `title="Secondary-Paragraph"` because of the hyphen between `Secondary` and `Paragraph`.

Likewise, when working with the `[Attribute|=Value]` selector, you must supply hyphenated terms. For example, `[title|="Sub"]` matches `title="Sub-Header"`, but it won't match `title="Sub Header"` because there's a space rather than a hyphen.

The odd thing is that these two examples work consistently across all of the test browsers and across all platforms. This behavior doesn't make sense, but you need to be aware that it exists — and then compensate for it when creating your site. A lot of people complain about these selector issues without realizing that they are consistently embedded in the browsers they use.

If you want to select terms without worry about precise formatting, then you need to rely on alternatives. For example, `[Attribute*=Value]` is the less specific version of `[Attribute~=Value]` and `[Attribute^=Value]` is the less specific version of `[Attribute|=Value]`. Using the correct selector is absolutely essential if you want to get the desired results.

8. **Type the following code after the existing styles and save the changes to disk.**

```
[title|="Sub"]
{
    text-align: right;
    background-color: rgb(128, 255, 128);
}
```

9. **Reload the test page.**

You see the effect of making the style change (as shown in Figure 2-8). Each object that has the word Sub somewhere in its title attribute is changed. Notice that this particular change affects both <p> and <h1> tags. This example also shows another way to define color selections. Each color: red, green, blue (rgb) is represented by a value between 0 and 255. You can read more about the rgb() approach to creating colors at www.w3schools.com/cssref/css_colors.asp.

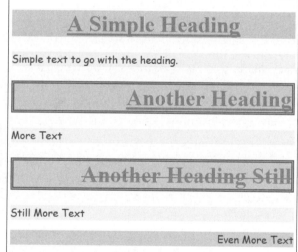

Figure 2-8: Here every object that has Sub in its title property is changed.

Working with pattern selectors

In some cases, a selection you need to make has nothing to do with either tags or attributes, but the pattern in which the objects appear on the page. For example, you might want to select just the first object, regardless of what that object might be. In some cases, you want to format with alternate members of a list or other repetitive data element in some manner to make it easier for the user to see each element individually. The following list tells you about pattern selectors that documents commonly use.

✔ **:first-letter:** Select the first letter of the specified object. This selector is useful in creating special textual effects, such as drop caps.

It's extremely rare to see most pattern selectors used alone because you normally don't want to specially format just the first letter of every object on the page in a certain way. Generally, you see pattern selectors used in combination with an attribute selector, such as the `class` selector, or with a particular tag selector. Using pattern selectors globally can have unexpected results or even cause an application to fail (depending on how the application's code and the CSS interact).

✔ **:first-line:** Selects the first line of the specified object.

✔ **:before:** Selects the area immediately before the specified object content. This selector is normally coupled with the `content` property to insert something special before the content in the existing object.

✔ **:after:** Selects the area immediately after the specified object content. This selector is normally coupled with the `content` property to insert something special before the content in the existing object.

✔ **:first-of-type:** Selects the first object of a specific type.

Even though the specification doesn't actually tell you that you must provide a type or a parent, some pattern selectors won't work without one. Typically you see the `:first-of-type` selector used with a tag selector, (for example, `p:first-of-type`), but it can also be used with an attribute selector. All of the other type and child pattern selectors work the same way.

✔ **:last-of-type:** Selects the last object of a specific type.

✔ **:only-of-type:** Selects the only object of a specific type. If there's more than one object of a particular type, then no selection is made.

✔ **:nth-of-type(*Number*):** Selects the specified object of a specific type.

✔ **:nth-last-of-type(*Number*):** Selects the specified object of a specific type, beginning from the end of the object list.

✔ **:first-child:** Selects the first child of a specified object. This selector is commonly used to apply special formatting to the first item in a list or table.

✔ **:last-child:** Selects the last child of a particular parent.

✔ **:only-child:** Selects the only child of a particular parent. When a parent object has more than one child, no selection is made.

✔ **:nth-child(*Number*):** Selects the specified child of a particular parent.

✔ **:nth-last-child(*Number*):** Selects the specified child of a particular parent beginning from the end of the list of children.

Pattern selectors can create some interesting effects on your site. The following procedure takes a quick look at what these selectors can do. It's important to remember that you'll see selectors, including pattern selectors, used in examples throughout the book, so consider this a starting point.

1. **Copy the** `ExternalCSS.HTML` **and** `ExternalCSS.CSS` **files you created in Chapter 1 to a new folder.**

2. **Open** `ExternalCSS.HTML`.

3. **Type the following code after the existing** `<p>` **tag in the file and save the changes to disk.**

```
<ul id="MyList">
    <li id="One" class="ListItem">One</li>
    <li id="Two" class="ListItem">Two</li>
    <li id="Three" class="ListItem">Three</li>
    <li id="Four" class="ListItem">Four</li>
    <li id="Five" class="ListItem">Five</li>
</ul>
```

In this case, you add a list to the page to allow easier detection of patterns. Of course, patterns aren't limited to lists or tables. You can use them with any arrangement of objects that could lend themselves to selection by a pattern.

3. **Open ExternalCSS.CSS.**

4. **Type the following code after the existing styles and save the changes to disk.**

```
.ListItem:first-letter
{
    font-size: xx-large;
}

.ListItem:after
{
    content: " \27A8";
    font-size: x-large;
    color: Red;
}

.ListItem:nth-child(odd)
{
    background-color: LightBlue;
}

.ListItem:nth-child(2n+2)
{
    background-color: LightGreen;
}
```

5. **Reload the test page.**

You see the effect of making the style change as shown in Figure 2-9. To begin, each bullet starts with an extra-large letter.

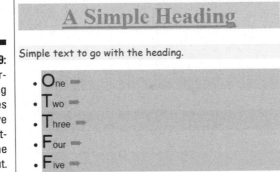

Figure 2-9:
The for-
matting
changes
have
created pat-
terns in the
output.

At the end of each bullet you see a special arrow character. Notice how the CSS uses \27A8 to create this character. When viewing charts such as the one at `http://ikwebdesigner.com/special-characters/` and the one at `www.petterhesselberg.com/charcodes.html`, you see these character codes presented with a &# combination at the beginning. CSS uses the same numeric codes, but relies on a backslash (/).

The `:nth-child()` selector can be used in a number of ways. Even though the example doesn't show it, you can provide a number to select one specific child element. However, this selector also accepts a number of other interesting inputs. For example, you can use the `even` and `odd` keywords to select the even or odd objects in a list. You can also provide an equation that uses n to indicate the current object. When the browser inputs 0 for n, for example, the equation becomes 2 * 0 + 2 or element 2. If you wanted to start with element 3 instead, you'd use 2n+3. The equation you provide can be of any complexity required to produce the desired result.

Working with event selectors

Most CSS changes are static — you ask the browser to look for specific tags, attributes, or patterns. However, event selectors choose objects based on a particular event, such as a mouse over. When the user hovers the mouse pointer over an object, the object's formatting changes to signify that the event has occurred. When the user moves the mouse pointer off of the object, the formatting returns to normal. The following list tells you about event selectors that documents commonly use.

✔ **:hover:** Selects an object when the mouse pointer is hovered over it. Developers commonly use this feature to show that an item is selected or to display details about an object. You see this feature used quite often with menu systems to display the submenu items.

✔ **:focus:** Selects an object when the object has the input (keyboard) focus. It's commonly used with forms to show which field is selected for input. One interesting use of this selector is to show the selected field in a larger-sized font to make input easier.

Event selectors are handy because you can use them to make it appear the page is interacting with the user without writing even one line of code. Everything happens as part of a style. The following procedure shows one way to use event selectors to produce a visual effect, but this particular trick appears relatively often in the book, so you'll see it used more than once.

1. **Copy the** `ExternalCSS.HTML` **and** `ExternalCSS.CSS` **files (created in Chapter 1) to a new folder.**

2. **Open** `ExternalCSS.CSS`.

3. **Type the following code after the existing styles and save the changes to disk.**

```
p:hover, h1:hover
{
    text-decoration: none;
    font-family: "Arial", sans-serif;
    font-size: xx-large;
    color: BlueViolet;
    background-color: Plum;
}
```

4. **Reload the test page.**

5. **Hover the mouse pointer over the paragraph text.**

You see the effect of making the style change as shown in Figure 2-10. The style of the text changes to match the selection criteria.

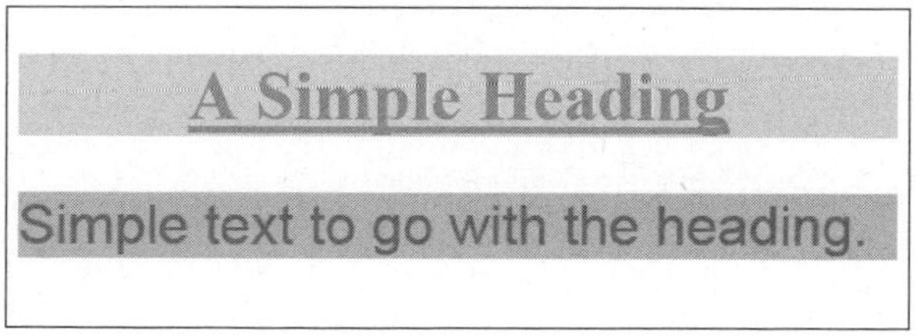

Figure 2-10: Events make it appear that your application is coded, when it really isn't.

A Simple Heading

Simple text to go with the heading.

6. **Hover the mouse over the header text.**

   The paragraph text returns to normal and the header text now matches the selection criteria. You can use this approach with any object on screen and make any kind of change desired.

Working with state selectors

There are some situations in which the dynamic state of an object is important in formatting it. For example, an object may have a link associated with it. When the user clicks that link, the state of the link changes to "visited." Using state selectors can help a user determine when goals have been achieved or a particular feature is unavailable (the object is disabled). The following list tells you about state selectors that documents commonly use.

✔ **:link:** Selects all of the unvisited links in a document.

It's common practice to combine state selectors with tag selectors. For example, you may not want to format all unvisited links in a document. The link for an `<img>` tag would most likely be formatted differently from the link for an `<a>` tag. Consequently, you commonly see state selectors as `a:link` where the formatting would affect all of the unvisited anchor links.

✔ **:visited:** Selects all of the visited links in a document.

✔ **:active:** Selects the link that the user currently has selected.

✔ **:empty:** Selects an object that has no content.

✔ **:target:** Selects the target of an object. For example, when the user clicks a link, the target of that link is selected.

✔ **:enabled:** Selects any object that's enabled.

✔ **:disabled:** Selects any object that's disabled.

✔ **:checked:** Selects any object that's checked.

✔ **::selection:** Selects the content that the user has highlighted in some way.

State selectors make it possible to change the appearance of the document to match activities that the user has performed. What this means is that the document becomes more interactive, without requiring any coding on your part. This effect is used in a number of the examples that follow, so you'll get plenty of practice working with state selectors. The following procedure shows one method for working with state selectors.

1. **Copy the** `ExternalCSS.HTML` **and** `ExternalCSS.CSS` **files (created in Chapter 1) to a new folder.**

2. **Open** `ExternalCSS.HTML`.

3. **Type the following code after the existing <p> tag in the file and save the changes to disk.**

```
<a href="#One">Select One</a><br />
<a href="#Two">Select Two</a>
<p id="One">One</p>
<p id="Two">Two</p>
```

This added code provides some state indicators for the example. When you click a link, the target of that link changes state.

3. **Open ExternalCSS.CSS.**

4. **Type the following code after the existing styles and save the changes to disk.**

```
::selection
{
    color: BlueViolet;
    background-color: Plum;
}
::-moz-selection
{
    color: BlueViolet;
    background-color: Plum;
}

:target
{
    border: solid;
    border-width: medium;
    border-color: Red;
    background-color: BlanchedAlmond;
}
```

Notice the use of the special -moz- preface for the second ::selection selector. This is one of your first exposures to browser compatibility issues. In order to make this selector work with Firefox, you must add this second ::-moz-selection selector with the preface.

5. **Reload the test page.**

6. **Select some of the first paragraph text.**

The color of the text and its background change.

7. **Click Select One.**

The paragraph containing One changes its appearance as shown in Figure 2-11.

8. **Click Select Two.**

The paragraph containing Two changes its appearance. The paragraph containing One returns to its original appearance.

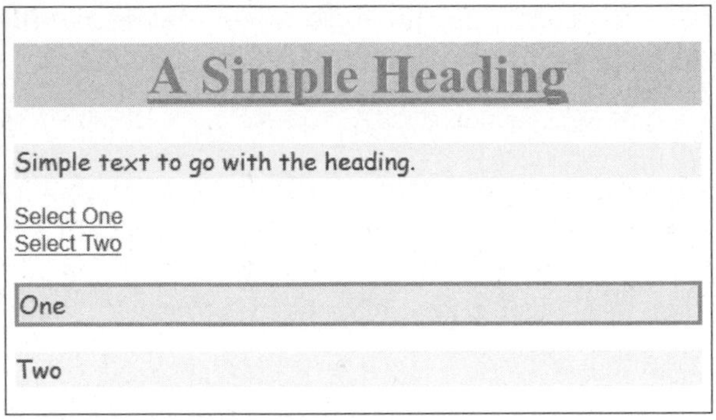

Figure 2-11:
Using a :tar-
get selector
can make it
clear which
link was
clicked.

Understanding Layout Using the Basic Box Model

Everything you view on a page is in a box. That box separates objects from each other and makes it possible to create various special effects. Using boxes makes it possible to position content onscreen, fill various areas with color, and create the sorts of separations that users expect. The following sections discuss the basic box model in more detail.

Viewing the box

The *basic box model* actually relies on a series of four boxes — each of which is placed inside the next. Figure 2-12 shows how these boxes appear and the names associated with each box.

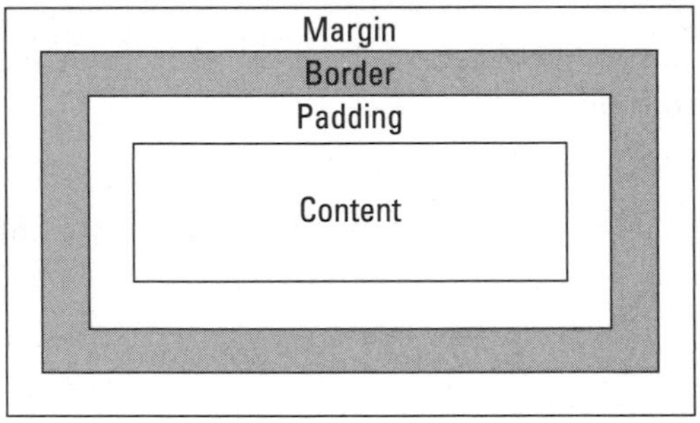

Figure 2-12:
Boxes make
it possible
to format
data in pre-
cisely the
way users
expect.

Each *region* or *box* has a specific purpose. For example, the margin serves to separate the entire boxed region from other boxed regions on the page. Of course, you can set the margin to zero so that there's no separation, but you can provide as much separation as needed to obtain the desired appearance.

Borders serve to provide visual separators between items of content. They are used all the time on web pages. What you may not realize is that each side of a border can be controlled separately. You may choose to display only the right border and not the top, bottom, or left when working on the left pane of a page. The border would end up looking like a line instead of a box.

Padding separates the border from the content, when the border is displayed. Otherwise, the border and content would appear directly next to each other and the content would appear cramped in some cases. This would be a serious problem when you're working with text. On the other hand, you may actually want the border directly next to an image to highlight the image and set it off on a page.

The result of all these regions is that you end up with a content area that's somewhat smaller than the box as a whole unless you eliminate the margin, border, and padding. The content is nestled securely in its box and presents information to the user in a form that's both usable and aesthetically pleasing.

Working with the box model

You've already seen a few examples of the box model in Chapter 1 and in this chapter. The use of a border is one such situation. In addition, setting the margin to zero removes the space between screen elements. All the examples so far have made use of content, but there's no requirement to do so. An object on the page can provide a visual function as well. The following procedure shows a few other ways in which to work with the margin, border, padding, and content used to create the basic box model.

1. **Copy the** `ExternalCSS.HTML` **and** `ExternalCSS.CSS` **files (created in Chapter 1) to a new folder.**

2. **Open** `ExternalCSS.CSS`.

3. **Change the existing styles by adding the code shown in bold:**

```
p
{
    font-family: cursive;
    font-size: large;
    color: #0000ff;
    background-color: #ffff00;
```

```
    border: outset;
    border-width: thick;
    border-radius: 6px;
    margin: 2px;
    padding: 5px;
}

h1
{

    font-family: "Times New Roman",Georgia,serif;
    font-size: 40px;
    text-align: center;
    text-decoration: underline;
    color: #ff0000;
    background-color: #00ffff;

    border-bottom-style: groove;
    border-left-style: ridge;
    border-right-style: ridge;
    border-top-style: groove;
    border-width: 15px;
    border-color: Gray;
    margin: 2px;
    padding: 6px;

}
```

These changes add various special effects to the text. You wouldn't actually use this many different kinds of styles all on one page. It's a bit overwhelming.

Notice that you can make the corners square or rounded. The amount of rounding is specified by the `border-radius` property. The `border-width` and `border` properties both affect the rounding as well. Certain border styles support round corners better than others do.

It's possible to control each border, margin, and padding side individually. This example also shows the effect of combining border styles to create a particular look. In order to combine styles, you must specify each side separately.

4. Type the following code after the existing styles and save the changes to disk.

```
body
{
    border: double;
    border-width: 20px;
    border-color: Blue Red Green Purple;
    margin: 0;
    padding: 20px;
}
```

Many developers forget that the document <body> tag is also an object onscreen — and that its appearance is controllable. This example adds a border around the entire content area. Notice that the border-color property is used to add a different color to each side: top, right, bottom, and left (in that order).

5. **Reload the test page.**

   You see the effect of making the style change as shown in Figure 2-13. As previously mentioned, you'd never use this many styles together, except in an example for comparison purposes.

Figure 2-13:
Using borders, margins, and padding to create an interesting effect.

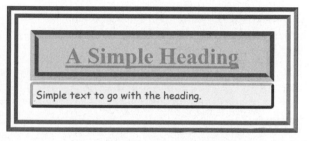

Designing Backgrounds

Most pages you look at have some sort of background. For example, vendor sites normally display pictures of the kinds of products they create or industries in which they participate. Other sites use other kinds of graphics to portray the overall feeling of the site at a glance. The following procedure shows how to add a background using CSS.

1. **Copy the** ExternalCSS.HTML **and** ExternalCSS.CSS **files (created in Chapter 1) to a new folder.**

2. **Create or obtain a background image in Joint Photographic Experts Group (JPEG) format and name it** Background.JPG.

   The downloadable source for this chapter includes a Background.JPG file for your use.

3. **Open ExternalCSS.CSS.**

4. **Type the following code after the existing styles and save the changes to disk.**

```
body
{
    background-image: url("Background.JPG");
    background-size: 100%;
    background-repeat: no-repeat;
}
```

The most common place to book background images is in the <body>. However, nothing prevents you from using backgrounds in other objects and in various other ways. The starting point for most backgrounds is the background-image property where you can specify the image you want to use with the url() method. It's possible to add multiple images to the background. If you do so, the browser combines the images into a single presentation.

The use of the background-size property determines how large the image appears onscreen. The example is a large picture, so you want it to take up the entire display area. Using 100% as the value means that the image automatically resizes to take up the entire client area.

You use the background-repeat property to determine whether the image repeats in the background. It's common for small images to repeat so they take up the entire display area. Repeating a large image tends to make the background look confusing and detract from the overall appearance of the display.

5. **Reload the test page.**

You see the effect of making the style change (as shown in Figure 2-14).

6. **Resize the browser window.**

You see that the background image automatically resizes to take up the entire display area.

Figure 2-14:
The for-
matting
changes
create pat-
terns in the
output.

Chapter 3

Working with Fonts and Colors

The first two chapters of this book introduce fonts and colors. You can't really create a page without these two features. What you've seen so far are some practical ways to use both fonts and color to create a basic page. Of course, there's always more to the picture than just the basics. This chapter extends your knowledge and helps you understand some interesting things you can do with both fonts and color.

Part of jazzing up a page effectively is knowing what to avoid and why you should avoid it. Instead of giving you a designer's knowledge of the topic, this chapter provides some useful tips that developers should know when working with pages. The third-party libraries that you work with later in the book tend to enforce these guidelines automatically, but you still need to know why these guidelines are in place.

The final part of this chapter deals with aural style sheets. The idea of *hearing* a page and then being able to speak to it were originally intended to help those with special needs. *Aural* technology includes the ideas of both hearing and comprehending the content on a page.

 The technology was designed not only for those who lack the ability to see, but also for those who have low vision capability or even cognitive requirements where hearing works better than reading. Today aural style sheets are gaining a significant new focus. For example, they come into play when working through turn-by-turn GPS instructions while driving a car. In fact, any task that requires hands-free operation while keeping the eyes focused somewhere else benefits from this sort of technology. As a developer, you'll be called on more often to provide some sort of aural and speech technology as a part of the pages you design.

Using Fonts

Text, as an abstract presentation of concrete concepts, ideas, and objects, requires fonts for presentation. The font chosen for the text often does as much to convey an idea as the text itself. Spend some time looking at greeting cards and you find that the purveyors of these missives use fonts to present the message in unique ways. A soft font accompanies a romantic message; a comical font helps us laugh at a funny message. The goal of this chapter isn't to provide you with a full history of font usage; you can find online sources such as `www.onextrapixel.com/2011/12/13/the-psychology-of-fonts/` that look at the psychology behind using a font. However, the following list does help you understand the standard CSS properties at your disposal for obtaining access to fonts and using them on a page (in your own pages, make sure you use the capitalization shown):

- `font-family`: Defines the name of the font. There are three font classifications typically used as part of CSS (and most CSS pages use all three unless you also specify the `src` property):

  - `Specific`: Provides a precise presentation wherever it's used. For example, when you specify Arial as a font, you know that it will have a specific presentation everywhere you use it. A specific font must be installed on a system or the browser will ignore it.

  - `Web safe`: This is a font type that provides a less-precise presentation but is more likely to appear on the user's machine. What you're actually requesting is one of several fonts that have similar appearances. The presentation is often close enough to the original that the user won't even notice.

  - `Generic`: A non-specific font that fits a general description of a type of font. Such font names include cursive, fantasy, monospace, sans-serif, and serif. What you actually end up seeing onscreen may not convey much of the original message at all, but these selections are guaranteed to work on every platform.

- `font-size`: Determines the size of the font when compared to other fonts on the page, or provides a specific font size. You can use one of these techniques for defining the font size:

  - `Specific size`: As with most CSS objects, you can specify an exact size for a font, using pixels, ems, or some other absolute or relative measurement. (The "Defining the CSS Units of Measure" section of Chapter 1 has details.)

  - `Percentage`: Defines the size of a font as a percentage of a parent element's font size. Specifying a size above `100%` increases the font size, specifying a value below `100%` decreases the font size.

- • Keyword: Specifies the font size using relative terms: xx-small, x-small, small, medium, large, x-large, xx-large, smaller, larger, and inherit (where the font size is inherited from the parent).

✔ font-style: Determines the style of font that the browser creates. The browser must support the style and the font must supply the style in order for this property to take effect. The font style keywords are: normal, italic, oblique (normally a stronger italic), and inherit.

✔ font-variant: Specifies whether the font should be presented in a variant form. Not all browsers and fonts support this feature. The keywords for this property are normal, small-caps, and inherit.

✔ font-weight: Determines the relative darkness of the font and the width of its strokes. There are two methods for defining the font weight:

- • Numeric: A value specifying the relative weight of the font where a value of 400 is normal and 700 is bold. The numeric values are: 100, 200, 300, 400, 500, 600, 700, 800, and 900. In most cases, you must use the numbers precisely as specified here — a browser may ignore a value of 150.

- • Keyword: Specifies the font weight using relative terms: normal, bold, bolder, lighter, and inherit.

Understanding Web Safe Fonts

Fonts provided as part of a graphic image never have any sort of restriction associated with them because the browser displays the text as an image and not as text. When working with actual text, you need to consider how the text is used and what conditions affect its presentation. Three factors come into play when using standard CSS methodologies to work with fonts:

✔ The browser must support the fonts you want to use.

✔ The font must appear on the user's system or you must find some method for downloading the font to the user's system.

✔ The font must be compatible with the user's platform.

This all means you can't be sure that any font choice you make will actually work unless the font is described in some standard or if the browser vendor has agreed to support the font by convention. This is where Web safe fonts come into play. Web safe fonts are guaranteed to work on any platform — and with any browser — that supports CSS. Consequently, when you use Web safe fonts, you can be certain that the user will see text presented in a manner similar to what you had originally intended. The following sections discuss Web safe fonts in more detail.

Using standard Web safe functionality

Hundreds of different devices use the Internet to access information. When you run a public site, you can't be guaranteed that a user will have any particular device. It's quite likely that your site will see use from all sorts of devices — everything from desktops to smartphones. People with Internet-equipped televisions and other personal electronics will also access your site. With this broad diversity of devices, you need to use `Web safe` fonts — those guaranteed to work on the Internet — when creating an application.

Actually, there's no one `Web safe` font for every platform unless you want to use the most generic font types. Developers want to maintain a certain appearance, so it's important to include specific fonts first, and then fallback fonts that are less specific. Using this approach ensures that everyone will be able to see your page as you originally intended to present it, at least to some degree. When you're working with a generic font, its appearance will vary slightly. With this in mind, here's a list of `Web safe` *serif* fonts (whose characters use a line to finish the main stroke of each character, such as the lines that appear under the main lines of an M); the most-specific font appears first and the least-specific font appears last.

- ✔ `Georgia, serif`
- ✔ `"Palatino Linotype", "Book Antiqua", Palatino, serif`
- ✔ `"Times New Roman" Times, serif`

Each of these fonts has a slightly different feel, but sometimes the best you can do is a simple serif font — the last choice in each list. The following list describes common *sans-serif* fonts (those whose characters lack serifs). Again, the most specific font appears first and the least specific appears last.

- ✔ `Arial, Helvetica, sans-serif`
- ✔ `"Arial Black" Gadget, sans-serif`
- ✔ `"Comic Sans MS", cursive, sans-serif`
- ✔ `Impact Charcoal, sans-serif`
- ✔ `"Lucida Sans Unicode" "Lucida Grande", sans-serif`
- ✔ `Tahoma Geneva, sans-serif`
- ✔ `"Trebuchet MS" Helvetica, sans-serif`
- ✔ `Verdana Geneva, sans-serif`

The last group of fonts is for monospace type, where each letter takes up precisely the same amount of space (as did the output of older typewriters). Monospace fonts are normally used for application code, but you can use them anywhere you want to create the appearance of the typewritten page as well. The following list presents common monospace fonts with the most-specific first and the least-specific last.

✔ `"Courier New" Courier, monospace`

✔ `"Lucida Console" Monaco, monospace`

These are common fonts. However, you might find that you want to use something a little less common. Fortunately, there are sites where you can see lists of accepted fonts. In fact, the CSS Font Stack (`http://cssfontstack.com/`) makes it easy to select a font by seeing how it looks first and then clicking a single button to copy the required code to the clipboard. For example, when you click on Arial at that site, what you actually get is `font-family: Arial, "Helvetica Neue", Helvetica, sans-serif;`. You might also want to look at sites such as WebDesignDev (`www.webdesigndev.com/web-development/16-gorgeous-web-safe-fonts-to-use-with-css`) and Vision {Widget} (`http://visionwidget.com/web-safe-fonts.html`).

Using .WOFF fonts

The CSS3 standard includes a new method for defining fonts using the `@font-face` style. The new method has a number of advantages, including the ability to use specific terms to define the font you want to use. In addition, this standard obviates the need to use `Web safe` fonts by considering every font to be `Web safe`. However, the browser must actually support the `@font-face` style — and many don't. An additional departure from standard CSS support is that you must provide certain properties for this style to work — even in browsers that support it. The following list describes the required and optional properties and the values you provide for them:

✔ `font-family` (required): Specifies the name of the font as provided by the source file (described with the `src` property). The font name is always specific when you're working with CSS3 techniques.

✔ `src` (required): Specifies the source of a font to download. Adding this property means that you aren't quite as limited on the fonts you can use because when a browser that supports this property sees that the font isn't available on the user's machine, it downloads the font from the source you specify. The problem, of course, is figuring out which browsers support what file formats. The following list describes the common file formats and which browsers support them.

  • `.WOFF` (Web Open Font Format): This is the preferred file format for browser-based applications because it enjoys broad support amongst browsers and across platforms. Of the most popular browsers, Internet Explorer 9+, Firefox, Chrome, Safari, and Opera all support `.WOFF` files.

- `.TTF` (TrueType Font): This is the preferred file format when you target Mac and Windows systems because these systems are apt to contain a large number of these files already. The Internet Explorer, Firefox, Chrome, Safari, and Opera browsers all support these font types. Some Linux systems do have a `.TTF` counterpart called FreeType that may work with `.TTF` files, but support is spotty at best (see www.freetype.org/freetype2/ for details).

- `.OTF` (OpenType Font): This is the successor to the `.TTF` standard. A problem with this file format is that it's newer and less supported than `.TTF` files. Generally, you find this file format only on Windows systems, despite the fact that it's marketed as cross-platform. Newer versions of the Internet Explorer, Firefox, Chrome, Safari, and Opera browsers all support these font types.

- `.SVG` (Scalable Vector Graphics): Most people associate these file types with graphics and animation. It's also possible to create fonts using this technology. However, only the Chrome, Safari, and Opera browsers support these fonts.

- `.EOT` (Embedded OpenType): In the interest of speed, Microsoft has created a compact version of the `.OTF` specification. However, only Internet Explorer 9+ supports this file type. It's really not a good option unless you're working exclusively with a newer version of Windows where it's guaranteed that the user has updated the operating system and browser regularly.

✔ `font-stretch` (optional): Specifies whether the font should be modified in any way to address specific special effects and host platform needs. The default setting is to present the font as it normally appears. However, you can also rely on these keywords to stretch the font in specific ways: `normal`, `condensed`, `ultra-condensed`, `extra-condensed`, `semi-condensed`, `expanded`, `semi-expanded`, `extra-expanded`, and `ultra-expanded`.

✔ `font-style` (optional): Determines the style of font that the browser creates. The browser must support the style and the font must supply the style in order for this property to take effect. The `font-style` keywords are `normal`, `italic`, `oblique` (normally a stronger italic), and inherit.

✔ `font-weight` (optional): Specifies the darkness of the font. However, you have fewer options in this case than when working with standard font definitions (see the "Using Fonts" section of the chapter). Your choices in this case are `normal`, `bold`, `100`, `200`, `300`, `400`, `500`, `600`, `700`, `800`, and `900`.

✔ `unicode-range` (optional): Defines the range of characters that the font supports. The default setting is `"U+0-10FFFF"`, which supports 1,114,111 different character combinations.

The new CSS3 method of supporting fonts generally works well with newer browsers on desktop, laptop, and tablet platforms. If your users also want to access the page using smartphones, you'll start to find that support is lacking — and that the page may appear in a plain font that won't serve your needs. Considerable testing for this problem is required when you're working with smartphones. A public site that has visitors using televisions and other personal electronics probably won't have much success using this new technique. In this case, use the older approach that uses `Web safe` fonts (described in the "Using standard Web safe functionality" section of this chapter).

Producing Text Effects

Text effects make text look dressy — give it emphasis and convey unspoken messages to the viewer. You've already seen a few text effects, such as bold and italics. Even the selection of a `font-family` is a kind of effect. However, you can do more to add effects to the fonts you use. The first approach is to decorate the text to convey additional meaning — and this approach works everywhere. The second approach is to actually add special effects, but this approach only works with systems that fully support CSS3. The following sections discuss both approaches.

Using the safe text decorations

The only safe text effect is the use of the `text-decoration` property to define the addition of a characteristic to the font. This property works everywhere, so you don't need to worry whether someone viewing your page on a television or using a smartphone will get your message. The following list describes the sorts of text decoration you can perform.

- ✔ `none`: Removes any text decoration that might already be in place.
- ✔ `underline`: Places a line under the text.
- ✔ `overline`: Places a line over the top of the text.
- ✔ `line-through`: Places a line through the text (often used to mark deletions).

- ✔ `blink`: Causes the text to blink. This particular feature is unsafe. People who have certain physical issues, such as photosensitive epilepsy (see `www.epilepsysociety.org.uk/aboutepilepsy/what isepilepsy/triggers/photosensitiveepilepsy`), could have a seizure just from viewing your page. Mind you, this effect isn't limited to those who have photosensitive epilepsy; it's been documented for other people as well (read www.ncbi.nlm.nih.gov/pmc/articles/ PMC1028775/ as an example). In fact, the only reason this book documents this particular feature is to help you avoid it. Blinking text isn't just annoying; it can have significant nasty side effects.

✔ inherit: Uses whatever decoration is employed with the parent element.

It isn't possible to combine text decoration effects. For example, if you try to combine an underline with an overline, you won't see either effect onscreen because the browser will be confused. In addition, text decoration effects won't appear in places where there's no text.

Adding the CSS3 text effects

Just being able to decorate the text doesn't offer much in the way of pizzazz; most people want a lot more, especially in this age of self-published works of all sorts. A CSS3 site can make use of a significant number of new effects, in addition to simple text decorations. Of course, the tradeoff is that you must know that the viewer has the required support — which means using newer browsers on a limited number of platforms. A few text effects are part of the specification, but so far remain unsupported by any browser — these entries are marked as such — and you shouldn't use them until the browser vendors catch up. The following list describes the special text effects that you can create using CSS3.

✔ hanging-punctuation (currently unsupported): Specifies whether punctuation can appear outside the start or end of a line of text when the text would otherwise need to be wrapped. Acceptable values are

- none: The punctuation can't appear outside the box. For more on how page content appears within the box, see Chapter 2.

- first: Punctuation can appear outside the box on the first line.

- last: Punctuation can appear on the outside of the box on the last line.

- allow-end: Punctuation can appear outside the box on any line if the punctuation wouldn't ordinarily fit after the text is justified.

- force-end: Punctuation can appear outside the box on any line. If the line is justified, the browser will force the punctuation to land outside the box.

✔ punctuation-trim (currently unsupported): Specifies whether punctuation is trimmed when it appears outside the start of the end of a line of text when the text would otherwise need to be wrapped. Acceptable values are

- `none`: The punctuation isn't trimmed.

- `first`: Trim any hanging punctuation on the first line.

- `last`: Trim any hanging punctuation on the last line.

- `allow-end`: Trim the punctuation on any line where it wouldn't fit after the line is justified.

- `adjacent`: Trim some types of punctuation that appears at the beginning, middle, or end of a line when the punctuation appears next to a full-width character.

✔ `text-align-last` (currently unsupported): Describes how to align the last line of text when the paragraph relies on a justified margin. Acceptable values are:

- `auto`: Relies on the value of the text-align property.

- `start`: Aligned to the start of the line, which depends on the direction the text is laid out (left-to-right or right-to-left).

- `end`: Aligned to the end of the line, which depends on the direction the text is laid out (left-to-right or right-to-left).

- `left`: Always aligned to the left side of the box (regardless of text direction).

- `right`: Always aligned to the right side of the box (regardless of text direction).

- `center`: Contents are centered within the text box.

- `justify`: Context are justified within the text box.

✔ `text-emphasis` (currently unsupported): Sets the `text-emphasis-style` and `text-emphasis-color` properties in a single call.

✔ `text-justify` (Internet Explorer only): Determines the alignment and spacing of text that has been marked as *justified* (where the right and left side of the text are even, rather than jagged). Acceptable values are

- `auto`: The browser determines the method in which text is justified.

- `inter-word`: Word spacing is used to justify the text.

- `inter-ideograph`: Symbol spacing is used to justify the text (spaces between words aren't counted). This setting is normally used with the Double-Byte Character Sets (DBCS) used with languages that rely on characters other than those used by Roman-alphabet languages such as English.

- `inter-cluster`: Only text that naturally lacks whitespace (such as material written in an Asian language) is justified.

- • `distribute`: Justification follows the model used by newspapers, except that the last line isn't justified when working with East Asian languages such as Thai.

- • `kashida`: Justification is accomplished by elongating individual characters.

- • `trim`: Justification is accomplished by shortening the amount of whitespace between letters.

- • `none`: Disable any form of justification.

✔ `text-outline` (currently unsupported): Creates an outline that follows the contours of the target character. The property supports three values:

- • `thickness`: The width of the outline.

- • `blur`: The radius of the outline.

- • `color`: The color used to create the outline.

✔ `text-overflow`: Defines the action that will take place when the text overflows the box used to contain it. Acceptable values are

- • `clip`: Removes any extra text.

- • `ellipsis`: Displays an ellipsis to show there's additional text.

- • *String*: Displays the specified string value to show there's additional text.

✔ `text-shadow`: Displays a shadow of the target characters at the same width as the target character. The positioning, strength, and color of the shadow are determined by the following properties:

- • `h-shadow`: Determines the horizontal positioning of the shadow.

- • `v-shadow`: Determines the vertical positioning of the shadow.

- • `blur`: Specifies the clarity of the shadow text. Using a value of `0` means that the shadow text has the same clarity as the original text.

- • `color`: Defines the color used to create the outline.

✔ `text-wrap` (currently unsupported): Determines how text is wrapped within the containing box. Acceptable values are

- • `none`: The text overflows the containing box when it's too long.

- • `normal`: Text is broken between words or other white space.

- • `unrestricted`: Text is broken between any two characters.

- • `suppress`: The browser can only break lines if there are no other valid places to break a line within the paragraph. The specification is unclear as to where the break will take place, but the assumption is that it will occur between words or in some other white space.

✔ word-break (no Opera support): Determines how text is wrapped within a containing box when working with a non-CJK (Chinese-Japanese-Korean) language. Acceptable values are

- normal: Break the text using the browser's standard rules, which normally means between words or other white space.

- break-all: Break the text between any two characters.

- hyphenate: Break the text at natural hyphenation points, between words, or in some other white space.

✔ word-wrap: Determines how text is broken and then wrapped to the next line in a containing box when working with a non-CJK language. Acceptable values are

- normal: Break words using the browser's standard rules, which normally means at natural hyphenation points.

- break-word: Allow breaking of words that normally don't allow breaking.

Adding Colors

Color is an essential component of most pages because color conveys emotion. Look at a red element and you might instantly think about danger. A yellow element might seem light and friendly. Green could signal peaceful conditions or nature. In short, color helps get your message across in ways that other elements on the page might not.

It's essential to choose colors carefully. For one thing, not everyone has the same level of natural color perception; colors that are too close to each other can prove difficult to see. Another issue is that about 8 percent of the male population and ½ percent of the female population is colorblind, which means that they can't easily see certain colors. For them, the colors appear shifted to other colors — red and green, for example, could look like brown. Always check your color combinations by using an application designed for the purpose or a site such as VisCheck (www.vischeck.com/vischeck/vischeck Image.php). The article telling how various forms of color blindness work at www.vischeck.com/examples/ is especially helpful.

Understanding how CSS colors work

CSS provides three methods you can use to define the color of any object: color value, color name, or hexadecimal value. (Chapters 1 and 2 introduce these techniques.) It doesn't matter to CSS — or to the browser — which form of color definition you use; choose the method that works best for you. It's important that you do not change techniques in a single style sheet; use the same color definition method consistently.

Most devices today can display millions of colors. In fact, the devices we use can display more colors than most of us can actually see. However, some devices are still limited in their ability to display color. When you're targeting a device with limited color capability, you need to rely on the Web safe color palette shown at www.techbomb.com/websafe/. Using this color palette makes CSS less likely to do problematic things like dither the colors so the viewer sees an unfortunate mix that may not look anything like the color choice you intended.

Using the Web safe color palette ensures that the viewer will see the color you intended — at least for the most part. There are some situations where a device supports some number of levels of gray and the viewer isn't going to see color at all. It's important to avoid using color alone to refer to objects onscreen; you can't be certain that the viewer can see the color. Instead, label objects and refer to the object's name as needed.

Using color values

The examples in the book have focused on Red Green Blue (RGB) color values. However, CSS actually supports a number of color value systems. The only requirement is that the browser also supports the color system. Here are the color systems that most browsers support:

- ✔ **Red Green Blue (RGB):** Use the rgb() method when describing this color value that uses three numbers between 0 and 255 to specify the amount of red, green, and blue to use.

- ✔ **Red Green Blue Alpha channel (RGBA):** Use the rgba() method when describing this color value. The first three numbers are simply red, green, and blue. The fourth number, *alpha channel* (relative transparency), is a value between 0.0 (fully transparent) and 1.0 (fully opaque). You must have IE9+, Firefox 3+, Chrome, Safari, or Opera 10+ to use this color value scheme.

- ✔ **Hue Saturation Lightness (HSL):** Use the hsl() method when describing this color value that consists of three numbers. *Hue* is a value between 0 and 360 that describes the position of a color on the color wheel: red is 0 (or 360), green is 120, and blue is 240. *Saturation* (the color intensity or darkness) is a percentage value between 0 (gray scale) and 100 (full color). Lightness is a percentage between 0 (black) and 100 (white).

✔ **Hue Saturation Lightness Alpha channel (HSLA):** Use the `hsla()` method when describing this color value that uses the same first three numbers as an HSL value. The fourth number, alpha channel, is a value between 0.0 (fully transparent) and 1.0 (fully opaque). You must have IE9+, Firefox 3+, Chrome, Safari, or Opera 10+ to use this color value scheme.

Trying to understand how color values interact can be hard. The color mixer at `www.w3schools.com/tags/ref_colormixer.asp` helps you see how various color choices interact, making it easier to choose good color combinations.

Using color names

For many people, the easiest way to manage colors is to specify a color name. There are 17 standard color names that will work on any browser, even when that browser displays only shades of gray: `aqua`, `black`, `blue`, `fuchsia`, `gray`, `green`, `lime`, `maroon`, `navy`, `olive`, `orange`, `purple`, `red`, `silver`, `teal`, `white`, and `yellow`. Use these color names when you must ensure the user's ability to see the difference between colors under any circumstance.

There are 130 additional color names that will work on any systems that can display them. The most accurate listing of all 147 color names (17 standard and 130 additional) appears at `www.w3schools.com/cssref/css_color names.asp`. This site also makes it possible to display various shades of the colors so you can mix and match color choices. Most importantly, you obtain access to the color's precise hexadecimal value so that you can tweak your color choices as needed.

You can find these colors displayed in a number of places online, but one of the more interesting places to view them is at `www.crockford.com/wrrrld/color.html`. Choosing a color displays that color outside the table. Selecting another color will add the color in the inner tier, while the first choice moves out one position. This site makes it relatively easy to compare various colors to see how they look with each other.

Using hexadecimal values for color

You define a hexadecimal value for a color by preceding the value with a hash sign (#), followed by three hexadecimal color values (red, green, and blue). For example, `#000000` is black, `#ff0000` is red, `#00ff00` is green, and `#0000ff` is blue. Many developers see this method as the most accurate and concise for creating colors. However, the results of using hexadecimal color values aren't really any different from those of the other techniques described in this section. (If you really like using hexadecimal values and need a good color picker for a Windows system, try the Color Cop color picker at `http://colorcop.net/`.)

Understanding Aural Style Sheets

Aural style sheets make it possible for users who rely on screen readers and other voice-driven technology to make better use of your site. You won't actually hear anything when your site is using an aural style sheet unless you have a screen reader enabled. In fact, without a screen reader, the aural style sheet won't seem to be in place at all. The aural style sheet offers cues to the screen reader that specify how to read the text on your site — and also provides hints about how to convert information to textual form.

Many operating systems today include a relatively basic screen reader as part of the product; you can enable this screen reader to test your aural style sheets. For example, Windows offers a screen reader as part of its accessibility features — and you'll find that the Mac has VoiceOver installed for the same purpose. However, most people who actually rely on screen readers use something a bit more robust, such as Jaws (`www.freedomscientific.com/products/fs/jaws-product-page.asp`). You can see a list of screen readers at `http://en.wikipedia.org/wiki/List_of_screen_readers`.

Creating an aural style sheet is precisely the same as creating any other CSS style sheet. You define aural styles for various objects by using exactly the same selectors as you use for creating visual effects. Aural style sheets do have their own set of properties, however, as described in the following list:

- ✔ `azimuth`: Defines the horizontal source of the sound. The acceptable values are:

    - *angle*: A value between 0 and 360 that determines the actual angle.

    - Keyword: `left-side`, `far-left`, `left`, `center-left`, `center`, `center-right`, `right`, `far-right`, `right-side`, `behind`, `leftwards`, or `rightwards`.

- ✔ `cue-after`: Specifies a sound to make after the content is read. You can use a value of `none` or provide a specific URL for a sound source.

- ✔ `cue-before`: Specifies a sound to make before the content is read. You can use a value of `none` or provide a specific URL for a sound source.

- ✔ `elevation`: Defines the vertical source of the sound. The acceptable values are

    - *angle*: A value between 0 and 360 that determines the actual angle.

    - Keyword: `below`, `level`, `above`, `higher`, or `lower`.

- ✔ `pause-after`: Specifies how long to pause after reading the content. You can provide a numeric value in seconds or a percentage based on the length of the content.

✔ pause-before: Specifies how long to pause before reading the content. You can provide a numeric value in seconds or a percentage based on the length of the content.

This setting is often used to provide cues about punctuation. For example, you'd provide a longer pause for an em dash or semicolon than you would for a space.

✔ pitch: Determines the frequency of the speaking voice. The acceptable values are

- *frequency*: The frequency of the speaking voice in hertz.

- Keyword: x-low, low, medium, high, or x-high.

✔ pitch-range: Determines the amount of modulation in the spoken voice where a value of 0 is monotone. Higher values produce more animation in the voice.

✔ play-during: Specifies a sound to make while the content is read (possibly background music or some other accompaniment. The acceptable values are

- none: Suppresses sound while reading the content.

- *url*: The location of the sound source to play.

- Keyword: auto, mix, or repeat.

✔ richness: Determines the depth of the spoken voice where a value of 0 is a thin voice and higher values make the voice deeper, more resonant.

✔ speak: Specifies how to speak the content. The acceptable values are

- normal: The content is spoken as words.

- none: The content isn't spoken at all.

- spell-out: The individual characters of the content are spoken, such as when handling abbreviations (where individual letters are spoken). For example, you'd use this setting for W3C (World Wide Web Consortium).

- Acronyms are always spoken as words, so you'd use the normal setting. For example, you'd use the spell-out setting for ACID (Atomic, Consistent, Independent, and Durable).

✔ speak-header: Indicates whether the readers should speak the heading for each cell as the individual cells are read. The acceptable values are:

- always: The headers are read for each cell, whether or not the heading has changed.

- once: The headers are only read once for each cell.

- ✔ speak-numeral: Determines how the reader handles numeric values. The acceptable values are
    - digits: The individual numbers are read, such as one, two, three for 123.
    - continuous: The number is read as a unit, such as one hundred twenty three for 123.

- ✔ speak-punctuation: Determines how the reader handles punctuation. The acceptable values are:
    - none: The reader doesn't do anything special with punctuation. Some higher end readers will add pauses automatically to match the differences in punctuation, such as using a longer pause for an em dash or semicolon.
    - code: The reader tells the viewer what punctuation appears in the content. This would be especially important when reading content such as source code, where punctuation is especially important or takes on atypical meanings.

- ✔ speech-rate: Indicates how fast the reader should read the content. The main reason to use this value is for emphasis or to make especially difficult passages clearer. The acceptable values are
    - *number*: A number indicating the speed in Syllables Per Minute (SPM). Some sources use Words Per Minute (WPM), but the rate is more along the lines of syllables per minute, with longer words taking longer to say.
    - Keyword: x-slow (80 SPM), slow (120 SPM), medium (180 SPM), fast (300 SPM), x-fast (500 SPM), faster (add 40 SPM to current rate), or slower (subtract 40 SPM from current rate).

- ✔ stress: Indicates how much emphasis the reader should place on certain syllables of a word — the higher the numeric value, the greater the amount of emphasis. Most readers pay no attention to this value.

- ✔ voice-family: Defines which voice to use when reading the content. As with fonts, the voice-family can be specific or generic. The most generic voice-family values are male, female, and child. Specific voice-family values require voice files that are supported by the reader.

- ✔ volume: Indicates how loud the reader should read the content. The acceptable values are:
    - *number*: A value between 0 and 100 to indicate absolute volume.
    - %: A percentage between 0 and 100 to indicate a relative increase in volume (with a maximum value of 100).
    - Keyword: silent (a value of 0), x-soft (a value of 0), soft (a value of 25), medium (a value of 50), loud (a value of 75), or x-loud (a value of 100).

Chapter 4

Working with Graphics

Content comes in a number of forms, but the two most common forms are text and graphics. CSS provides a number of methods for dealing with both of these forms. Earlier chapters of this book focused on text. This chapter begins your foray into graphics.

Most developers rely on premade graphics to create sites. So this chapter focuses on the mechanics of working with graphics — the techniques used to present them onscreen, rather than on any design or aesthetic element of graphics. Of course, the starting point for most graphic elements is the `<img>` tag. Even though the `<img>` tag isn't strictly a CSS element, knowing about the tag is essential if you want to use CSS to control the presentation of graphics.

An object can contain any number of foreground images and a single background image. (The background can actually consist of multiple images, but these images are combined into a cohesive whole — you see a composite of the various image elements.) The chapter also discusses techniques for positioning graphics onscreen and using repetitive images to create special effects.

The one artistic technique I discuss in this chapter is the *transformation* because it has a mechanical element to it. Transformations can subtly or radically change the appearance of your image. For the most part, the transformations change the way the image is presented onscreen — the way it's zoomed, rotated, positioned, or skewed. These are the sorts of transformations that the chapter will focus on — nothing of a completely radical nature.

The transformation features of CSS3 can work with any presentation object. For example, you can use transformations with a `<div>` to modify the presentation of text onscreen. It's also possible to use transformations with the `<canvas>` tag to change the appearance of drawn elements. When it comes to transformations, thinking about the box (refer to Chapter 2) is a plus. Any element that consumes space can be transformed in some way.

Understanding the `<img>` Tag

The `<img>` tag has been around for a long time — so long, in fact, that it has picked up a bit of baggage along the way. Developers who think that the `<img>` tag supports certain attributes may be surprised to find that it doesn't — at least not anymore — because those attributes have been *deprecated* (removed) as new HTML versions have appeared on the scene. For example, the `align` attribute isn't available in HTML5 — it was deprecated in HTML4 because CSS already provided good transformation alternatives to the `align` attribute. Unfortunately, one casualty of deprecation, `longdesc`, affects people with special needs, but few sites actually implemented this useful feature anyway. Because you need to know the attributes used with HTML5 in order to work with the examples in this book, the following list provides you with an updated list of attributes that you can use for reference.

✔ `alt`: Provides a textual description of the image for those who can't see it. A screen reader will describe the image to the person. It's important to keep the description short and focused. Even though a picture is worth a thousand words, the viewer likely won't have time to hear them all.

✔ `crossorigin`: Allows usage of images located on another server as specified within an `<img>` tag enclosed in a `<canvas>` tag. The browser will act as if the image is served by the local server, rather than the foreign server. Because the image is on another server, the `src` attribute is normally modified to include additional server details. To use this feature, you must also provide an `origin` HTTP header that describes the location of the server. You can also use JavaScript to access this information (see http://saltybeagle.com/2009/09/cross-origin-resource-sharing-demo/ or https://developer.mozilla.org/en-US/docs/HTML/CORS_Enabled_Image for an example of performing this task). This attribute can have the following values:

   • `anonymous`: The foreign server doesn't require any special login to use the image.

   • `use-credentials`: The foreign server requires a username and password to gain access to the image. The credentials are supplied using a variety of means, including a cookie, x.509 certificate, or HTTP basic authentication.

✔ height: Specifies the height of an image using any supported unit of measure (see Chapter 1 for details).

✔ ismap: Specifies that the image is a server-side map when included (there's no value associated with this attribute). Mapped images can be used to perform all sorts of tasks, such as acting as a site map (redirecting viewers to other places on the site).

✔ src: Defines the source of the image. Normally, this attribute contains a simple URL. When you're working with the crossorigin attribute, however, src takes on new meaning (see the crossorigin attribute entry for details).

✔ usemap: Specifies that the image is a client-side map. You provide the name of the <map> tag to use with the image.

✔ width: Specifies the width of an image using any supported unit of measure (see Chapter 1 for details).

Working with Foreground Images

You may have noticed that there are some interesting attributes missing from the <img> tag in the previous section. For example, it's no longer possible to define a border around your image using the border attribute (see http://www.w3schools.com/tags/tag_img.asp for a discussion of other deprecated attributes). This section of the chapter focuses on the sorts of decoration that you can perform on an image that doesn't include transforming the image in any way (Chapter 5 discusses transforming graphics).

Before you can do anything, you need a basic page to work with. The following procedure gets you started.

1. **Create an image file of any sort that you want to see while working on the example. Give this image file a name of** CuteCat.JPG.

   The downloadable source code includes a sample file containing a 400 × 378 pixel image that you can use. The filename and extension are important because you need a specific name when writing the code.

2. **Create a new HTML5 file with your text editor.**

   Your editor may not support HTML5 files. Any text file will do.

3. **Type the following code for the HTML page.**

```
<!DOCTYPE html>

<html>
```

```
<head>
    <title>Simple Graphics Example</title>
</head>

<body>
    <h1>Interact with an Image </h1>
    <div id="ImageContainer">
        <img alt="A Picture of a Cute Cat."
             title="A Picture of a Cute Cat."
             name="CuteCat"
             id="CuteCat"
             src="CuteCat.JPG" />
    </div>
</body>
</html>
```

This example displays a heading and an associated picture. The page looks like the one shown in Figure 4-1 when you use the image supplied with the downloadable source code.

Interact with an Image

Figure 4-1:
Create a
page that
contains an
image that
you'll work
with in the
sections
that follow.

4. **Save the file as SimpleGraphics.HTML.**

The sample will appear in other chapters, so naming is important.

Now that you have a page to work with, it's time to try interacting with the image. The following sections discuss some common tasks you perform.

Creating a border

One of the more common changes you can make to an image is to add a border. This sets off the image from the other content on the page. Of course, CSS offers a broad range of border types. The trick is to get the border to display around the image in such a way that you can perform other tasks with that border later. That's where the <div> in the HTML code comes into play. It provides a container that can hold all sorts of things (such as the <div> used as a container for the <img> tag shown in the previous example) — and you can interact with that container in various ways. The following procedure helps you add a border around the image.

1. **Create a new CSS file with your text editor.**

   Your editor may not support CSS files. Any text file will do.

2. **Type the following CSS style information.**

   ```
   #ImageContainer
   {
       border-style: groove;
       border-width: thick;
       border-color: gray;
       padding: 5px;
       float: left;
   }
   ```

   The majority of this style information is about the border. Adding padding to the border makes it stick out more like a frame. The float value keeps the <div> around the image, rather than having it follow the right side of the browser, when a user resizes the browser window.

    If you want the image on the right side of the page, rather than the left, substitute float: right;. The entire container, image included, will reside on the right side of the page, rather than the left. As the user changes the browser window, the image will remain the same size, but it will move with the right side of the browser window.

3. **Save the file as** SimpleGraphics.CSS.

   The sample will appear in other chapters, so naming is important.

4. **Add the following code to the** <head> **area of the HTML file.**

   ```
   <link rel="stylesheet" href="SimpleGraphics.CSS" />
   ```

   This code creates the link between the HTML file and the CSS file.

5. **Save the HTML file and reload the page.**

   You see the border shown in Figure 4-2.

Interact with an Image

Figure 4-2:
Create a
page that
contains an
image with
a border
that you'll
work with in
the sections
that follow.

Centering the image

One of the most commonly asked questions is how to center an image on the page. Unfortunately, most of the answers you receive discuss just the `<img>` tag, without showing how to center a container. Using a container is important because you may want to add other items to that image later. The following procedure tells how to center the image.

1. **Add the following style to the** `SimpleGraphics.CSS` **file.**

```
#ImageContainer img
{
    height: 400px;
    width: 400px;
    margin: 0px;
}
```

The purpose of this style is to create an image of a specific size. There are a number of ways to deal with images of various sizes. This is one of them. It works well when most of your images are about the same size.

In some cases, such as when you're centering images of widely different sizes, you must resort to using JavaScript. In order to place an image in the center of the page, you must know the size of the image. Many third-party libraries make it easy for you to center images onscreen — the CSS-only technique does have limits.

2. Add the following code to the `#ImageContainer` **style.**

```
position: absolute;
height: 400px;
width: 400px;
left: 50%;
margin-left: -205px;
```

This code sets the `<div>` position as absolute and gives it the same size as the image, so that the `<div>` and `<img>` tags are linked. It then places the left side of the `<div>` 50% across the page, so that no matter how the user changes the browser window, the left side of the `<div>` will remain center. Of course, you don't want to center the left side of the `<div>` — you want to center the image. The `margin-left` setting moves the left margin 205 pixels to the left (half the overall size of the image, plus the padding), so that the center of the image is now in the center of the page.

3. Save the CSS file and reload the page.

You see the image and its frame centered on the page as shown in Figure 4-3.

Interact with an Image

Figure 4-3:
The image
is now
centered on
the page.

Adding a caption

You might be wondering what sort of content could go with an <img> tag. You could add buttons, say, to move from one image to another in a gallery. However, it's more common to add a caption so that people looking at the site have some idea of what the image is all about. The following procedure describes how to add a caption to the image.

1. **Add the following tag (in bold) to the** <div> **found in the** SimpleGraphics.HTML **file and save the file.**

```
<div id="ImageContainer">
    <img alt="A Picture of a Cute Cat."
        title="A Picture of a Cute Cat."
        name="CuteCat"
        id="CuteCat"
        src="CuteCat.JPG" />
    <p>A picture of a cute cat!</p>
</div>
```

2. **Add the following style to the** SimpleGraphics.CSS **file.**

```
#ImageContainer p
{
    text-align: center;
    height: 20px;
    width: 400px;
    margin: 0px;
}
```

It's possible to add any amount of text formatting desired. However, you must provide a text element of a specific size or else the border might appear in a place other than where you'd like it to appear.

3. **Modify the** #ImageContainer height **property to accommodate the new text element. The property should look like this:**

```
height: 420px;
```

Any time you add new features to the container, you must resize the container to hold them. The original container size was 400 pixels. You've added 20 pixels worth of text, so the new size is 420px.

4. **Save the CSS file and reload the page.**

The image now includes a caption as shown in Figure 4-4.

Interact with an Image

A picture of a cute cat!

Figure 4-4:
Adding a
caption
makes the
intent of
the image
clearer.

Adding Background Images

Background images add flavor to a site. People may not think users pay much attention to them, but the right background image can have a major impact on your site. Working with background images is a little different from foreground images. For one thing, there's normally only one background image for any given object on the site and the background image is usually limited to the main object, which is the body of the page.

The background should be pleasing, but should not detract from the content in the foreground. A good background image adds flavor to a site — some background images are quite targeted, but most merely suggest the overall theme of the site. In fact, some backgrounds are simply patterns and have no real meaning by themselves. The following sections discuss various techniques you can use to interact with background images.

Using CSS alone

There are a number of ways to create a background for your page using CSS alone. The easiest method is to simply define a background color. Of course, having just a single background color would be boring. However, you see sites that use a simple background color as a palette for adding content — and it does work.

Another technique is to provide a frame for the entire page. You create a border around the <body> tag. A combination of multiple layers and special effects can create amazing border effects for your page. Using borders with other objects increases the number of things you can do with regard to framing effects.

The following sections describe how to create interesting backgrounds using CSS alone. Some of these examples don't work in Internet Explorer 9, but they will work with all newer versions of Chrome, Firefox, and Internet Explorer 10. Incompatibility is one of the issues you face when using techniques like these, but the payoff is also good, so it's important to weigh the costs against the benefits.

Working with linear gradients

Most people will want something a little more exciting than a background color or a frame for their sites. For example, you can rely on a linear-gradient() function to perform the task. Using a linear-gradient(), you can create lines (horizontal, vertical, and angled), diamonds, and squares. When you combine the linear-gradient() with other gradient methods (such as the radial-gradient()) you can create all sorts of patterns (as described later in this section). For now, create a simple linear-gradient() using the following procedure to get a feel for how they work.

1. **Create a new HTML5 file with your text editor.**

2. **Type the following code for the HTML page.**

```
<!DOCTYPE html>

<html>
<head>
    <title>A Non-image Background</title>
    <link rel="stylesheet"
          href="PatternedBackground.CSS" />
</head>

<body>
    <h1>A Simple Heading</h1>
    <p>Simple text to go with the heading.</p>
</body>
</html>
```

The main purpose of this example is to focus on backgrounds, so the content is quite simple. All you see is a simple header and paragraph.

3. **Save the file as** PatternedBackground.HTML.

The sample will appear in other chapters, so naming is important.

4. **Create a new CSS file with your text editor.**

5. **Type the following CSS style information.**

```
body
{
    background: linear-gradient(
        45deg, Crimson, Transparent, RoyalBlue);
    background-color: #00ff00;
    background-size: 100px 100px;
}
```

The focal point of this pattern is the `background` property, which relies on the `linear-gradient()` function. You can use this function in a number of ways; the example shows one simple way. It begins by telling the `linear-gradient()` function to draw the line at 45 degrees. There are three colors in the gradient: `Crimson`, the background color (`Transparent` shows the background), and `RoyalBlue`. The gradient will begin with `Crimson`, transition to the background color, and end with `RoyalBlue`, all in equal proportions.

The `background-color` property defines a value of green in this case. The `background-size` property defines the size of the gradient pattern. It would be easy to obtain a number of different effects using the same `linear-gradient()` and varying these last two properties.

6. **Save the file as** PatternedBackground.CSS.

The sample will appear in other chapters, so naming is important.

7. **Save the HTML file and reload the page.**

You see the background shown in Figure 4-5, which is actually quite dramatic. The background automatically repeats no matter how the user resizes the window.

Figure 4-5:
Using linear-gradients helps you create interesting backgrounds.

 It's possible to combine graphics and gradients to create even more unusual effects without resorting to programming. Simply replace one of the color entries with the URL for a downloadable graphic using the `url()` function. The resulting gradient will combine color, graphics, transparency, and transition effects to create an unusual background for you.

Experimenting with linear gradients

You could work for quite some time trying to figure out which color combinations look best and how best to present your gradient to the world. In addition, you can use more than just two or three colors, so gradients can become complex color undertakings. Gradients can also have special settings, such as controlling the amount of each color to use. Fortunately, there's a fast way to discover the settings to use: the CSS3 Gradient Generator (http://gradients.glrzad.com/) shown in Figure 4-6.

To use the CSS3 Gradient Generator, begin by setting the colors you want to use under Color Swatches. The plus sign (+) next to this heading lets you add more colors. Likewise, the red X button on the slider lets you remove colors, which isn't very obvious. The Gradient Sample shows a color swatch of the selections you've made. The Gradient Direction settings let you create angled and vertical variations of your color swatch. You can also set the kind of color settings to use with the Color Format settings. The result of your manipulations appear in The Code, which you can copy to your editor and use as part of your application.

The CSS3 Gradient Generator is simply a tool that helps you play with colors and angles. It's not always going to produce the final version of your gradient. When you finish working through your selections, you still need to tinker with the settings to ensure that the display is optimal for the user.

Figure 4-6: The CSS3 Gradient Generator helps you experiment with gradients.

Obtaining CSS patterns online

Creating simple effects using gradients is easy. However, creating something truly spectacular takes time and artistic ability. Most developers really don't have the time or skills required to create something dazzling using CSS3 alone (or CSS3 combined with graphics) — that's where designers come into play. Many designers allow you to use their designs. You can find a number of sites with simple examples, such as those found at `http://lea.verou.me/demos/css3-patterns.html`. As you can see in Figure 4-7, these patterns all rely on the CSS `linear-gradient` function.

In order to use these designs, you need to right-click your browser and choose the option for viewing the source code. The designs are all documented in the `<style>` tag that appears at the top of the page. All you need to do is copy the desired design from the page source to your application.

Figure 4-7:
Many sites will provide you with free CSS3 designs you can use as backgrounds.

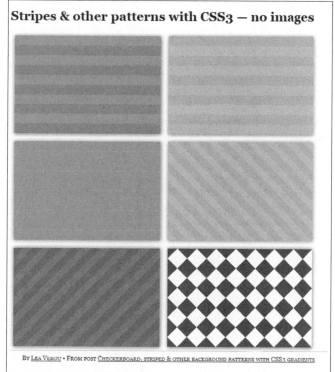

Stripes & other patterns with CSS3 — no images

BY LEA VEROU • FROM POST CHECKERBOARD, STRIPED & OTHER BACKGROUND PATTERNS WITH CSS3 GRADIENTS

The site at `http://lea.verou.me/css3patterns` provides a much larger group of significantly more complex designs, as shown at Figure 4-8. These patterns are all labeled so you know what the designers have named them. Click a pattern and you go to a page with that pattern as a background. In addition, the code for that pattern appears in a window with the pattern. You can simply copy it from this window to your application. Believe it or not, all of these gorgeous designs use gradients alone — none of them rely on down-loaded art to achieve their goals.

The advantages of using CSS3 patterns are that you get an interesting background for your site quickly and easily. In addition, patterns require few resources and they're extremely fast to display. However, it's also important to realize that only people who own CSS3-capable browsers will be able to use this solution — everyone else will see a blank background, which is why you always provide a complementary color for the background as a minimum. Although CSS3 patterns are long on pizzazz, they're also quite short on compatibility, so you should consider using them only in situations where you know the user will actually see them onscreen.

Figure 4-8:
A few sites provide you with truly amazing backgrounds you can use for your page.

Getting the gradient details

For the most part, you really don't need to know the gritty details of gradients unless you want to design complex gradient schemes of your own. Most developers rely on simple gradient patterns of the sort I describe in the "Working with linear gradients" section, earlier in this chapter, or they download gradient patterns that were designed by one of many designers out there. However, if you want to know a little more information, you can find it on the CSS3 Files site at `www.css3files.com/gradient/`.

You may still find though that you want to know more. You can get significant information about linear-gradients on the Mozilla site at `https://developer.mozilla.org/docs/Web/CSS/linear-gradient`. The associated site at `https://developer.mozilla.org/docs/Web/CSS/radial-gradient` provides details about the radial-gradients used in some of the downloadable examples in this chapter. You can find out additional details about gradients as a whole at `https://developer.mozilla.org/docs/Web/Guide/CSS/Using_CSS_gradients`.

Using a single image

The simplest, most compatible way to create a background that has at least a little pizzazz is to use a single image. The right image says a lot about your site and provides continuity between pages. Because this approach is so standard, you see it used on a lot of sites. All you really need to know to use it is the `background-image` property, as shown in the following procedure.

1. **Create a new HTML5 file with your text editor.**

2. **Type the following code for the HTML page.**

```
<!DOCTYPE html>

<html>
<head>
    <title>A Single Image Background</title>
    <link rel="stylesheet"
          href="SingleImage.CSS" />
</head>

<body>
    <h1>The Cute Cat</h1>
    <p>A page that has a cute cat as a background.</p>
</body>
</html>
```

3. **Save the file as** SingleImage.HTML.

The sample will appear in other locations, so naming is important.

4. **Create a new CSS file with your text editor.**

5. **Type the following CSS style information.**

```
body
{
    background-image: url("CuteCat.jpg");
    background-color: SaddleBrown;
    color: SeaGreen;
    font-size: x-large;
    text-shadow: 1px 1px Yellow;
}
```

This is the simplest form of a single background image. The `background-image` property has a single `url()` function associated with it. Just in case the user can't display the image (or chooses not to), you need to set an appropriate background color. Depending on the image (the example uses one that's particularly hard to work with when it comes to text), you may need to set the text color and size to make the content easy to read.

This is one place where using the `text-shadow` property may make the difference between user joy and user complaints. Use contrasting colors for the font and shadow so that the two work together to make the content viewable against an image with a range of colors.

6. **Save the file as** SingleImage.CSS.

The sample will appear in other locations, so naming is important.

7. **Load the** `SingleImage` **page.**

You see the background shown in Figure 4-9. Notice that the graphic starts in the upper-left corner and automatically repeats as needed to fill the entire window.

Figure 4-9: Background images can lend just the right level of interest to a page.

Using multiple images

It's possible to combine multiple images into a single image when working with CSS3-capable browsers. At least one of the images must have transparent regions that allow the second image to peek out from behind it. The following procedure modifies the SingleImage example to contain two images. The second image is supplied with downloadable source as PawPrint.GIF. However, you can easily substitute an image of your liking instead (as long as the image has the required transparent regions).

1. **Open the** `SingleImage.CSS` **file.**

2. **Modify the** `body` **style so that the** `background-image` **property now contains two images, as shown here.**

```
body
{
    background-image: url("PawPrint.gif"),
                      url("CuteCat.jpg");
    background-color: SaddleBrown;
    color: SeaGreen;
    font-size: x-large;
    text-shadow: 1px 1px Yellow;
}
```

Notice that the two image entries are separated by a comma — not many multi-entry properties require commas, but this is one of them. The order in which the images appear is also important. The image containing the transparency must appear first because it appears over the top of the second image. If you reverse the entries, the image lacking transparencies will be on top and you'll see only one image.

3. **Save the CSS file as** MulitpleImage.CSS.

4. **Open the** `SingleImage.HTML` **file.**

5. **Modify the** `<title>` **and** `<link>` **tags so they look like this:**

```
<title>A Multiple Image Background</title>
<link rel="stylesheet"
      href="MultipleImage.CSS" />
```

6. **Save the HTML file as** MultipleImage.HTML.

7. **Load the** `MultipleImage` **page.**

You see the background shown in Figure 4-10. Notice how the paw prints overlay the original image but don't conceal it completely.

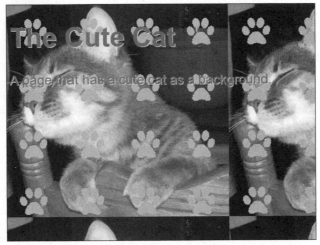

The Cute Cat

A page that has a cute cat as a background.

Figure 4-10:
It's possible
to combine
multiple
images into
a single
background.

Positioning Graphics

You can find techniques for positioning foreground graphics in the "Centering the image" section of this chapter. In essence, you use the combination of the `left`, `right`, `top`, and `bottom` properties to provide basic positioning. Tweaking the position involves using the `margin-left`, `margin-right`, `margin-top`, and `margin-bottom` properties. To ensure that the image stays in one place, normally you set the `position` property to `absolute`. Of course, all positioning is relative to image size, which you set by using the `height` and `width` properties.

Background images also have positioning functionality. You can also control the background image position, margin, and size. The following procedure provides an example of how you might modify the `SingleImage` example to place a single copy of the image in the center of the page (and keep it there no matter how the page is scrolled).

1. **Open the** `SingleImage.CSS` **file.**

2. **Modify the** `body` **style so that the image is fixed in the center, as shown here.**

```
body
{
    background-image: url("CuteCat.jpg");
    background-color: SaddleBrown;
    color: SeaGreen;
    font-size: x-large;
```

```
    text-shadow: 1px 1px Yellow;

    background-position: center;
    background-attachment: fixed;
}
```

The `background-position` property makes it possible to define the placement of the primary copy of a background image. The default setting places the image in the upper-left corner, which may not be very pleasing to the eye.

The `background-attachment` property defines how that image is attached to the browser's background. Setting this value to `fixed` means that the image stays in the same location even when the user resizes the display or scrolls the content.

3. **Save the CSS file as** BackgroundPosition.CSS.

4. **Open the** `SingleImage.HTML` **file.**

5. **Modify the** `<link>` **tag so it looks like this:**

```
<link rel="stylesheet"
      href="BackgroundPosition.CSS" />
```

6. **Save the HTML file as** BackgroundPosition.HTML.

7. **Load the** `BackgroundPosition` **page.**

You see the background shown in Figure 4-11. Notice that the initial image is now centered and the copies radiate out from it.

Figure 4-11:
Centering a background image often makes the page more pleasing.

Working with Repetitive Images

There are a number of ways you can use repetitive images — or keep from using them. For example, when you work with a background, you automatically get repeating images. If you'd prefer not to see multiple copies of the image, you need to tell the browser to display only one. Likewise, you may encounter situations where you really do want repeating images, but in a specific way, such as creating a border around a graphic. The following sections discuss these two scenarios, but you can use the information you obtain to control image repetition in other ways.

Changing repetitive backgrounds

There are situations where you only want a single copy of a background picture. It may be that the image you've used is something that doesn't repeat well or is large enough that you really don't want it repeated. The following procedure demonstrates a technique you can use to tell the browser to use just one copy of a background image.

1. **Open the** `BackgroundPosition.CSS` **file.**

2. **Modify the** `body` **style so that the image doesn't repeat, as shown here.**

```
body
{
    background-image: url("CuteCat.jpg");
    background-color: SaddleBrown;
    color: SeaGreen;
    font-size: x-large;
    text-shadow: 1px 1px Yellow;

    background-position: center;
    background-attachment: fixed;

    background-repeat: no-repeat;
    background-size: 80%;
}
```

The `background-repeat` property is set to `no-repeat` so that the browser knows to display just one copy. Because there's just one copy and the image may not be the right size to provide a good presentation when the user resizes the browser, you should also set the `background-size` property to resize the image automatically.

3. **Save the CSS file as** NoRepeat.CSS.

4. **Open the** `BackgroundPosition.HTML` **file.**

5. **Modify the** `<link>` **tag so it looks like this:**

```
<link rel="stylesheet"
      href=" NoRepeat.CSS" />
```

6. **Save the HTML file as** NoRepeat.HTML.

7. **Load the** `NoRepeat` **page.**

   You see the background shown in Figure 4-12. There's just one image in the center now — and when you resize the browser, the image automatically resizes as well.

Figure 4-12: Use just one image when presenting larger images.

Creating repetitive borders

One of the more common uses for repetitive images is to create borders made of images. Unfortunately, this technique doesn't work well with Internet Explorer 9. It does work, however, with all newer versions of Chrome, Firefox, and Internet Explorer 10. The following procedure takes the `SimpleGraphics` example created earlier and adds a paw-print border to it.

1. **Open the** `SimpleGraphics.HTML` **file.**

   You need to modify the page so that there's a new `<div>` to hold the margin, which really isn't part of the image. If you try to attach the margin graphics to the existing image container, the graphics will appear centered on the image container's margin, rather than as full images.

2. **Add a new** `<div>` **to the page as shown here.**

```
<div id="BorderContainer">
    <div id="ImageContainer">
        <img alt="A Picture of a Cute Cat."
             title="A Picture of a Cute Cat."
             name="CuteCat"
             id="CuteCat"
             src="CuteCat.JPG" />
        <p>A picture of a cute cat!</p>
    </div>
</div>
```

3. **Modify the** `<link>` **tag so it looks like this:**

```
<link rel="stylesheet"
      href="BorderGraphics.CSS" />
```

4. **Save the HTML file as** BorderGraphics.HTML.

5. **Open the** `SimpleGraphics.CSS` **file.**

   You need to change the styles so that they'll work with the new containers found in the HTML file. Think about the border being a box that encloses a box holding the image and caption. What you get instead of a single image box is a box within a box.

6. **Add a new** `#BorderContainer` **style like the one shown here.**

```
#BorderContainer
{
    border-style: solid;
    border-width: 20px;
    border-image:
        url(PawPrint.GIF) 25 22 23 fill round;

    padding: 24px;
    float: left;

    position: absolute;
    height: 465px;
    width: 440px;
    left: 50%;
    margin-left: -244px;
}
```

Most of these properties are the same as those originally used for the #ImageContainer style. The BorderContainer <div> is now the outer container, so you position it rather than the ImageContainer <div>. There are some changes in measurements to accommodate the size of the border.

The biggest change is the addition of the border-image property. You supply the URL of the image you want to use, along with the inward offset of the border image, the width of the image, and the image outset. The fill value tells the browser to fill the <div> with copies of the image and the round value tells the browser to resize the image so that an even number of images fill the <div>.

Figuring out the numbers for a border image can be difficult and time-consuming. Fortunately, you can use the border-image-generator (http://border-image.com) to do the work for you. Simply provide the location of the border image you want to use and then use the sliders to figure out optimal values for placing that image around a <div>. You can copy the results directly from the page to your application.

7. **Modify the** #ImageContainer **style so that it reflects its new role as an inner container.**

```
#ImageContainer
{
    margin: 20px;
    height: 420px;
    width: 400px;
    background-color: White;
}
```

8. **Save the CSS file as** BorderGraphics.CSS.

9. **Load the** BorderGraphics **page.**

You see the page shown in Figure 4-13. Notice that the border graphics surround both the image and its caption.

Chapter 5

Using CSS Shortcuts

*E*veryone likes shortcuts — methods of doing something quickly without any loss of quality. In fact, there are entire industries that are focused solely on the shortcut. Just think about the number of ads you see every day that tell you about a product, service, or technique that reduces the time you spend doing something — they're all shortcuts. So it shouldn't surprise you too much to discover that CSS has shortcuts as well. In this case, shortcuts are techniques you can use to reduce your workload and make life easier. Many of these techniques help you when you write the code, and then a second time when you need to perform updates. That's the best kind of shortcut — the kind that keeps providing a dividend for little time spent up front.

Many of these techniques focus on the fact that the true purpose of CSS is to separate content from formatting. Chapters 2, 3, and 4 show you all sorts of interesting new techniques — and you've probably gotten away from this core idea a little. This chapter brings that idea back to the forefront — it's all about the concept of keeping things separate so you can interact with the part you need and leave the other part undisturbed.

As part of the separation of content and formatting, this chapter discusses some special effects, and then shows you how to present your content in columns. Special effects make it possible to communicate information in non-verbal ways, but they only work when the person using your site has the ability to interact with them. When you use CSS to build your site, users with special needs can remove your site's special effects and still enjoy the content you provide. Likewise, columnar presentations work for people with normal vision who want to review content more quickly or see it grouped in certain ways. By using CSS, you allow someone who requires larger text to see the content in a single column, but with a larger font size. Again, the person can still enjoy the content, even if the presentation isn't quite the same as you envisioned.

Understanding Style Inheritance

All of the chapters so far have worked around the idea of style inheritance. The *cascading* part of Cascading Style Sheet (CSS) tells it all. A style at the uppermost part of the page hierarchy will cascade down into the lower parts of the page. By defining a style at the right level of the hierarchy, you reduce the work required to implement that style in all the places that the style is needed. For example, a style that is defined with the <body> tag will flow down into the <div> tag that is a child of the <body> tag. If you defined the style at the <div> level, you would need to define it for each <div> that requires the style. By defining it at the <body> level, you employ a shortcut in the form of a cascading style.

The use of a cascading architecture means that you define styles that affect the page as a whole at a higher level than the specific styles used to define particular elements. For example, if your page relies mainly on a single font, then you should define that font at the <body> tag. Even though the Document Object Model (DOM) hierarchy starts with the document, moves toward the root (the <html> tag), and only then splits into the <head> and <body> tags, the <body> tag is the first displayable element.

Inheritance also comes in another form. You can define styles in three different places. The location of that definition modifies the priority of that style. Here are the three style locations and their priorities:

- **Inline (top priority):** An *inline style* appears specifically with a particular object. It modifies only that object and no other object in the document or in any other document. You haven't seen an inline style used so far in the book because they tend to cause problems. Locating and changing an inline style is time-consuming and error-prone, so you should avoid them whenever possible.

- **Internal:** An *internal style* appears as part of the <style> tag in the <head> of the document. It affects all of the objects in the document, but no other document on the site. Using internal styles can help you provide special pizzazz to a particular page, but you should use an internal style only when the style is unique to that page, and you never intend to use that style anywhere else. Given that you normally can't make such a guarantee, it's best to avoid internal styles whenever possible, but even so, they're preferable to inline styles.

✔ **External (lowest priority):** An external style appears in an external .CSS file. You must create a reference to this file by using a <link> tag in the <head> of a document. The styles affect every document linked to the .CSS file. Using this approach makes updates easier and gives your site a uniform appearance overall. In addition, using external styles makes it easy for people with special needs to supply an alternative style sheet that better meets their needs.

You can associate as many external style sheets as needed with a page by using multiple `<link>` tags. This approach lets you use styles from diverse sources so that you can format your page with the least amount of effort. External style sheets are processed in the order in which they appear. If two .CSS files contain the same style name that modify the same properties, the style processed last is the style that has precedence.

The final level of inheritance to consider is the selector itself. You can create selectors that act only on objects contained within other objects or that meet special criteria (as discussed in Chapter 2). A specific selector will always override the settings provided by a generic selector, so you should only use this technique when necessary (imagine trying to find all of those specific changes in all the files on your site). The more specific the selector, the greater its priority becomes. However, you need to consider the effects of the selector's level within the document — and the manner in which the style is defined — as part of the overall picture.

Cascading Styles — Using Multiple Styles Together

Understanding the rules of inheritance helps you create interesting sites that require a minimum of maintenance. By following these rules, when maintenance is required, you normally have to make just one change, rather than changing hundreds of items individually. It pays to experiment, though, so you can understand the full effects of inheritance and the effects of using multiple styles together. The following procedure helps demonstrate these techniques.

1. **Create a new HTML5 file with your text editor.**

   Your editor may not support HTML5 files. Any text file will do.

2. **Type the following code for the HTML page.**

```
<!DOCTYPE html>

<html>
<head>
    <title>Inheritance Example</title>
```

```
    <style>
        p
        {
            font-family: Arial, Helvetica, sans-serif;
            color: Blue;
            background-color: Yellow;
            margin: 0;
            font-style: italic;
            font-size: medium;
        }

        div p
        {
            font-style: italic;
            font-size: larger;
        }
    </style>
</head>

<body>
    <h1>An Example of CSS Inheritance</h1>
    <p>A paragraph outside a
        <span style="font-family: monospace">
            &lt;div&gt;</span>.</p>
    <div id="Container"
        style="text-align: left;">
        <p>A paragraph inside a container.</p>
    </div>
</body>
</html>
```

This page contains a number of inline styles, which always have the highest inheritance precedence. For example, the `<span>` provides a `font-family` of `monospace` for the `<div>` tag part of the sentence. You could accomplish the same thing by assigning the `<span>` a `class` attribute for code, but this example uses the inline style instead.

The `<div>` uses an inline style to set the `text-align` style to `left`. Because the default style sets the alignment to left, you won't see any difference. However, if another style change modifies the text alignment, this style will take effect and prevent movement of this paragraph.

The internal style modifications all appear within the `<style>` tag in the `<head>` element. The first style sets the general characteristics for a `<p>` tag. Notice that the style specifically sets the `font-style` to `italic` and the `font-size` to `medium`.

The second style is more specific. It sets the characteristics for `<p>` tags that appear as a child of a `<div>`. Consequently, inheritance rules say that this style will take precedence when the rules of inheritance are met, which means the `font-style` and `font-size` styles will be different in this case. Figure 5-1 shows how these styles play out.

4. **Save the file as Inheritance.HTML.**

   The sample will appear in other chapters, so naming is important.

5. **Load the Inheritance example into your browser.**

   You see the role that inheritance and cascading styles play, as shown in Figure 5-1.

Figure 5-1:
Inheritance
and cascad-
ing styles
interact
to format
this page.

An Example of CSS Inheritance

A paragraph outside a `<div>`.
A paragraph inside a container.

6. **Create a new CSS file with your text editor.**

   Your editor may not support CSS files. Any text file will do.

7. **Type the following CSS style information.**

```
body
{
    text-align: center;
    color: DarkRed;
    background-color: Khaki;
    border: inset;
    border-color: Green;
}

h1
{
    border: outset;
    border-color: Brown;
}

p
{
    text-decoration: underline;
    font-family: "Times New Roman", Times, serif;
    font-style: oblique;
    font-size: xx-large;
}
```

The <body> tag appears as the topmost object in a page, so the changes noted in the body style should affect everything not specifically overridden later. In this case, the example changes the text alignment to center and places a dark red border around any content. The background color is also changed. Finally, the style adds a green border around every object.

The h1 style overrides any body styles. In this case, that means modifying the border styles.

The p style also overrides any body styles. However, there aren't any properties that are the same in this case, so the p styles enhance the styles inherited from the body style.

8. **Save the file as Inheritance.CSS.**

The sample will appear in other chapters, so naming is important.

9. **Add the following code to the <head> area of the HTML file.**

```
<link rel="stylesheet" href="Inheritance.CSS" />
```

This code creates the link between the HTML file and the CSS file.

10. **Save the HTML file and reload the page.**

You see the changes shown in Figure 5-2.

Figure 5-2:
Modifying the external style produces both inheritance and cascading changes.

An Example of CSS Inheritance

A paragraph outside a <div>.
A paragraph inside a container.

Notice that all the expected changes are in place. For example, the text is centered, except for the one paragraph that has an inline style overriding the centered text. The heading text is now in dark red — the paragraph text overrides that color selection, so it remains blue. Even though there is an external p style for the size of the text, the internal style overrides it.

You should notice something else about the example. The body contains an inset border of the correct color (where the left and top lines are green and the border appears to sink the content below the surface of the rest of the page) and the heading contains an outset border of the correct color, because it has overridden the default. The right and bottom lines in the heading border are brown, but that the left and top lines are a lighter color due to the effect of the outset border (giving the appearance that the heading is raised above the surface of the background). However, the paragraphs have no border. At one time, `<body>` tag changes affected the entire document and some of them still do. However, other changes affect only the body and not other block elements. Block elements don't inherit some settings from the `body` style.

11. **Delete the** `h1` **style from the** `Inheritance.CSS` **style sheet.**

    You can also comment out the `h1` style by adding the starting (`/*`) and ending (`*/`) comment symbols to it like this:

    ```
    /* Commented out to show block settings.
    h1
    {
        border: outset;
        border-color: Brown;
    }
    */
    ```

12. **Save the CSS file and reload the page.**

    You see the changes shown in Figure 5-3.

Figure 5-3:
Take care not to assume that your body-style changes affect other block-level objects.

An Example of CSS Inheritance

A paragraph outside a `<div>`.
A paragraph inside a container.

Notice that the heading now lacks a border. It turns out that the heading wasn't overriding the body-level border — it was adding a new border. Never assume that a `body` style will carry through to other block-level styles — some settings simply don't. When you find that your page doesn't look as you expected it to look, try configuring the setting at a lower block level.

You may also see some style sheets that access the `html` style, which affects the `<html>` tag that contains the `<body>` tag. It's true: You can work with the html style to achieve some effects. For example, you may want to create a raised border around the page, which would require accessing the html style.

13. **Add the html style shown here to the** Inheritance.CSS **style sheet.**

```
html
{
    border: outset;
    border-color: Green;
    background-color: White;
}
```

14. **Save the CSS file and reload the page.**

You see the changes shown in Figure 5-4.

Figure 5-4:
The html
style can
help you
achieve spe-
cific special
effects.

You rarely have to rely on the html style because it simply isn't neces-sary. The html block is a level above the body block, as shown by this example. The html block doesn't give you access to anything that the body block can't change in most cases, except for special effects like the one shown here.

Using Additional Basic User Interface Features

The book discusses a number of user interface features so far and you'll find even more details in later chapters. The user interface is the hardest part of your application to get right. It's not a matter of coding or of presentation — it's a matter of perception. The way you perceive the user interface is com-pletely different from that of your users because you approach it from the viewpoint of a developer — it's unavoidable.

Users commonly have problems figuring out what to put in fields. Most of this book's user interface suggestions help you create an environment where the user has few questions. For example, using drop-down list boxes helps eliminate user confusion over what to include in fields. However, the second most common problem is finding an application feature, a page of content, or a resource. The following sections address this problem by presenting methods of defining a document outline (that is, a method for navigating a single page) and site navigation. You'll see other techniques for addressing these issues as the book progresses.

Performing quick navigation

Most sites provide some sort of site navigation aid. If you don't provide this sort of support, the user may get lost and you'll lose business or at least activity. Site navigation makes information easier to find and use. In addition, you really need it in order for the user to make good use of your site. The following procedure describes how to add site navigation without programming to a page. It doesn't do anything fancy, but it does work well with most browsers.

1. **Create a new HTML5 file with your text editor.**

2. **Type the following code for the HTML page.**

```
<!DOCTYPE html>

<html>
<head>
    <title>Navigating User Interfaces</title>
    <link rel="stylesheet" href="Navigation.CSS" />
</head>

<body>
    <ul id="MainMenu">
        <li>
            <a href="Navigation.HTML">Home</a>
        </li>
        <li>
            <a href="Navigation.HTML">Products</a>
            <ul>
                <li>
                    <a href="Navigation.HTML">One</a>
                </li>
                <li>
                    <a href="Navigation.HTML">Two</a>
                </li>
                <li>
                    <a href="Navigation.HTML">Three</a>
                </li>
```

```
            <li>
                <a href="Navigation.HTML">Four</a>
            </li>
        </ul>
    </li>
    <li>
        <a href="Navigation.HTML">Events</a>
        <ul>
            <li>
                <a href="Navigation.HTML">Red</a>
            </li>
            <li>
                <a href="Navigation.HTML">Green</a>
            </li>
            <li>
                <a href="Navigation.HTML">Blue</a>
            </li>
            <li>
                <a href="Navigation.HTML">Orange</a>
            </li>
        </ul>
    </li>
    <li>
        <a href="Navigation.HTML">About</a>
        <ul>
            <li>
                <a href="Navigation.HTML">Contact</a>
            </li>
            <li>
                <a href="Navigation.HTML">Founding</a>
            </li>
            <li>
                <a href="Navigation.HTML">Privacy</a>
            </li>
        </ul>
    </li>
    </ul>
</body>
</html>
```

The menu system consists of a number of lists. Each unordered list represents another layer of menus. This example has just two layers, but you can easily apply the concepts to any number of layers desired. The overall menu is enclosed with an unordered list element (`<ul>`) named `MainMenu`. The name is important because you'll use it extensively when creating the required styles.

3. Save the file as Navigation.HTML.

The sample will appear in other chapters, so naming is important.

4. Create a new CSS file with your text editor.

5. Type the following CSS style information.

```
#MainMenu
{
    margin: 0;
    padding: 0;
}

#MainMenu li
{
    margin: 0;
    padding: 0;
    list-style: none;
    float: left;
}

#MainMenu li a
{
    display: block;
    margin: 0 1px 0 0;
    padding: 4px 10px;
    width: 80px;
    background: Black;
    color: White;
    text-align: center;
}

#MainMenu li a:hover
{
    background: Green;
}

#MainMenu li:hover ul
{
    visibility: visible;
}

#MainMenu ul
{
    position: absolute;
    visibility: hidden;
    margin: 0;
    padding: 0;
    background: Grey;
    border: 1px solid White;
    width: 80px;
}

#MainMenu ul a
```

```
{
    position: relative;
    display: block;
    margin: 0;
    padding: 5px 10px;
    width: 80px;
    text-align: left;
    background: LightGrey;
    color: Black;
}


#MainMenu ul a:hover
{
    background: Violet;
}
```

REMEMBER

Wow, that's a lot of code! Styles can become complex as you try to do more with them. That's why many developers rely heavily on third party libraries and tools, which is the focus on most of this book. Trying to come up with all that style information on your own is time consuming. In fact, the kind of menu we're creating here is easily made using a tool such as CSS Menu Maker (http://cssmenumaker.com/), Menucool. com (www.menucool.com/), or CSS3Menu (http://css3menu.com/index.html). However, it's important to go through this exercise at least once so you know how things work.

The styles begin with the MainMenu, an unordered list (<ul>) element. Everything is referenced to this element. The MainMenu consists of a number of list items (<li>), which are set using the #MainMenu li style. You don't want the list items to actually look like a list — you want them to look like menus — so it's essential to set the list-style to none. Setting float to left will also help give the menu a professional appearance. Within each list item is an anchor (<a>) that points to the location to which the user goes after selecting the menu item. The #MainMenu li a style creates the required appearance, which includes displaying the item as a block. When the user hovers the mouse over one of the MainMenu items, the #MainMenu li a:hover style turns the entry green.

The #MainMenu li:hover ul requires a little explanation. Normally, the secondary menu has its visibility set to hidden, so that you don't see it. When a user hovers the mouse over a MainMenu list item, you want the submenu displayed. This style performs that task. It creates the appearance of using code without actually using any code.

The submenus will appear vertically, below the horizontal main menu. In order to do this, the #MainMenu ul style sets the width to 80px, the size required to hold a single menu entry. This setting must match the width setting for the #MainMenu ul a style. Notice that this second level of menus has its visibility property set to hidden because you don't want to see it until the user clicks the associated main menu item. As with the main menu, you want users to know when they have selected a particular item, so the `#MainMenu ul a:hover` style changes the menu's `background` value to `Violet`.

6. **Save the file as** Navigation.CSS.

   The sample will appear in other chapters, so naming is important.

7. **Load the Navigation example.**

   You see the menu similar to the one shown in Figure 5-5 (your menu won't have anything selected initially and will appear as a black bar across the top of the page).

Figure 5-5:
You don't need any code at all to produce a useful menu for your site.

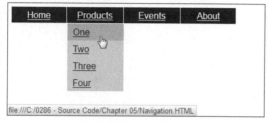

Try selecting various items. The example uses the existing site for each of the links, but if you want, you can try using other links. Clicking a link will take you to the desired location. The point of this menu is that you can create quite a few user interface items that look like they're coded, but really aren't, using CSS. This CSS-only approach will work with most browsers without having to ask the user to enable JavaScript. Most browsers support the level of CSS required to make this menu system work.

Providing a document outline

A document outline is useful when a page contains a lot of material and you want the user to navigate it easily. The outline relies on the various tags you provide. The current method of creating a document outline is to use the `<h1>` through `<h6>` tags. This approach works great when the material comes from the same page or you have control over the formatting of the content. It doesn't work quite so well when the content comes from another location, which is why the standards groups had to come up with an entirely new way to do things (see the "Discovering HTML5 Document Outlining" sidebar for details). The following procedure demonstrates a technique for adding an outline to a page that already contains a menu. You use the Navigation example created in the previous section as a starting point.

1. **Open the** `Navigation.HTML` **file and add the following code to the end of the** `<body>` **section (after the existing menu).**

```html
<div id="DocOutline">
   <ul>
      <li>
         <a href="Navigation.HTML#MainHeading1">
            Main Heading 1
         </a>
         <ul>
            <li>
               <a href="Navigation.HTML#SubHead1a">
                  Sub Heading 1
               </a>
            </li>
            <li>
               <a href="Navigation.HTML#SubHead1b">
                  Sub Heading 2
               </a>
            </li>
         </ul>
      </li>
      <li>
         <a href="Navigation.HTML#MainHeading2">
            Main Heading 2
         </a>
         <ul>
            <li>
               <a href="Navigation.HTML#SubHead2a">
                  Sub Heading 3
               </a>
            </li>
            <li>
               <a href="Navigation.HTML#SubHead2b">
                  Sub Heading 4
               </a>
            </li>
         </ul>
      </li>
   </ul>
</div>

<div id="DocContent">
   <br />
   <h1 id="MainHeading1">Main Heading 1</h1>
   <p>Introductory Material</p>
   <h2 id="SubHead1a">Sub Heading 1</h2>
   <p>Article</p>
   <h2 id="SubHead1b">Sub Heading 2</h2>
   <p>Article</p>
   <h1 id="MainHeading2">Main Heading 2</h1>
```

```
    <p>Introductory Material</p>
    <h2 id="SubHead2a">Sub Heading 3</h2>
    <p>Article</p>
    <h2 id="SubHead2b">Sub Heading 4</h2>
    <p>Article</p>
</div>
```

The entries consist of a document outline and the associated content. The outline specifically follows the <h1> and <h2> objects in this example. There are methods for generating this sort of content automatically, but all of them require coding. This is one case where using CSS does involve some manual coding that you wouldn't have to perform when using other techniques, such as including JavaScript. However, the advantage is that the example will work fine with any browser that supports CSS.

2. Save the HTML file.

3. Open Navigation.CSS **and type the following styles at the end of the file.**

```
#DocOutline
{
    font-family: Arial, Helvetica, sans-serif;
    font-size: 14px;
    width: 145px;
    height: 800px;
}

#DocOutline ul
{
    margin-bottom: 20px;
    list-style: none;
    margin-left: -40px;
}

#DocOutline ul ul
{
    margin-left: -20px;
}

#DocContent
{
    margin-top: -800px;
    margin-left: 150px;
}
```

The main focus is on the document outline where you need to provide formatted links to the content found on the remainder of the page. Notice that the outline is set to a specific height. The reason for this setting is to make it easier to position the document content once the links are displayed.

The example sets the #DocOutline ul style list-style property to none. You could just as easily use numbers, letters, or any other outlining index you prefer. This list will automatically indent half of the distance of the individual menu elements you created earlier. In order to place the links at the left side of the page, you must reverse the list's indentation by setting margin-left to -40px, which is half the 80px width of the individual menu elements.

Each level will require some additional amount of indentation so the user can see the relative levels of each entry. The #DocOutline ul ul changes the indentation for the second-level headings. If you had a third level of headings, you'd create a #DocOutline ul ul ul style to format it.

The document content will start after the document outline unless one of two things happens. First, you can use actual columns as described in the "Working with Multiple Columns" section, later in this chapter. However, this functionality requires CSS3. Second, you can use pseudo-columns. You set the margin-top property value equal to the height of the document outline. The technique shown in this example will work with any browser that fully supports CSS. Notice that you must also set margin-left to a value that equals the width of the document outline (plus a few pixels for spacing.

4. **Save the CSS file.**

5. **Reload the Navigation example.**

   You see the document outline and associated content as shown in Figure 5-6. This outline actually works — you can click links to go to the various headers presented in the outline.

Figure 5-6:
Using a document outline on complex pages makes it easier to find specific content.

Discovering HTML5 document outlining

Document outlining isn't anything new. HTML was created to organize content through the use of various tags. The <h1> through <h6> tags have existed since early versions of HTML. However, what has changed over the years is how these tags are perceived by the browser — and how add-on software uses these tags when interacting with the user. In addition, many sites now mash content together from multiple locations; how the content was organized originally on the other sites no longer makes sense when viewed as a composite with other content from other sites.

HTML5 adds functionality to make sense of content that is mashed together from multiple locations. Instead of using the heading tags alone, you now have a selection of sectional tags: <article> (content that is self-contained and could appear separately from the rest of the content on the site), <aside> (content, such as a sidebar, that is related to other content in the section, but not actually part of that content), <nav> (a collection of navigational links of any sort), and <section> (items such as chapters, headers, and footers). If you find that you really don't understand the latest outlining features completely, reading "HTML5 And The Document Outlining Algorithm" (http://coding.smashingmagazine.com/2011/08/16/html5-and-the-document-outlining-algorithm/) will help quite a lot.

The change that most developers don't quite understand is that all the tags used to outline and organize material on a page are now part of the HTML5 specification — and you use these special tags to describe the outline. If you're already familiar with the way HTML4 did things, reading "Document Outlines" (http://html5doctor.com/outlines/) provides you with a quick update that will prove helpful, especially when it comes time to update existing pages. You should also check the more detailed article at https://developer.mozilla.org/en-US/docs/Web/HTML/Sections_and_Outlines_of_an_HTML5_document.

There are also tools available to help you create better documents. For example, the HTML5 Outliner (http://gsnedders.html5.org/outliner/) shows how your document would look when outlined using HTML5 specifications. You can use this tool to look for and fix organizational errors. A number of browsers also come with plug-ins you can use to inspect the HTML5 view of your document outline directly in the browser; an example is HTML5 Outliner for Chrome (https://chrome.google.com/webstore/detail/html5-outliner/afoibpobokebhgfnknfndkgemglggomo).

The reason that you don't see the HTML5 document outlining tags used very often in this book is that few browsers actually support them yet; even assistive technologies haven't caught up. Before you begin using the new tags in your next project, you should also read some alternative viewpoints such as "Don't Style Headings Using HTML5 Sections" (www.stubbornella.org/content/2011/09/06/style-headings-using-html5-sections/). It does pay, at least, to know about these tags so you can start preparing your site to use them.

Creating Special Effects

You can create so many special effects by using CSS that it would require a book or two to list them all. The following paragraphs discuss two of the more interesting special effects. You'll find a considerable array of special effects in other examples in this book.

Transforming objects, including graphics

A *transform* changes the appearance of objects onscreen in a specific way. For example, you might rotate the object or skew its dimensions. Transforms make it easy to create unique presentations from common objects — effects that ordinarily you'd need a designer or graphic artist to create for you. The following list describes the kinds of transformations you can perform.

✔ matrix(a, b, c, d, tx, ty): Skews the object using a matrix defined by points a, b, c, and d. It then translates the object's position on screen by a value denoted by tx and ty. (You can try the matrix() transform out at www.w3schools.com/cssref/playit. asp?filename=playcss_transform_matrix.)

There are versions of many of these functions that work on three-dimensional objects. For example, there is a matrix3d() function. These functions add a *z*-axis to the equation, so that you can manipulate three-dimensional objects in three-dimensional space. A full discussion of precisely how the 3D versions work is outside the scope of this book, but you can read more at https://developer.mozilla.org/docs/Web/CSS/transform-function and http://css-tricks.com/missing-documentation-for-matrix3d-transforms/.

✔ translate(tx, ty), translateX(tx), translateY(ty): Modifies the position of the object on screen by a horizontal amount defined by tx, a vertical amount defined by ty, or both. (You can try the translate() transform at www.w3schools.com/cssref/playit. asp?filename=playcss_transform_translate.)

✔ scale(x, y), scaleX(x), scaleY(y): Stretches the object horizontally by the amount specified by x, vertically by the amount specified by y, or both. (You can try the scale() transform at www.w3schools. com/cssref/playit.asp?filename=playcss_transform_scale.)

✔ rotate(angle), rotateX(angle), rotateY(angle): Rotates the object by the number of degrees specified in the desired axis. (You can try the rotate() transform at www.w3schools.com/cssref/playit.asp?filename=playcss_transform_rotate.)

Internet Explorer doesn't support all of the transforms. For example, you'll find that Internet Explorer 9 doesn't support the `rotateX()` and `rotateY()` functions.

✔ `skew(angleX, angleY)`, `skewX(angleX)`, `skewY(angleY)`: Skews the object by the number of degrees horizontally specified by `angleX`, the number of degrees vertically specified by `angleY`, or both. (You can try the `skew()` transform at www.w3schools.com/cssref/ playit.asp?filename=playcss_transform_skew.)

The best way to understand these transformations is to see them in action. The following procedure helps you create a sample application that demonstrates the transformations you can perform.

1. **Create a new HTML5 file with your text editor.**

2. **Type the following code for the HTML page.**

```
<!DOCTYPE html>

<html>
<head>
    <title>Examples of Transforms</title>
    <link rel="stylesheet" href="Transforms.CSS" />
</head>

<body>
    <p id="Matrix">Matrix</p>
    <p id="Translate">Translate</p>
    <p id="Scale">Scale</p>
    <p id="Rotate">Rotate</p>
    <p id="RotateY">Rotate Y</p>
    <p id="Skew">Skew</p>
</body>
</html>
```

The example demonstrates the transformations listed as paragraphs. You can try other transformations by modifying the example (a great idea).

3. **Save the file as** Transforms.HTML.

4. **Create a new CSS file with your text editor.**

5. **Type the following CSS style information.**

```
#Matrix
{
    border: solid;
    border-color: Black;
    border-width: thin;
    font-size: 30px;
    margin: 50px;
```

```
       width: 140px;
       height: 40px;
       transform: matrix(0.866,0.5,0.4,0.866,5,15);
       -ms-transform: matrix(0.866,0.5,0.4,0.866,5,15);
       -webkit-transform: matrix(0.866,0.5,0.4,0.866,5,15);
}

#Translate
{
       border: solid;
       border-color: Black;
       border-width: thin;
       font-size: 30px;
       margin: 50px;
       width: 140px;
       height: 40px;
       transform: translate(20px, 30px);
       -ms-transform: translate(20px, 30px);
       -webkit-transform: translate(20px, 30px);
}

#Scale
{
       border: solid;
       border-color: Black;
       border-width: thin;
       font-size: 30px;
       margin: 50px;
       width: 140px;
       height: 40px;
       transform: scale(1.6, 0.75);
       -ms-transform: scale(1.6, 0.75);
       -webkit-transform: scale(1.6, 0.75);
}

#Rotate
{
       border: solid;
       border-color: Black;
       border-width: thin;
       font-size: 30px;
       margin: 50px;
       width: 140px;
       height: 40px;
       transform: rotate(140deg);
       -ms-transform: rotate(140deg);
       -webkit-transform: rotate(140deg);
}

#RotateY
{
```

```
    border: solid;
    border-color: Black;
    border-width: thin;
    font-size: 30px;
    margin: 50px;
    width: 140px;
    height: 40px;
    transform: rotateY(140deg);
    -ms-transform: rotateY(140deg);
    -webkit-transform: rotateY(140deg);
}

#Skew
{
    border: solid;
    border-color: Black;
    border-width: thin;
    font-size: 30px;
    margin: 50px;
    width: 140px;
    height: 40px;
    transform: skew(15deg, 30deg);
    -ms-transform: skew(15deg, 30deg);
    -webkit-transform: skew(15deg, 30deg);
}
```

Each of these transforms uses precisely the same paragraph format so that you can better understand how they work. The use of a border makes it easier to understand the transform because the combination of words and an onscreen object convey more information (something to remember when you create your own test applications).

Transforms are considered experimental, even though they appear as part of the specification. In order to use them with Internet Explorer 9+, you must include the -ms- prefix. Both Safari and Chrome require the -webkit- prefix. This is why you see each transform listed three times. The transforms should also work with both Opera and Firefox without any problem.

6. **Save the file as** Transforms.CSS.

   The sample will appear in other chapters, so naming is important.

7. **Load the Transforms example.**

   You see the transformation effects shown in Figure 5-7. All these transforms are using the same font, font size, and box size, so the differences you see are due solely to the transformation taking place. Notice that the rotateY() transformation actually shows the text backward.

   Try modifying the transform values to see how the changes affect the output. You'll be surprised at just how flexible these functions are.

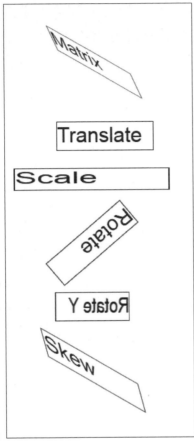

Figure 5-7:
Transfor-
mations
produce
special
effects
that create
interesting
pages.

It's possible to combine transforms to create even more unusual effects. Simply separate them with a space. For example, to combine a `rotate()` with a `skew()`, you'd type **transform: rotate(25deg) skew(15deg, 30deg);**.

Using the attr() function

The `attr()` function is interesting because it lets you interact with any attribute of an object as part of a style. You see this function used in a number of unique ways on the Internet, even though it seems to be a well-kept secret for the most part. One site that demonstrates a quick application that relies on `attr()` is The New Hotness: Using CSS3 Visual Effects (`http://coding.smashingmagazine.com/2010/01/25/the-new-hotness-using-css3-visual-effects/`). The following procedure demonstrates the `attr()` function in a simpler way so that you can better understand the few examples online that demonstrate it in a detailed way.

Transforms and JavaScript

Many special effects that you see online are the combination of transforms and JavaScript. This chapter doesn't discuss how to use transforms and JavaScript together, but there are many interesting sites that discuss them and provide examples you could potentially copy onto your own site without modification. One of the most interesting examples is 50 Awesome Animations made with CSS3 (`www.1stwebdesigner.com/css/50-awesome-css3-animations/`). A lot of the examples on this site don't even require any complex coding because they rely on third party libraries to perform the heavy lifting. Another good place to look for interesting examples is 50 Useful Coding Techniques (CSS Layouts, Visual Effects and Forms) (`http://coding.smashing`

`magazine.com/2010/02/18/50-css-and-javascript-techniques-for-layouts-forms-and-visual-effects/`), which contains a wealth of useful techniques you want to know, even if you use them as a way to look for third-party libraries.

CSS3 can also help things along when you include transitions with the transforms. The result is a type of animation that relies more on CSS and less on coding. However, even in this case, you need to perform some level of coding in order to obtain the special effect. (You can see some uses for these sorts of special effects in Chapter 6.) It's important to note that these kinds of animations are different from the movie-like animations created using technologies such as animated Graphic Interchange Format (.GIF) files.

1. **Create a new HTML5 file with your text editor.**

2. **Type the following code for the HTML page.**

```
<!DOCTYPE html>

<html>
<head>
    <title>Using the attr() Function</title>
    <link rel="stylesheet" href="Attr.CSS" />
</head>

<body>
    <h1>Using the attr() Function</h1>
    <p id="TestMe"
      TestText="Hello">
       World
    </p>
</body>
</html>
```

All you have here is a heading and paragraph. Notice that the paragraph defines a standard attribute, id, and a non-standard attribute, TestText. The attribute you use for the attr() function need not be standard — you can define any attribute desired.

3. **Save the file as** Attr.HTML.

4. **Create a new CSS file with your text editor.**

5. **Type the following CSS style information.**

```
#TestMe:before
{
    content: attr(TestText);
}
```

The style begins by saying that the output from the style should appear before the tag referenced by TestMe as an id. It then sets the content of that area to the current value of the TestText attribute by using the attr() function.

6. **Save the file as** Attr.CSS.

The sample will appear in other chapters, so naming is important.

7. **Load the Attr example.**

The output is pretty much what you'd expect, Hello World, as shown in Figure 5-8. The attr() function can make it possible for you to hide and use all sorts of information in your pages, reuse information in different ways, or even perform debugging tasks.

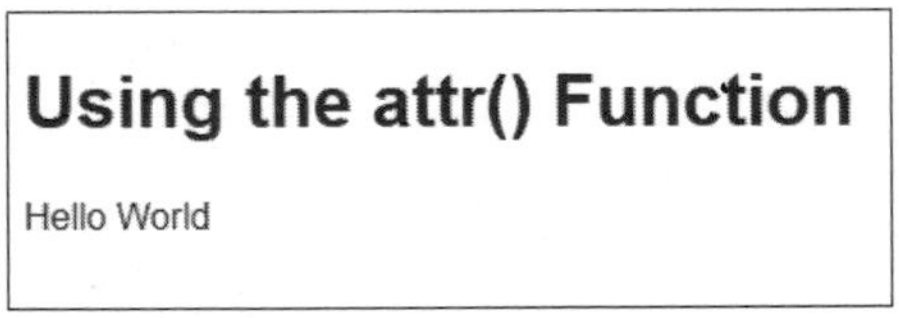

Figure 5-8:
Use the attr()
function to
output the
value of
attributes.

Using the attr() Function

Hello World

Working with Multiple Columns

CSS3 provides a new method for working with columns that doesn't require you to have a math degree and perform test setups with arcane styles. The column styles provide the means to create multiple columns on a page without a lot of effort on your part. Depending on the specific style you use, you can obtain various layouts or simply create a newspaper-type setup where content flows from column-to-column based on the user's browser setup.

As with anything CSS3-specific, you need to test your application with the browsers that your users intend to use. In addition, this feature is considered experimental — and you have to jump through a few hoops to make it work with some browsers. While Internet Explorer and Opera support the column properties directly, you must prepend -moz- to make them work with Firefox and -webkit- to make them work with Safari and Chrome. The following list provides a brief overview of the column properties.

- ✔ column-count: Specifies the number of columns to create. The width of the columns automatically fluctuates as the user resizes the browser window (or the browser displays a horizontal scrollbar to make it possible to scroll across columns when a specific width is set as well).

- ✔ column-fill: Determines how the browser fills the columns (either filling one column at a time or filling all columns simultaneously with an even amount of content).

- ✔ column-gap: Creates a gap between columns to make it easier to determine where one column ends and another begins.

- ✔ column-rule: Creates a rule between columns so the user can see a physical separator. This property consists of color, style, and width.

- ✔ column-rule-color: Determines with color of the rule used between columns.

- ✔ column-rule-style: Determines the style of the rule used between columns.

- ✔ column-rule-width: Determines the width of the rule used between columns.

- ✔ column-span: Specifies the number of columns that an object can span.

- ✔ column-width: Specifies a column width.

- ✔ columns: Provides a shorthand method for defining both the column-count and column-width properties.

One of the easiest ways to begin experimenting with columns is to create some content and then use a newspaper-style layout to present it. The following procedure helps you create a multiple column newspaper layout for some dummy text.

1. **Create a new HTML5 file with your text editor.**

2. **Type the following code for the HTML page.**

```
<!DOCTYPE html>

<html>
<head>
    <title>Creating a Newspaper Layout</title>
    <link rel="stylesheet" href="NewspaperLayout.CSS" />
</head>

<body>
    <h1>Creating a Newspaper Layout</h1>
    <p id="Text">
```

```
            Lorem ipsum dolor sit amet, consectetuer
            adipiscing elit, sed diam nonummy nibh euismod
            tincidunt ut laoreet dolore magna aliquam erat
            volutpat. Ut wisi enim ad minim veniam, quis
            nostrud exerci tation ullamcorper suscipit
            lobortis nisl ut aliquip ex ea commodo consequat.
            Duis autem vel eum iriure dolor in hendrerit
            in vulputate velit esse molestie consequat, vel
            illum dolore eu feugiat nulla facilisis at vero
            eros et accumsan et iusto odio dignissim qui
            blandit praesent luptatum zzril delenit augue
            duis dolore te feugait nulla facilisi. Nam liber
            tempor cum soluta nobis eleifend option congue
            nihil imperdiet doming id quod mazim placerat
            facer possim assum. Typi non habent claritatem
            insitam; est usus legentis in iis qui facit eorum
            claritatem. Investigationes demonstraverunt
            lectores legere me lius quod ii legunt saepius.</p>
    </body>
    </html>
```

All you have here is a heading and paragraph. The paragraph contains the dummy text used for content in the newspaper layout.

If you're wondering what Lorem ipsum is all about, you can read more at www.lipsum.com/. In fact, the site provides a dummy-text generator that won't distract a viewer's attention from an underlying layout or other technical consideration.

3. **Save the file as** NewspaperLayout.HTML.

4. **Create a new CSS file with your text editor.**

5. **Type the following CSS style information.**

```
#Text
{
    column-count: 3;
    column-rule: 4px ridge Blue;
    column-gap: 20px;

    -moz-column-count: 3;
    -moz-column-rule: 4px ridge Blue;
    -moz-column-gap: 20px;

    -webkit-column-count: 3;
    -webkit-column-rule: 4px ridge Blue;
    -webkit-column-gap: 20px;
}
```

REMEMBER

The example creates a style that includes three columns, with a blue rule between columns. Of course, you need to repeat the styles three times — once for each of the browser requirements.

6. **Save the file as** NewspaperLayout.CSS**.**

   The sample will appear in other chapters, so naming is important.

7. **Load the NewspaperLayout example.**

   You see a newspaper-style format as shown in Figure 5-9. This format will be easier to read when you work with a lot of text on a site. In the past, you'd have had to work pretty hard to get a layout as nice as this one, but now all you need is a few simple styles.

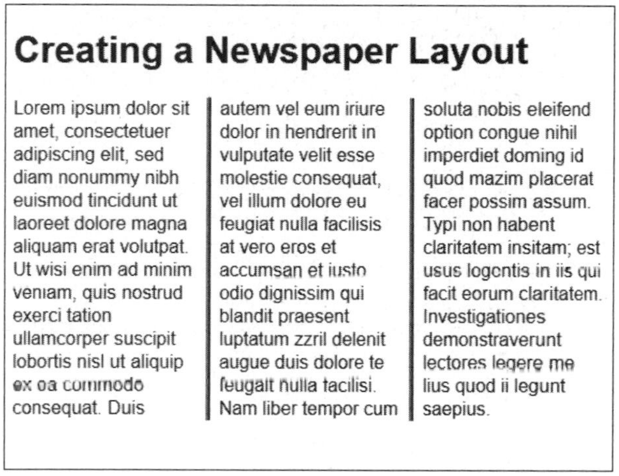

Figure 5-9:
It's easy
to create
a news-
paper style
layout with
columns.

Creating a Newspaper Layout

Lorem ipsum dolor sit amet, consectetuer adipiscing elit, sed diam nonummy nibh euismod tincidunt ut laoreet dolore magna aliquam erat volutpat. Ut wisi enim ad minim veniam, quis nostrud exerci tation ullamcorper suscipit lobortis nisl ut aliquip ex ea commodo consequat. Duis

autem vel eum iriure dolor in hendrerit in vulputate velit esse molestie consequat, vel illum dolore eu feugiat nulla facilisis at vero eros et accumsan et iusto odio dignissim qui blandit praesent luptatum zzril delenit augue duis dolore te feugait nulla facilisi. Nam liber tempor cum

soluta nobis eleifend option congue nihil imperdiet doming id quod mazim placerat facer possim assum. Typi non habent claritatem insitam; est usus legentis in iis qui facit eorum claritatem. Investigationes demonstraverunt lectores legere me lius quod ii legunt saepius.

Part II
Making Layouts Fast and Simple with Libraries

CSS Library: Horizontal CSS Menus: Links & Buttons: CSS3 demos: **Here**

Flipboard CSS buttons

Author: Dynamic Drive

Flipboard creates a series of CSS buttons that flip horizontally on themselves when the mouse rolls over them, creating an elegant, eye catching effect. It employs CSS3 transform and transitions to do the heavy work. The menu works in IE10+, and all modern versions of FF, Chrome, Safari, and Opera. It degrades perfectly with older browsers, down to IE7.

On a technical note, each button consists of 3 levels deep of markup, specifically: LI -> A -> SPAN. This is necessary to create the desired effect. When the mouse rolls over the outer LI parent, we rotate **both** the inner A and SPAN elements 180 degrees using CSS3 transform's rotateY(180deg) value. The key here is to declare this value on both of the inner elements, so while the child A element causes any content inside to appear as a mirror of itself when rotated, the grand child SPAN element restores the content back to its proper orientation.

⊞ Demo:

D R I V E N

www.dynamicdrive.com

In this part . . .

- ✔ Discover how jQuery makes it easy to add advanced functionality to a site
- ✔ Enhance your user interface using jQuery UI widgets and special effects
- ✔ Rely on Dynamic Drive to add structure to your site using layouts and menus
- ✔ Use the Google API to access all your favorite libraries and generators from one location

Chapter 6

Creating a Test Site with jQuery and jQuery UI

hird-party libraries are a cornerstone of creating web-based applications today because most developers (and even many designers) simply don't have the time to perform every task required to create a new site by hand. In fact, it doesn't make sense to create everything by hand when someone else already has done most of the work for you. The day of the Application Programming Interface (API), as libraries are often called, is at hand. This chapter is about two of the most popular libraries: jQuery and jQuery UI. Of course, there are many other libraries out there and you'll work with a number of them as the book progresses.

Third-party libraries differ in what they can do for you. Both jQuery and jQuery UI are JavaScript libraries. Up to this point in the book, you haven't used any JavaScript at all. In most cases, you'll use at least some JavaScript or another language on your site, but, as the examples in previous chapters prove, there are situations when all you need is CSS to accomplish a task. The jQuery and jQuery UI examples in this chapter focus on the sorts of tasks that you can't perform using CSS, such as discovering what kind of browser a user has.

In order to use some of the features of jQuery UI, you need to know a little more about the special selectors it uses and the way it interacts with the page. This chapter provides a short section that presents the essentials of working with jQuery UI to produce some really interesting special effects on a page. More importantly, once you know the way that jQuery UI works, you'll find that you can create some pretty amazing pages with very little JavaScript code.

This book is not a tutorial on using JavaScript. In fact, it would take another book to perform that task. My book, *HTML5 Programming with JavaScript for Dummies* (which you can find at `www.dummies.com`), provides a detailed guide for working with JavaScript. The book starts simply and moves through a number of topics, including using third-party libraries for a wealth of tasks. You can also find a number of helpful JavaScript tutorials online. The best of these tutorials is on the W3Schools.com site at `www.w3schools.com/js/`. If you really don't do well with online tutorials, you can watch the JavaScript video, "Learn JavaScript in 30 Minutes," at `www.youtube.com/watch?v=_cLvpJY2deo`.

Using the jQuery Core Features

The jQuery library (`http://jquery.com/`) helps you perform non-graphical tasks, such as detecting a user's browser, with relative ease. This library is designed to work with a broad array of browsers and doesn't rely on any particular platform to do its work. The library automatically handles browser and platform differences for you, so you don't have to worry about whether a particular bit of CSS requires a `-moz-` or a `-webkit-` prefix to work. All you need to think about is getting your work done.

The examples in this book show you how to access jQuery directly from the Internet, so you don't have to do anything special to use it except provide the required link on the page (much as you already do for CSS). However, if you want to use a local copy of jQuery to make your page work faster and to handle some security issues for your users, you can download a copy of the jQuery library from `http://jquery.com/download/`. The API is also fully documented online at `http://api.jquery.com/`. You can also get help with questions about issues not discussed in this book at `http://forum.jquery.com/`. Mobile device support is something that many API vendors haven't really tackled yet, so your Android (or other mobile device) may not work well with the examples in this chapter. The list of browsers that jQuery supports appears at `http://jquery.com/browser-support/`.

Detecting the user's browser type

In most cases, developers don't get to choose a user's browser. To determine whether a particular user can work with your application, then, you need first to detect the user's browser — and then determine whether that browser is acceptable.

Pros and cons of accessing libraries online

Many libraries such as jQuery provide both downloadable and direct Internet access versions of the code. Each method has pros and cons that you must consider. This book uses the Internet access technique because of the advantages it provides. You gain access to the most recent version of the library this way to ensure that the code you're using has all of the latest fixes in it. In addition, all you need is the page source — there is no need to download the JavaScript code. Trying to send JavaScript to some clients proves difficult because the client firewall prevents the transfer.

However, there are also disadvantages to using the Internet approach that are addressed by the downloadable code. For instance, a library vendor can update a library in a way that makes your application break, or the vendor may decide to remove the library altogether. Another problem is that using the Internet approach means that a heavily loaded server could slow your application to a crawl — using a local download doesn't incur this problem.

Creating the code required to perform this task by hand isn't impossible, but it can be hard. Articles like the one at www.javascripter.net/faq/browsern.htm tell you how to perform this task, but one look at the code should tell you that it's a complex task. (You can see the output from this example code at www.javascripter.net/faq/browserv.htm.)

jQuery makes it possible to perform the detection with relative ease. The following example shows one method to detect the name and version of the user's browser. It relies on the latest 1.*x* version of jQuery, which is version 1.10.1 at the time of this writing. (You can find complete code for this example in the \Chapter 06\jQuery folder of the downloadable code as BrowserDetect.html.)

```
<!DOCTYPE html>
<html>
   <head>
      <title>Detect a Browser</title>
      <script
         src="http://code.jquery.com/jquery-latest.js">
      </script>
      <script
         src="http://code.jquery.com/jquery-migrate-1.2.1.js">
      </script>
   </head>
   <body>
      <h1>Browser Information</h1>
      <p id="name"></p>
      <script language="JavaScript">
         var browser =
```

```
                    $.uaMatch(navigator.userAgent).browser;
            $('p[id="name"]').html(
                "Browser Name: <span>" + browser + "</span>");
        </script>
        <p id="version"></p>
        <script language="JavaScript">
            $('p[id="version"]').html(
                "Version Number: <span>" + $.browser.version +
                "</span>");
        </script>
    </body>
</html>
```

This is an HTML5 page, so it starts with the HTML declaration, <!DOCTYPE html>. As with the examples in Chapter 1, this example begins with a basic structure that includes the <html>, <head>, <title>, and <body> tags.

The code begins with the first <script> tag that uses the src attribute to tell the browser where to find the jQuery library. You can copy this information as shown to any page where you want to use jQuery. Anyone who uses the application will automatically have access to jQuery as long as the browser can access the Internet. (You can also download a copy of jQuery for local access from the jQuery site.)

The latest 1.*x* version of jQuery doesn't support the browser detection feature directly. You can read about this omission at http://api.jquery.com/jQuery.browser/. In order to make the feature work with anything newer than jQuery 1.8.3, you must also include the link for the jQuery Migrate library (http://code.jquery.com/jquery-migrate-1.2.1.js) as shown in the example.

The <body> of the page starts out with a <h1> tag that contains the page's heading. The next step is to provide a place for jQuery to put the browser's name. In this case, the example uses a <p> (paragraph) tag that has an id of name. The first <script> creates a var (variable) named browser and places the browser's name in it. The browser name is always provided to your application as part of the JavaScript navigator.userAgent object, but working with this object is time-consuming, so this code shows a one-line method for obtaining the information.

It's time to display the name onscreen. The $ (dollar sign) is a special symbol that refers to the jQuery library, which is also called an Application Programming Interface (API). The bit of code that says, $('p[id="name"]').html, tells jQuery to use the <p> tag with an id value of name to hold some HTML. This is a kind of selector. You can read about jQuery selectors in general in the "Selecting elements" section, later in this chapter, or in specific online at http://api.jquery.com/category/selectors/.

Using feature detection

An alternative to detecting the browser's name and version is to detect the features it supports directly by testing for them. For example, instead of inferring that a browser supports Asynchronous JavaScript and XML (AJAX) by verifying the browser name and version, you can test the browser's ability to use AJAX by executing code that relies on AJAX. In fact, this is the technique currently recommended by the makers of jQuery (`http://api.jquery.com/jQuery.support/`). The library automatically runs the required tests for you and then places the results in properties that you can check. You can check the `ajax` property to determine whether the browser supports AJAX.

Although this technique is directly supported in the latest version of jQuery, there are problems using it as well. The most important issue to consider is that the site tells you outright that the library might have certain detection features pulled without notice or without a long deprecation cycle, which means that your code could simply stop working at some point. You could wake up some morning to find that the `ajax` property is no longer available and that your application is failing as a result. The jQuery testing technique is a poor way to detect the functionality of the browser that you're using because it's unreliable.

You now have a specific tag selected. The code then tells jQuery to create some text, a `<span>`, and then place the name of the browser within that span. All this information appears in the `<p>` tag after the script executes.

Next comes a second `<p>` tag. This one has an `id` attribute of `version`. The accompanying script starts out the same as before. The `$('p[id="version"]').html` entry tells jQuery to place some HTML in the `<p>` tag with an `id` attribute of `version`. In this case, jQuery provides what you need as a property. All the code has to do is tell jQuery to place the value in `browser.version` within the `<p>` tag to display the browser's version number. When you run this example, you see output similar to what's shown in Figure 6-1.

Figure 6-1:
Detecting the browser name and version is made easier when using jQuery.

Browser Information

Browser Name: mozilla

Version Number: 21.0

A library can detect only the browsers it's designed to detect. Consequently, jQuery detects some browsers, but not others. For example, you can't currently use it to detect an Android browser because Android isn't in the list of browsers supported by jQuery (which focuses on desktop browsers). Most browser detection methods rely on user agent strings that contain information about the browser (see http://msdn.microsoft.com/library/ms537503.aspx for details). To see the user agent string for your browser, check out What's My User Agent? (www.whatsmyuseragent.com/). You can generally find lists of user agent strings for devices online. For example, the Android user agent strings appear at www.gtrifonov.com/2011/04/15/google-android-user-agent-strings-2/. With enough knowledge, you can usually modify third party libraries to detect other browser types, but that topic is well outside the scope of this book.

Selecting elements

You can use jQuery to perform a vast array of object selections in your application, but for the most part, you use the basic selectors. You can read more about them at http://api.jquery.com/category/selectors/basic-css-selectors. Here's a list of basic selectors that you commonly use:

- **All selector** ("*"): Selects all the elements in the document.
- **Object selector** (object): Selects the specific object types. The most commonly used object is document.
- **Class selector** (".class"): Selects a specific class as specified by the class attribute for an element. This selector always appears within quotes and is preceded by a period.
- **Element selector** ("element"): Accesses all the elements with a particular tag name, such as *p* for the <p> tag. This selector always appears within quotes.
- **ID selector** ("#id"): Chooses a specific element with the id attribute value specified. This selector always appears within quotes and is preceded by a pound sign (#).
- **Multiple selector** ("selector1, selector2, selector*N*"): Selects each of the elements specified in the comma delimited list.

One of the more commonly used selectors is the element selector. After you select an element, you can change it in a number of ways. For example, you might choose to change the text associated with that element in some way (later examples will show all sorts of other ways to manipulate output). The following example shows how to select elements and modify their associated text. (You can find complete code for this example in the \Chapter 06\ jQuery folder of the downloadable code as SelectingElements.html.)

```
<!DOCTYPE html>

<html>
<head>
    <title>Selecting Elements</title>
    <script
        src="http://code.jquery.com/jquery-latest.js">
    </script>
</head>

<body>
    <h1></h1>
    <p></p>

    <script type="text/javascript">
        $("h1").text("A Sample Header")
        $("p").text("This is a sample paragraph.")
    </script>
</body>
</html>
```

The example begins with simple <h1> and <p> tags that don't contain any text. If you displayed this page without the script, you'd see a blank page. However, with the script in place, the page now contains information as shown in Figure 6-2. It's also possible to use the text() method to obtain the current value of an object of any sort (assuming the object actually contains text).

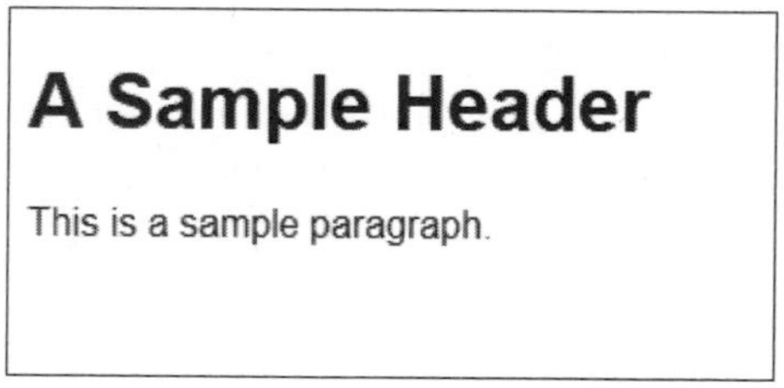

Figure 6-2: jQuery provides a number of methods for selecting objects, including element selection.

A Sample Header

This is a sample paragraph.

Changing an element's CSS

The previous two sections about jQuery have described various mechanical ways in which you can use the library to obtain specific results. The jQuery library is mostly used to perform these sorts of necessary, but low-level tasks. You can, however, use jQuery to perform some fancier tasks by incorporating CSS. There's an actual `.css()` method you can use to access the CSS associated with an object or to modify the CSS used by that object. You always see the change made to the CSS because the jQuery changes are inline, rather than internal or external CSS.

Imagine that you want to create a formatted multiplication table that automatically changes the color of a selected cell to make it easier to see. The example uses JavaScript to generate the table. Of course, you could also manually generate the table using standard code, but this approach is simpler. (You can find complete code for this example in the `\Chapter 06\jQuery` folder of the downloadable code as `NestedLoop.html`.)

```javascript
// Start the table.
document.write("<table>");

// Start a heading row.
document.write("<tr>");

// Create a heading.
for (var i = 0; i <= 10; i++)
{
   if (i == 0)
   {
      document.write("<th />");
   }
   else
   {
      document.write("<th>" + i + "</th>");
   }
}

// End the heading row.
document.write("</tr>");

for (var i = 1; i <= 10; i++)
{
   // Start a data row.
   document.write("<tr>")

   // Create the row header.
   document.write("<th>" + i + "</th>");

   for (var j = 1; j <= 10; j++)
   {
      // Add each data element.
      document.write("<td>" + i * j + "</td>");
   }

   // End a data row.
   document.write("</tr>")
```

```
    }

    // End the table.
    document.write("</table>");
```

This code starts by creating a `<table>` and creating a heading row, `<tr>`, for it. The loop simply adds the numbers 1 through 10 to the header using heading, `<th>`, tags. After the header row is complete, the code then begins to create the data rows. Each data row begins with a heading, followed by the multiplied values. The double loop creates a square table that shows the multiplied values all the way up to 10 * 10.

In order to make this example pleasant to look at, you'd want to use CSS to differentiate the rows and columns. The highlighted cell would use a larger font size and a different font color. In order to make this change, the example uses the `.Selected` internal CSS style shown here.

```
<style type="text/css">
   .Selected
   {
      color: blue;
      font-size: 30px;
      font-weight: bold;
   }
</style>
```

The example now contains a table with multiplied values and a special style for the selected cell. However, it still lacks any formatting for the rows and there isn't any way to select a specific cell so that it will have the required special formatting. The following code presents one way to accomplish these goals.

```
// Perform some basic formatting.
$("th:even").css("background-color", "lightblue");
$("th:odd").css("background-color", "lightgreen");
$("td:even").css("background-color", "lightgreen");
$("td:odd").css("background-color", "lightblue");
$("th, td").css("width", "50px");

// Add a special effect.
$("td").mouseover(
   function()
   {
      $(this).toggleClass("Selected");
   });
$("td").mouseout(
   function()
   {
      $(this).toggleClass("Selected");
   });
```

The formatting consists of selecting the `<th>` and `<td>` elements and then using a basic filter to choose between odd and even elements. The odd elements receive one background color, and the even elements receive another. The code then uses a multiple selector to apply the same width formatting to each of the cells. By combining selectors and selector filters, you can create some interesting effects with little programming. It's important to remember that this table is programmatically generated, so applying formatting to it could be difficult.

The special effect starts with the `<td>` elements. When a user hovers the mouse pointer over a particular element, the code applies the `.Selected` CSS formatting to it. Likewise, when the user places the mouse pointer somewhere else, the effect is toggled back to the original formatting used by the `<td>` element. Toggling the formatting is a quick way to create a `mouseover` effect. Figure 6-3 shows typical output from this example.

Nesting Loops - Multiplication Table

	1	2	3	4	5	6	7	8	9	10
1	1	2	3	4	5	6	7	8	9	10
2	2	4	6	8	10	12	14	16	18	20
3	3	6	9	12	15	18	21	24	27	30
4	4	8	12	16	20	24	28	32	36	40
5	5	10	15	20	25	30	35	40	45	50
6	6	12	18	24	30	36	42	48	54	60
7	7	14	21	28	35	42	49	56	63	70
8	8	16	24	32	40	48	56	64	72	80
9	9	18	27	36	45	54	63	72	81	90
10	10	20	30	40	50	60	70	80	90	100

Figure 6-3: The table is a little nicer and includes a special effect now.

Understanding jQuery UI

Although jQuery is interesting, it lacks pizzazz. For the most part, you can't use it to create any sort of special visual effect (at least, aside from the sorts of visual effects you could use CSS to perform). The jQuery UI library (`http://jqueryui.com`), on the other hand, works with the user interface. You use it to add new kinds of interactions, expand the number of controls at your disposal, create special effects, and perform utilitarian tasks, such as positioning user interface elements precisely.

All the examples in this section require that you provide a link to the jQuery UI as well as jQuery. They also use the jQuery Cascading Style Sheet (CSS) that helps create a pleasant presentation. These external elements make the coding task easier. Make sure you include the following entries in the heading of the file for each of the examples:

```
<script
   src="http://code.jquery.com/jquery-latest.js">
</script>
<script
   src="http://code.jquery.com/ui/1.9.2/jquery-ui.js">
</script>
<link
   rel="stylesheet"
   href="http://code.jquery.com/ui/1.9.2/themes/base/jquery-ui.css" />
```

You can always download the required files if desired. However, this approach makes it easier for your application to receive required updates. The following sections introduce you to jQuery UI and help you understand how you can use these features to create more interesting applications.

Using a third-party library doesn't limit your ability to personalize the output. A number of sites show how to modify the CSS, for example, to create some interesting results (see `http://benknowscode.wordpress.com/2012/10/18/exploring-the-new-jquery-ui-spinner-beyond-the-basics/` as an example). Chapter 13 demonstrates techniques you can use to modify the CSS for jQuery and jQuery UI to produce your own customizations. For now, all you really need to know is that many of the effects that you see in this chapter owe their special nature to the use of CSS.

Using the jQuery UI Controls

Widgets are specialty controls you can use to create special effects on a page. The advantage of these controls is that they can make your application easier to use and more appealing as well. The disadvantage of widgets is that they can be overused or used incorrectly.

A widget is a good idea only when it materially adds to the usefulness and accessibility of your application. When you find yourself admiring the pizzazz that a widget adds to the application — rather than how it makes the user work faster or with greater ease — reconsider using the widget. Your application may work a lot better without it.

HTML5 already comes with a number of useful generic controls of all sorts. For example, if you need a standard check box for your application, rely on HTML5 to provide it. The controls described in the following sections are special in some way. For example, the `Accordion` widget makes it easy to focus user attention by hiding unused elements from sight. The jQuery UI library does provide access to additional widgets that aren't discussed in the sections that follow. Most widgets, such as `Button`, have HTML5 counterparts and therefore aren't that useful.

Working with Accordion

You use the accordion to hide any page element from view. When a user selects a category, the elements in that category become visible, and the elements from all other categories are hidden. The effect is to focus user attention and make the user more efficient in performing specific tasks. The following code is all you need to make this feature usable. (You can find complete code for this example in the `\Chapter 06\Widgets` folder of the downloadable code as `Accordion.HTML`.)

```
$(function()
{
    $("#Configuration").accordion();
});
```

The code is concise, but the secret in this case is the way you create the tags for your page. Figure 6-4 shows how the form appears to the user. Notice that the `Accordion` widget hides from view the settings that the user isn't focusing on. When the user clicks Background Color, the Foreground Color options are hidden from view. Likewise, clicking Options reveals the Options controls.

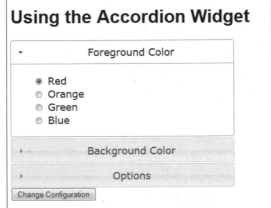

Figure 6-4:
The
Accordion
widget
focuses
user
attention.

The controls in each area don't matter to the `Accordion` widget, but the HTML5 formatting does. This form also includes a submit button. If you don't configure the controls properly, the submit button becomes part of the accordion effect, and clicking it no longer submits the form. Here's a condensed view of the HTML5 for this example:

```
<form id="ConfigForm"
      method="get"
      action="Accordion.html">
   <div id="Configuration">
       <h2>Foreground Color</h2>
       <div>
           <input id="FGRed"
                  type="radio"
                  name="Foreground"
                  value="Red"
                  checked="checked" />
           <label for="FGRed">Red</label><br />
... More inputs and labels ...
       </div>
       <h2>Background Color</h2>
       <div>
           <input id="BGRed"
                  type="radio"
                  name="Background"
                  value="Red"
                  checked="checked" />
           <label for="BGRed">Red</label><br />
... More inputs and labels ...
       </div>
       <h2>Options</h2>
       <div>
           <input id="Sounds"
                  type="checkbox"
                  name="Sounds"
                  value="SpecialSounds" />
           <label for="Sounds">Use Special Sounds</label>
           <br />
           <input id="Effects"
                  type="checkbox"
                  name="Effects"
                  value="SpecialEffects" />
           <label for="Effects">Use Special Effects</label>
       </div>
   </div>
   <input id="ChangeConfig"
          type="submit"
          value="Change Configuration" />
</form>
```

Notice that you must place the headings control groups within a separate `<div>` and then label that `<div>` as the one you want to use for the accordion effect. A separate `<div>` houses the individual controls for a specific group. The `submit` button is part of the form, but it's outside the `Configuration` `<div>`. When you click the Change Configuration button, you see that the form works as it should — by examining the address field content. Using the defaults, the resulting URL contains `Accordion.html? Foreground=Red&Background=Red` when you click Change Configuration.

Working with Datepicker

There are situations where HTML5 currently provides a solution for a particular need, but few vendors have implemented it yet. This is the case with the date and time support for HTML. Only Opera and Chrome provide support for the date and time features. For example, if you want to add a date to a form, you can use the date input type as shown here:

```
<label for="Date">Enter a Date: </label>
<input id="Date"
       type="date" />
```

The default date is today. When the user clicks the field, the application displays a date picker control, but only when you use Opera or Chrome. Until the other vendors provide date and time support, it's still necessary to use the jQuery UI Datepicker widget to ensure that all of your users can enter a date with ease. The following code shows how to use the Datepicker widget. (You can find complete code for this example in the \Chapter 06\ Widgets folder of the downloadable code as Datepicker.HTML.)

```
$(function()
  {
      $("#DateEntry").datepicker();
  })
```

DateEntry is a standard <input type="text"> control. When the user clicks the control, jQuery UI automatically displays a calendar like the one shown in Figure 6-5.

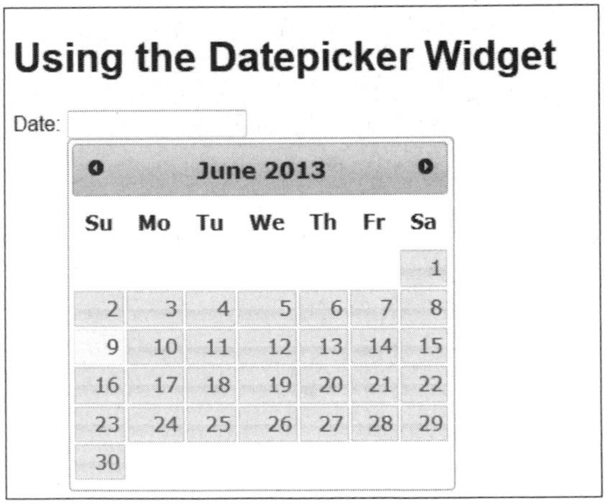

Figure 6-5:
The
Datepicker
widget
makes
entering
dates much
easier.

Working with Dialog

Both HTML5 and JavaScript make it possible to display dialog boxes. For example, you can see a combination of an HTML5/CSS3 dialog box that doesn't require the use of JavaScript at `www.codeproject.com/Tips/170049/ Pure-HTML-5-CSS-3-Modal-Dialog-Box-no-JavaScript`. Adding JavaScript means you have instant access to the `alert()`, `confirm()`, and `prompt()` functions for limited direct dialog box display. You also have all of the functionality that JavaScript can provide to create truly amazing custom dialog boxes. The problem with all of these approaches is that you may need to write a considerable amount of code to obtain the desired result. On the other hand, using jQuery UI makes it possible to create these dialog box types without much coding at all:

- Basic
- Animated
- Modal
- Modal with confirmation
- Modal form
- Modal message

Additionally, even a basic jQuery UI dialog box provides better functionality than the JavaScript `alert()` function. You can move the dialog box around, resize it, and close it by using the X in the upper-right corner. The text can also be decorated in various ways because it uses standard HTML input. The following example begins by creating an internal style to use to decorate the text. (You can find complete code for this example in the `\Chapter 06\ Widgets` folder of the downloadable code as `DialogBox.HTML`.)

```css
<style type="text/css">
 .Normal
 {
     font-family: Arial, Helvetica, sans-serif;
     color: SaddleBrown;
     background-color: Bisque;
 }
 .Emphasize
 {
     color: Maroon;
     font-style: italic;
     font-size: larger;
 }
</style>
```

This code provides a few simple changes to the text — just enough so you can see the custom CSS at work. The following code creates the dialog box on screen automatically when you load the page.

```
<h1>Creating a Simple Dialog Box</h1>
<div id="DialogContent"
    title="Simple Dialog Example"
    hidden>
    <p class="Normal">
        This is some
        <span class="Emphasize">interesting</span>
        text for the dialog box!
    </p>
</div>
<script type="text/javascript">
    $("#DialogContent").dialog();
</script>
```

The dialog box requires two elements — a container, such as a <div>, to hold the caption in the title attribute and a textual element, such as a <p>, to hold the content. Notice that the paragraph text includes a <span> in this case to provide emphasis to the word interesting. You can format the content in any way desired without modifying the call to jQuery UI at all.

The script uses an id selector to access the <div>. It then makes a simple call to dialog() to display the dialog box on screen. Figure 6-6 shows the output from this example. Notice that it provides a pleasing appearance and it contains formatted content, unlike the alert() function, which provides an austere, square dialog box that lacks any formatting.

Figure 6-6:
Creating
custom
dialog boxes
is easier
when using
jQuery UI.

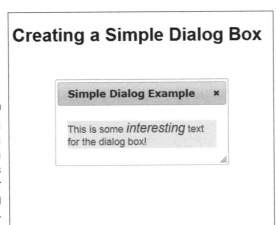

Working with Progressbar

Users are impatient, and sometimes a process takes a while to complete. A file downloads only so fast, and some transactions become bogged down on the server. A progress bar makes it possible for the developer to keep the user informed about the progress of a task. Modern programming strategies try to keep the user from waiting at all by performing longer tasks in the background, but sometimes a user can't proceed until the task is done. This is the time you need to rely on a progress bar to keep the user from attempting to stop the process before it completes.

The following example shows how to use a progress bar. In this case, the progress bar is updated through a timing loop. Each time the timer expires, the progress bar is updated, and the timer is reinstituted. The result is that the progress part indicator moves from left to right and that the timer eventually stops when the indicator moves all the way to right. (You can find complete code for this example in the \Chapter 06\Widgets folder of the downloadable code as Progressbar.HTML.)

```
// Configure the progress bar.
$(function()
  {
      $("#Progress").progressbar({value: 0});
  })

// Create a variable to hold the timer object.
var Timer;

// Create a variable to hold the total timeout.
var Timeout;

function StartTimer()
{
   // Initialize the timeout.
   Timeout = 0;

   // Set the progress bar maximum value.
   $("#Progress").progressbar(
      "option", "max", parseInt($("#StartValue").val()));

   // Create the timer variable.
   Timer = window.setTimeout(UpdateTimer, 100);
}

function UpdateTimer()
{
   // Get the maximum value.
   var MaxTime =
      $("#Progress").progressbar("option", "max");
```

```
    // Check for the end of the timing cycle.
    if (Timeout >= MaxTime)
        return;

    // Update the Timeout value.
    Timeout += 100;

    // Update the percentage completed.
    $("#PercentDone").text(
        Math.round((Timeout/MaxTime)*100));

    // Set the progress bar value.
    $("#Progress").progressbar("value", Timeout);

    // Create the timer variable.
    Timer = window.setTimeout(UpdateTimer, 100);
}
```

The first task is to create the progress bar itself by calling `progressbar()`. Notice that you must provide an initial value as input. However, the progress bar configuration isn't complete — the call to `StartTimer()` later will perform some additional configuration tasks.

The `StartTimer()` function is called when the user clicks the Start Timer button on the form. This function initializes two global variables. `Timer` is a timer object used to animate the progress bar. `Timeout` is the current elapsed time in milliseconds. This function also configures the `max` option for the progress bar. The indicator is a percentage of the current `value` and the `max` value properties. The maximum value is provided by the user through an `<input type="text">` control, `StartValue`.

Whenever `Timer` expires, it calls `UpdateTimer()`. `UpdateTimer()` obtains the maximum time value from the progress bar and places it in `MaxTime`. It then verifies that `Timeout` is less than `MaxTime`. When `Timeout` finally reaches `MaxTime`, the progress bar has reached 100 percent and it's time to stop the timer.

The next step is to update `Timeout` to the next value. Every iteration advances `Timeout` by 100 milliseconds.

After updating `Timeout`, the example updates the onscreen percentage, which is stored in a `<span>` with an `id` of `PercentDone`. It also updates the progress bar's `value` attribute so that the bar moves to the next position.

A timer fires only once. To create the next loop of the iteration, the example must reset `Timer`. When the next 100 millisecond wait is over, `UpdateTimer()` is called again and the process begins anew. Figure 6-7 shows typical output from this example.

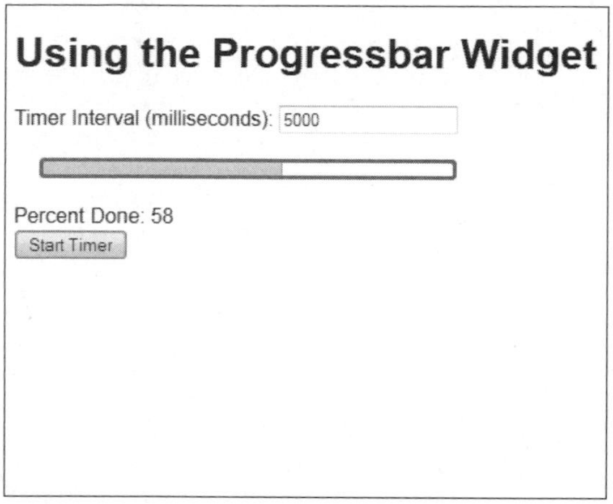

Using the Progressbar Widget

Timer Interval (milliseconds): 5000

Percent Done: 58

Start Timer

Figure 6-7:
Use progress bars
to show
the user
how far a
process has
completed.

Working with Slider

Sliders give the user the capability to input a value visually — as part of a whole. A slider ensures that the user inputs a correct value within a range of values, so you don't need to worry about security issues or incorrect values. As a result, sliders provide a valuable means of allowing variable input. The following example shows how to use a slider in your application. It begins with the HTML used to define the location and basic appearance of the slider. (You can find complete code for this example in the \Chapter 06\Widgets folder of the downloadable code as Slider.HTML.)

```
<h1>Using the Slider Widget</h1>
<div id="Slider">
    <span id="Left">0</span>
    <span id="Right">50</span>
</div>
<div>Value: <span id="Value"></span></div>
```

The slider has a minimum value of 0 and a maximum value of 50. The slider also uses the following CSS to give the output a more pleasing appearance and to make it possible to mark the beginning and ending of the scale.

```
<style type="text/css">
    #Slider
    {
        width: 50%;
        margin: 30px;
    }

    #Left
    {
```

```
        position: absolute;
        top: 15px;
        left: -5px;
    }

    #Right
    {
        position: absolute;
        top: 15px;
        left: 99%;
    }
</style>
```

As you can see, the CSS places the beginning and end of the scale in a particular position so that it matches the size of the slider. As far as the user
knows, the scale and the slider are one piece, but they're actually two pieces
in the code. The remaining piece of the code is the script shown here.

```
$(function()
{
    $("#Slider").slider(
        {
            // Set the maximum slider value.
            max: 50,

            // Perform tasks when the value changes.
            change: function(event, ui)
            {
                // Display the current slider value.
                $("#Value").text(
                    $("#Slider").slider("value"));
            }
        });
})
```

In this case, the code sets the maximum slider value to 50. The minimum
value defaults to 0. However, you can set both the maximum and minimum
values to any starting or stopping position. Even though the example doesn't
show it, the Slider can have more than one handle, so it can represent a
range. This flexibility means that you can ask the user to input both a starting
and a stopping point.

One of the most commonly used events is change. The example displays the
new value each time the user finishes moving the handle. However, the way in
which you use the output depends on your application. Generally, you use the
output to provide data input or application control. However, it's a good idea
to display the actual slider value so the user knows the actual input value.
(See Figure 6-8.)

Figure 6-8:
Sliders
make it
possible to
obtain pre-
cise input
in a given
range from
the user.

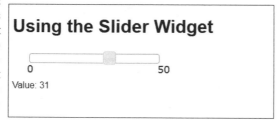

Working with Tabs

Many developers use tabbed interfaces to reduce application complexity. If you can focus the user's attention on one item at a time, you reduce the potential for errant input. This example provides an alternative to the example shown in the "Using the `Accordion` widget" section, earlier in this chapter. As with that example, you begin with a simple function call. (You can find complete code for this example in the `\Chapter 06\Widgets` folder of the downloadable code as `Tabs.HTML`.)

```
$(function()
  {
      $("#Configuration").tabs();
  });
```

The trick for this example is in the HTML tags, just as it was for the `Accordion` widget example. There are some important differences in how you create the two pages to obtain the desired appearance, as shown in the following code:

```
<form id="ConfigForm" method="get" action="Tabs.html">
   <div id="Configuration">
      <ul>
         <li><a href="#Tab1">Foreground Color</a></li>
         <li><a href="#Tab2">Background Color</a></li>
         <li><a href="#Tab3">Options</a></li>
      </ul>
      <div id="Tab1">
         <input id="FGRed"
                type="radio"
                name="Foreground"
                value="Red"
                checked="checked" />
         <label for="FGRed">Red</label><br />
... More inputs and labels ...
```

```
        </div>
        <div id="Tab2">
            <input id="BGRed"
                    type="radio"
                    name="Background"
                    value="Red"
                    checked="checked" />
            <label for="BGRed">Red</label><br />
... More inputs and labels ...
        </div>
        <div id="Tab3">
            <input id="Sounds"
                    type="checkbox"
                    name="Sounds"
                    value="SpecialSounds" />
            <label for="Sounds">Use Special Sounds</label>
            <br />
            <input id="Effects"
                    type="checkbox"
                    name="Effects"
                    value="SpecialEffects" />
            <label for="Effects">Use Special Effects</label>
        </div>
    </div>
    <input id="ChangeConfig"
            type="submit"
            value="Change Configuration" />
</form>
```

Notice that the <h2> elements are gone in this case. Instead of using headings to define the separation between elements, you provide an unordered
list (<ul>) instead. The list must contain a href to each of the <div> elements in the page. There isn't any difference in the page content. You also
need to provide some CSS to format the control as shown here.

```
<style>
    #Configuration
    {
        width: 90%;
        text-align: center;
    }
    #Configuration div
    {
        text-align: left;
    }
</style>
```

In this case, the #Configuration style defines the overall size of the
tabbed interface and the fact that the tabs have centered text. The
#Configuration div changes the content alignment to left. Figure 6-9
shows typical output from this example.

Figure 6-9:
Tabs focus
the user's
attention,
just as the
accordion
interface
does.

To make a change, you click the tab that contains the information you want to see. You make changes as normal. Clicking the Change Configuration button sends the changes to the server. If you test this example by using the same process you did for the accordion example, you get precisely the same results — only the interface appearance has changed.

Performing jQuery UI Interactions

The way in which a user interacts with an application is important. When a set of interactions seems contrived or proves inconvenient, users have to concentrate too hard on what the application should be able to do and how to obtain that result, which makes them lose focus on their work goal. Many business users are currently in the process of moving from desktop applications to browser-based applications for at least part of their work. Consequently, these users often anticipate having desktop-like features in their browser-based application solutions. The following sections describe some jQuery UI features that help you provide that desktop experience to your users.

Creating a Draggable Interface

Sometimes a user needs to reposition screen elements to make them easier to see or work with. Creating an environment in which the user can move items around need not involve writing reams of code. In fact, all you really need is a single method called `draggable()`. The following code shows the method used to create a draggable paragraph in this example. (You can find complete code for this example in the `\Chapter 06\Interactions` folder of the downloadable code as `DragContent.HTML`.)

```
$(function()
  {
     $("#MoveMe").draggable();
  });
```

This code is interesting because it actually creates a jQuery anonymous function that extends the jQuery environment rather than working with any particular page feature. The focus of this call is a paragraph (<p> tag) with an id of MoveMe. All you need to do is access that member and call draggable() to make it move around. Try the downloadable example and you find that you can move the paragraph anywhere you want on the page.

To create a movable box, this example relies on a custom style. The style creates a border, allows plenty of room for the text, and then centers the text both horizontally and vertically. Here's the style used for this example:

```
#MoveMe
{
    border: solid;
    width: 200px;
    height: 5em;
    text-align: center;
    line-height: 5em;
}
```

Many developers experience problems vertically centering text within a <p> tag. You can find a number of ways to perform this task. However, one of the easiest ways to get the job done in a platform- and browser-consistent manner is to use the line-height style as shown in the example. The trick though is to set the height and line-height styles to the same value — the text will always appear in the middle.

Creating a Droppable Interface

Sometimes a user needs to drag an item to a container and drop it in the container. There are many instances of this process in current applications. For example, the concept of dragging an item to a trash can and dropping it to delete it is consistent across all platforms. If you want to send an item to the printer, you drag its icon to the printer icon and drop it there.

Of course, to create this effect, you must have one item that's draggable and another item that's droppable. The preceding section describes how dragging works. As with that previous example, this example relies on some custom CSS to create a particular effect onscreen.

```
#FillMe
{
   border: solid;
   width: 400px;
   height: 10em;
   text-align: center;
   line-height: 10em;
   position: absolute;
   top: 250px;
   left: 250px;
}
.Filled
{
   background-color: lightblue;
}
```

There are two states for the `droppable` container: empty and filled. It starts out empty and uses the `#FillMe` style. When the `draggable` paragraph is dropped into the `droppable` paragraph, the style changes to `.Filled`. The following code shows how dragging and dropping can work together to create this desirable user interaction. (You can find complete code for this example in the `\Chapter 06\Interactions` folder of the downloadable code as `DropContent.HTML`.)

```
$(function()
  {
    $("#MoveMe").draggable();
    $("#FillMe").droppable(
      {
        drop: function(event, ui)
          {
            $(this)
              .addClass("Filled")
              .html("Filled!");
          }
      });
  });
```

This example uses the same code for the `MoveMe` <p> tag. A second <p> tag, with the `id` of `FillMe`, acts as a container. When a user drags `MoveMe` to `FillMe`, the code calls the anonymous function associated with the `drop` event. Notice how the example begins with the event name, followed by a colon (`:`), followed by the anonymous function to handle that event. Notice how the code uses `addClass()` to modify the class of `FillMe`. The `droppable()` method supports these events:

✔ `create`: Indicates that the `droppable` item has been created.

✔ `activate`: Indicates that a `draggable` item is active. You can use this event to change the droppable item style so that the user can see where to drop an item.

✔ deactivate: Indicates that the user has stopped dragging an item. You can use this event to change the droppable style back to its original state.

✔ over: Fires when the draggable item is over the top of the droppable item. You can use this event to indicate when the user should release the mouse to drop the item into the container.

✔ out: Fires when the draggable item has moved out of the droppable item container. You can use this event to tell the user that it's no longer possible to drop an item into the container.

✔ drop: Tells the droppable item (the container) that it has received a draggable item.

You can create an event handler for any of the events you want to handle in your code. In fact, there are several opportunities for special effects that would focus the user's attention.

Creating a Resizable Interface

The wide variety and types of screens used to display information make it necessary to allow the user to resize elements as needed. In most cases, you can simply allow the user to make the element any size. However, there may be situations where you need to monitor the amount of resizing so that you can tailor content to meet the needs of the container. The following example shows how to resize an object and monitor its size. (You can find complete code for this example in the \Chapter 06\Interactions folder of the downloadable code as ResizeContent.HTML.)

```
$(function()
  {
      $("#ResizeMe").resizable(
          {
              minWidth: 200,
              minHeight: 60,
              resize: function(event, ui)
              {
                  $("#Content")
                      .html("Width: " +ui.size.width +
                          "<br/>Height: " + ui.size.height);
              }
          });
  });
```

This example is interesting because it shows how to set properties as well as respond to events. In this case, the minWidth and minHeight properties keep the element a specific minimum size — the user can't make the element smaller.

The code also responds to the `resize` event. There's a special requirement for resizing you need to know about. The resizing container is separate from the content element. Here's the HTML for this example:

```
<div id="ResizeMe">
   <p id="Content">
      Resizable Paragraph
   </p>
</div>
```

The associated style, `#ResizeMe`, provides a border around the `<div>`, sets the starting height and width, and centers the content in the container. When you want to write content to the screen, you must use the content element, not the container element. Otherwise the sizing handles will disappear, and the user won't be able to resize the element after the first time. In this case, the current size of the container appears as part of the `ui` object passed to the `resize` event handler. You access the information though the `size.width` and `size.height` properties, as shown in the code.

Creating a Selectable Interface

Making it possible to select from a list of items reduces the chance that the user will enter incorrect information. Fortunately, HTML5 already comes with a number of selection controls, but you may find that these controls don't quite fulfill your needs at times. In this case, a custom selection technique implemented with jQuery UI might answer the need. A selection mechanism can consist of a `<div>` and a series of `<p>` tags, as shown here. (You can find complete code for this example in the `\Chapter 06\Interactions` folder of the downloadable code as `SelectContent.HTML`.)

```
<div id="Selections">
   <p id="Red">Red</p>
   <p id="Green">Green</p>
   <p id="Blue">Blue</p>
   <p id="Purple">Purple</p>
</div>
```

Notice that the `<div>` acts as a container and the `<p>` tags act as items within the container. (The example includes CSS styles to format each of the selectors, such as using a red background for the `Red` element — a `#Selections` style defines the width of the selectors, along with the margin and padding used to display them.) No matter how you implement your custom list (and it need not be the arrangement shown), it must have a container/item arrangement like the one shown here. When you have the arrangement in place, you can create a selection and tracking mechanism like the one shown in the following code:

```
// Create an array to track the selections.
var Selections = new Array();

// Handle the selects and unselects.
$(function()
  {
    $("#Selections").selectable(
      {
        selected: function(event, ui)
        {
          // Verify the item hasn't already
          // been added.
          if (Selections.indexOf(ui.selected.id ) ==
              -1)

              // Add the id of the selected item
              // to the array.
              Selections.push(ui.selected.id);
        },

        unselected: function(event, ui)
        {
          // Find the location of the unselected
          // item in the array.
          var Index =
              Selections.indexOf(ui.unselected.id);

          // Remove that item.
          Selections.splice(Index, 1);
        }
      });
  })

// Display the results.
function ShowResults()
{
   alert("You have selected: " + Selections);
}
```

The `Array`, `Selections`, keeps track of the current selection list. To make the `<div>`, `Selections`, selectable, you use the `selectable()` method. This example uses two events, `selected` and `unselected`, to keep track of the current selections. When the user selects a new item, the `selected` event handler verifies that the item doesn't already appear in `Selections`, and then it pushes the new item onto `Selections`.

The `unselected` event handler must perform two tasks. First, it must locate the unselected item using the `indexOf()` method. Second, it must use `splice()` to remove that item from `Selections`.

This example doesn't provide any fancy output, but you can see for yourself how well the selection methodology works. Click Show Selections to display the list of selected items. The `ShowResults()` event handler displays a list of the selections for you. In a production application, you could just as easily process each of the selected items.

A final piece to this particular application is the need to define one special style. You must provide a means for the display to register the selected state of a particular item, which means providing values for the `#Selections .ui-selected` style, as shown here:

```
#Selections .ui-selected
{
   background: black;
   color: white;
}
```

When a user selects an item, the background turns black with white text so the user can see a visual change. You could also modify the text as a second means of helping the user see the selection.

Creating a Sortable Interface

Certain kinds of sorting are easy for computers to do. For example, a computer can put items in alphabetical order much faster than a human can, especially when the list is long. However, sorts aren't always logical. You may want the user to sort a list of items by personal preference or other criteria that the computer can't even understand. In these cases, you need a means of allowing manual sorts — and this example gives you just what you need. The following example lets a user sort items by unspecified criteria. (You can find complete code for this example in the `\Chapter 06\Interactions` folder of the downloadable code as `SortContent.HTML`.)

```
$(function()
  {
     $("#SortMe").sortable();
  })

function ShowResults()
{
   // Create the ouput string.
   var Output = "The sort order is:\n        ";

   // Locate each of the required items and
   // add them to the string.
   $("#SortMe p").each(
     function(index, element)
```

```
        {
            Output += element.innerHTML.substr(74);
        });

    // Display the result.
    alert(Output);
}
```

The `sortable()` call is all that you need to do to make the list visibly sort-able. The user can place the elements, whatever those elements might be, in any order desired. To make this call work, however, you do need to create a container — a `<div>` in this case — and a list of items, specifically `<p>` tags. The `SortMe` id goes with the `<div>`.

Accessing the items in order is also a requirement. Otherwise there's no point in letting the user sort the items. In this case, it's actually easier to use other jQuery functionality to obtain the list of elements in the order in which they appear and process them that way. `ShowResults()` demonstrates one tech-nique for performing this task. You begin by creating the appropriate selector, which begins with the `<div>`, `SortMe`, and ends with each `<p>` tag it contains. The anonymous function receives both an `index` and an `element` argument. By checking the `innerHTML` property of the element, you can obtain the mon-iker for that `<p>` tag. The result is displayed in a dialog box.

This example also makes use of a special jQuery UI CSS style. This style cre-ates a double-ended arrow that helps the user understand that each item can move up or down in the list. You create it using a `<span>` like this:

```
<span class="ui-icon ui-icon-arrowthick-2-n-s"></span>
```

You can find a list of these icons at `http://jquery-ui.googlecode.com/svn/tags/1.6rc5/tests/static/icons.html`. It's important to create icons that match the way your list appears onscreen.

Creating jQuery UI Special Effects

Special effects can add pizzazz to your site. They can turn mundane informa-tion into something with that special sparkle that people will remember long after they've read the material you provide. Using special effects correctly can draw the user's attention to a particular area of the page or help the user understand a process when using an animated sequence. The point is that effects are normally an addition to the page, not the main focus of it. Effects normally don't present any sort of information, but they can enhance the impact of information you do present. The following sections describe some of the more interesting effects that you can create using jQuery UI.

Adding color animations

If you want to perform an actual color animation in your application, you need to use the `animate()` method. This method seems to be a work in progress because the documentation for it isn't nearly as well-written as the other documentation for jQuery UI. The method does seem to work for all the target platforms and browsers for this book, but you'll want to experiment to ensure that it will work for every browser you need to target. The color will actually transition in this case. It's also possible to control the text colors to a large degree. The following example shows the most commonly used transitions. (You can find complete code for this example in the `\Chapter 06\ Animations` folder of the downloadable code as `Animate.HTML`.)

```
$(function()
  {
    // Track the normal state.
    var State = true;

    $("#ChangeColors").click(
      function()
      {
        if (State)
        {
          // Set to the changed state.
          $("#SampleText").animate(
            {
              backgroundColor: "#0000ff",
              color: "white",
              borderColor: "#ff0000",
              height: 100,
              width: 600
            }, 1500);
        }
        else
        {
          // Set to the normal state.
          $("#SampleText").animate(
            {
              backgroundColor: "#7fffff",
              color: "black",
              borderColor: "#00ff00",
              height: 50,
              width: 400
            }, 1500);
        }

        // Change the state.
        State = !State;
      }
    )
  })
```

If you're thinking that this code looks like it works similar to CSS, it does, but the `animate()` method provides a significantly reduced list of features it can change. You can change many features of the text and the container that holds it, including both the width and height. However, you can't change things like the kind of border used to hold everything — even though you can change the color of the border. The jQuery UI documentation states that `animate()` supports these properties:

- `backgroundColor`
- `borderBottomColor`
- `borderLeftColor`
- `borderRightColor`
- `borderTopColor`
- `color`
- `columnRuleColor`
- `outlineColor`
- `textDecorationColor`
- `textEmphasisColor`

The library-supplied examples (those provided by the vendor on the vendor's site) show that a few other properties are supported, including `width`, `height`, and `borderColor`. Use these non-published properties with care. Even though they work now, they may not be supported in future releases of the library.

Employing class transitions

Using CSS classes can have an interesting effect on the presentation of information onscreen. jQuery UI makes it possible to use CSS classes to perform animations in four different ways:

- Adding a class
- Removing a class
- Switching between classes
- Toggling a class

In all four cases, the effect doesn't occur immediately — you provide a time delay to make the transition between presentations slow enough for the user to see. (You can find complete code for this example in the `\Chapter 06\ Animations` folder of the downloadable code as `ManageClasses.HTML`.)

```
$(function()
  {
    $("#ChangeClass").click(function()
      {
        $("#SampleText").addClass(
          "Effect", 1500, RemoveClass);
        return false;
      });

    function RemoveClass()
    {
      $("#SampleText").removeClass(
        "Effect", 1500, "easeOutBounce");
    };

    $("#SwitchClass").click(function()
      {
        $(".Normal").switchClass(
          "Normal", "Effect", 1500, "easeInElastic");
        $(".Effect").switchClass(
          "Effect", "Effect2", 1500,
          "easeOutElastic");
        $(".Effect2").switchClass(
          "Effect2", "Normal", 1500,
          "easeInOutElastic");
        return false;
      });

    $("#ToggleClass").click(function()
      {
        $(".Normal").toggleClass("Effect", 1500);
        return false;
      })
  })
```

There are three buttons on the front of the page: Add/Remove Class, Switch Between Classes, and Toggle Between Classes. Each of these buttons is assigned an event handler as shown. The RemoveClass() function is a callback for the Add/Remove Class button. After the transition for the event handler has ended, the code automatically calls this function.

All of these animations work in precisely the same way — they add or remove classes to or from the specified element. In this case, a <div> named SampleText is the target of the animations. The difference between the method calls is how they perform their task. The addClass() method performs a straightforward addition of a class. You supply the name of the class to add as the first argument. If the class already exists for the element, nothing happens. Likewise, the removeClass() method removes the specified class from the element. Again, you supply the name of the class to remove as the first argument.

The switchClass() method switches between one class and another. You can use it to create multiple transitions. For example, this example shows how to switch between three transitions. The Normal class is replaced with Effect, Effect is replaced with Effect2, and Effect2 is replaced with Normal. Consequently, you see the animations rotate between three classes. You supply the name of the class to remove as the first argument and the name of the class to add as the second argument.

The toggleClass() method adds or removes a class depending on whether the class is assigned to the element. In this case, the code adds Effect when SampleText lacks it and removes Effect when SampleText has it applied. You supply the name of the class to toggle as the first argument.

jQuery UI can't animate all styles. For example, there's a transition between having the text left justified and having it centered in this example. This transition can't be animated. What you see is that the effect occurs at the end of the animation. In addition, some effects are animated, but they aren't animated in the way you might expect. For example, if an element changes color, the new color is used throughout the animation, but you see it gradually fade in.

Each of these method calls includes a time delay of 1500 milliseconds. This value indicates the amount of time in which the animation occurs. The default setting is 400 milliseconds, which is a little hard for most people to see. However, this argument is optional, and you don't have to supply it to make the method work.

The addClass() method includes another optional argument, a callback function. The callback function is called when the animation is over. The example uses the callback function to toggle the effect. However, a callback could be used for any of a number of purposes. For example, you could use it to create a validation sequence to ensure that users enter the correct data for form fields that have incorrect information.

An animation can also use an *easing function*. This function determines how the animation appears onscreen. The default setting is to use the swing easing function, which provides a gentle transition from the starting point to the end point that most users will appreciate (the animation starts a tiny bit slow, becomes a bit faster and more linear in the middle, and then ends a bit slow). However, you might want a little more pizzazz or at least a different effect. You can see a list of easing functions at http://api.jqueryui.com/easings. This example uses a number of different easing functions so that you get an idea of how they work.

Working with advanced easing

Many applications require that you show or hide elements at different points of application execution. It may be something as simple as not needing the element at that particular time (such as a progress bar). In most cases, you simply want the element to go away. Whether the user notices the disappearance is immaterial to the application's functionality. However, you may want the user to notice the change in some situations. For example, a user might select an option that makes other options inaccessible. Using a special effect to make this more noticeable could be helpful.

The jQuery UI library provides several means of controlling element visibility in an animated manner. The fact that the element is shown or hidden doesn't change, but the way in which the application shows or hides it does. For example, you could use a slide effect to show that a new element has been added due to a choice the user has made. There are four main methods of animating elements by using this technique:

- Use an effect where the element visually changes.
- Show a hidden element by using an effect.
- Hide an element by using an effect.
- Toggle an element's visibility by using an effect.

The effect that you choose for working with an element controls how jQuery UI visually manages it. For example, an explode effect causes the element to break into pieces, with each piece moving in a different direction off screen. The following keywords define the sorts of effects that you can use (you can find additional details at `http://api.jqueryui.com/category/effects`):

blind	bounce	clip
drop	explode	fade
fold	highlight	puff
pulsate	scale	shake
size	slide	transfer

In addition to the actual effect, you can use an easing function to make the effect more pronounced or special in other ways. You can see a list of easing functions at `http://api.jqueryui.com/easings`. The following example shows how to use all four approaches for working with element visibility. There are actually four buttons used for the example, but element visibility limits you to seeing just three at a time because you can't show an element that's already visible or hide an element that's already hidden. (You can find complete code for this example in the `\Chapter 06\Animations` folder of the downloadable code as `Visibility.HTML`.)

```
$(function()
  {
      // Keep track of the element hidden state.
      var Hidden = false;

      $("#Effect").click(
          function()
          {
              $("#SampleText").effect(
                  "bounce", "easeOutBounce", 1500);
          });

      $("#Show").click(
          function()
          {
              Hidden = false;

              $("#SampleText").show(
                  "slide", 1500, ChangeButtonState);
          });

      $("#Hide").click(
          function()
          {
              Hidden = true;

              $("#SampleText").hide(
                  "explode", 1500, ChangeButtonState);
          });

      $("#Toggle").click(
          function()
          {
              Hidden = !Hidden;

              $("#SampleText").toggle(
                  "scale", {percent: 0}, 1500,
                  ChangeButtonState);
          });

      // Set the button state as needed.
      function ChangeButtonState()
      {
          if (Hidden)
          {
              $("#Show").attr("hidden", false);
              $("#Hide").attr("hidden", true);
          }
          else
          {
              $("#Show").attr("hidden", true);
```

```
            $("#Hide").attr("hidden", false);
        }
    }
})
```

The example begins by creating a variable, `Hidden`, to track the state of the element. When the element is hidden, the `Show` button is displayed. Likewise, when the element is displayed, the `Hide` button is displayed as well. This functionality is controlled by a callback function, `ChangeButtonState()`.

The code for the `Effect` button simply performs an effect on the element, `SampleText`. In this case, you see the `bounce` effect. The performance of this effect is modified by the `easeOutBounce` easing function, and the entire animation lasts 1500 milliseconds. The actual visibility is unchanged, but the user sees an animation of the element onscreen. You could use this technique to point out fields that have incorrect information or require additional information. Of course, you can also use it to perform any other sort of simple animation desired — including a looped animation, where the animation is constantly replayed.

The `Show` and `Hide` button code work hand-in-hand to hide or display `SampleText`. The `Show` button uses the `slide` effect, and the `Hide` button uses the `explode` effect. Both perform the task over 1500 milliseconds. Notice that both event handlers set the state of `Hidden` directly because the state is an absolute based on the task that the button performs. The event handlers also provide `ChangeButtonState()` as a callback function. The animation calls this function after the animation has completed to set the button state correctly.

The `Toggle` button works like a combination of the `Show` and `Hide` buttons — the event handler simply toggles the `SampleText` visual state. Because the state isn't known, the value of `Hidden` is also toggled. In this case, the event handler calls the `scale` effect, which requires an additional argument in the form of `percent`. Make sure you check the effects to determine whether they require additional arguments — most don't. When the animation completes, the application calls `ChangeButtonState()` to reconfigure the user interface as needed.

Performing transforms

It's possible to use jQuery to perform transformations and these transformations are often more powerful, yet easier to use, than the native CSS transformations I discuss in Chapter 5. However, in order to gain this functionality, you must download a *jQuery plug-in* — a special kind of library that extends the native jQuery functionality. The best plug-in to perform the task is jquery.transform.js (`http://louisremi.github.io/jquery.transform.js/index.html`). You can go to this page and see the transformations demonstrated.

The host page doesn't contain a link for downloading the plug-in, unfortunately. In order to obtain a copy of this plug-in, you go to `www.downscripts.com/jquery.transform.js_javascript-script.html` and click the Click Here to Download link. You receive a `.ZIP` file containing a number of files, including the `jquery.transform.js` file that you must copy into your application directory. (You must perform the download and obtain access to `jquery.transform.js` to work with the example in this section.) To gain access to this plug-in, you add the following `<script>` tag after all of the other jQuery entries (position is important).

```
<script
    src="jquery.transform.js">
</script>
```

Using this plug-in works much like any other jQuery function call. This example relies on a `<div>` that contains a `<p>` with the required content. In this case, the example simply rotates the content, but you have access to all of the usual CSS transformations. The interesting part is the simplicity of the script used to perform the task. (You can find complete code for this example in the `\Chapter 06\Animations` folder of the downloadable code as `Transform.HTML`.)

```
<script type="text/javascript">
    $("#TransformMe").css("transform", "rotate(45deg)");
</script>
```

This script simply says to perform a standard CSS transformation of rotating the `TransformMe` `<div>` 45 degrees. In addition to static transformations, this plug-in also provides animated transformations using the `animate()` function with a timing function that defines how long to perform the animation. It's also quite easy to combine transformations to create various special effects. Make sure you try the examples in the test folder of the downloaded plug-in to see the full range of effects that this plug-in provides.

Defining the Basic Page Layout

You'll find quite a few more examples throughout this book of working with jQuery plug-ins, but one requires a special mention. The jQuery UI Layout Plug-in (`http://layout.jquery-dev.net/`) makes it incredibly easy to create various kinds of layouts for your site without spending a lot of time. The layouts can incorporate all sorts of interesting features, such as the ability to resize partitions dynamically. That's right; the user can choose how to make each section of a page in order to focus on the content of interest.

The examples on the site can be complex, but it pays to review them at `http://layout.jquery-dev.net/demos.cfm`. This plug-in can help you create amazingly functional sites with very little programming. Of course, a simpler example is always welcome. This example demonstrates the simplest layout you can create using this plug-in. The starting point is to add a reference to the plug-in library. This is one case where you don't have to download anything. (You can find complete code for this example in the `\Chapter 06\ Layout` folder of the downloadable code as `Layout.HTML`.)

```
<script
   src="http://layout.jquery-dev.net/lib/js/jquery.layout-latest.js">
</script>
```

In order to create the panes used for this example, you define `<div>` tags for `North`, `South`, `East`, `West`, and `Center` panes. Of all the panes, the `Center` pane is the only one that's required.

```
<div class="ui-layout-center">
   Center
</div>
<div class="ui-layout-north">
   North
</div>
<div class="ui-layout-south">
   South
</div>
<div class="ui-layout-east">
   East
</div>
<div class="ui-layout-west">
   West
</div>
```

Notice that each pane has a specific `class` value associated with it. In order to create a pane in a particular location, you must use the associated predefined class. Otherwise the layout plug-in won't recognize the `<div>` as a pane. The object within each `<div>` defines the content for that pane.

The example also requires use of a script to associate the panes with the plug-in. The following script is all you need to make this example functional.

```
<script type="text/javascript">
   $(document).ready(
      function ()
      {
         $('body').layout({ applyDemoStyles: true });
      });
</script>
```

The arguments you supply to the layout() function determine the appearance of the panes. The applyDemoStyles argument provides the simplest
layout method. Figure 6-10 shows the output from this example.

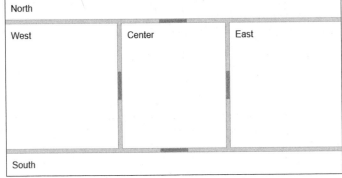

Figure 6-10:
The user
can resize
or toggle
individual
panes in this
layout.

You can perform two tasks with the example. Notice the dark area in the
middle of each line separating the panes. Clicking this dark area will close
that pane. Clicking it again will reopen the pane. When you hover the mouse
cursor over one of the lines, it turns into a double-pointed arrow. This arrow
lets you resize the pane as needed.

Chapter 7

Creating Pages Using Dynamic Drive

Dynamic Drive (www.dynamicdrive.com/) is a library composed of many resources — only some of which appear in this chapter. This site provides more than an API and it offers selections in more than just CSS3 or JavaScript. Of course, for this book, what you're really interested in is CSS3 — along with perhaps a little JavaScript to perform some additional tasks. With this in mind, the chapter discusses:

✔ Layouts

✔ Menus

✔ Image management

✔ Form management

✔ Icon usage

When you get an opportunity, you should also check out the other resources this site provides (especially the tools). For example, the site provides access to seven different kinds of calendar widgets you can add to your application (as of this writing — there may be more by the time you read this). The tools are really interesting as well. For example, ::Email Riddler (www.dynamic drive.com/emailriddler/) transforms your e-mail address into a series of incomprehensible numbers and letters — making it hard for spam harvesters to grab it. Yet the address is still usable by users of your site.

Each of the sections that follow will explore a different area of Dynamic Drive. Most focus exclusively on CSS3, which should amaze you because it turns out that CSS3 can do more than expected for a simple method of defining page style. Make sure you check the site relatively often for updates. The new items appear at www.dynamicdrive.com/new.htm.

Working with Layouts

The layout you use on a site determines its usability. Choose the wrong layout and the user will have a hard time interacting with your site. Frustrated users are always just a click away from the next site — one that uses a layout that works better with the information being presented. Dynamic Drive presents two basic kinds of layout: two-column and three-column. These two layouts can be further subdivided into *fixed* (the column size always remains the same) and *liquid* (the column size changes to match the amount of content displayed). A third layout type supports frames within pages.

This section provides a common set of instructions you can use to work with any of the layouts that Dynamic Drive provides. All of the layouts provide the same presentation, which makes them easy to review, compare, and use with your own code. After you create a page containing a layout, you'll want to modify it. The "Modifying the layouts" section, later in this chapter, provides instructions for performing this task. The following sections describe these layouts and how to use them in detail.

Developing with fixed layouts

Some content requires that you provide specific positioning and maintain columns of a particular size. For example, forms require this kind of precision, because otherwise you can't be sure that a user can even see which fields to fill out.

A *fixed column* doesn't change size with the browser. When the browser window becomes too small to hold the width of the columns, a horizontal scrollbar appears so that the user can scroll right and left within the content. Likewise, when the browser window becomes larger than the content width, the page displays blank areas to the right and left of the two columns.

Fixed columns are typically used when the presentation of the content requires it. For example, a site with pictures (such as my blog at http://blog.john muellerbooks.com/) may use a fixed column to ensure the pictures are always placed correctly on the page. You can find the Dynamic Drive fixed layouts at www.dynamicdrive.com/style/layouts/category/C12/.

Developing with liquid layouts

Liquid layouts, also called *fluid layouts* (the site uses both terms interchangeably), rely on content without particular dimensions. It doesn't matter if news is printed in a wide format or a tall format. All that really matters is that the user can access all the words in a story in order to read the information.

A *fluid* column is one that automatically resizes to take advantage of the browser window size. This format works best when the content is mainly text-based or store sites, such as `Amazon.com`. Store sites especially want you to see as much content as possible (hoping to make additional sales). You can find the Dynamic Drive liquid layouts at `www.dynamicdrive.com/style/layouts/category/C13/`.

Using two-column layouts

A *two-column* layout is great for a site where you want to create a list of links on either the left or right side of the page and then have a wide area for content on the other side. For example, many blogs use this type of setup. The two-column layouts all appear at `www.dynamicdrive.com/style/layouts/category/C9/`. Figure 7-1 shows a typical view of the layouts on this page.

Each listing provides an overview of what you can expect as output from the layout. For example, the first entry is a two-column layout where both columns are fixed.

Figure 7-1:
A listing of the two-column layouts on the Dynamic Drive site.

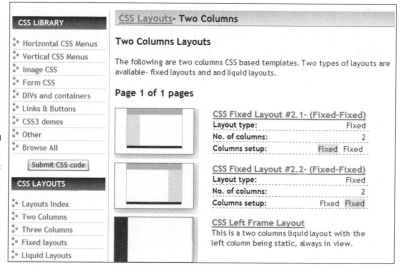

The second entry is a repeat of the first, but notice that the narrow column (the one that typically holds the links) is on the right rather than on the left. Many forums (such as `http://stackoverflow.com/`) use this format to present answers to questions. Placing the links on the right tends to put additional emphasis on the content because people look on the left side of the page first (for the most part).

Some of the entries in this list have fluid columns. In every case, the fluid column contains the content. All that happens, in this case, is that the content expands to fill the browser window so you can see more information without scrolling. The left or right pane remains the same size so that the links (or other content) continue to take up the same amount of space.

Working with layouts

To choose a particular layout, click its link. You see a page that contains a better presentation of the layout at the top as shown in Figure 7-2. The text contained in the layout is filler so that you can better judge how the layout will feel with content in it. You can try resizing the browser to see how the layout will look at different sizes.

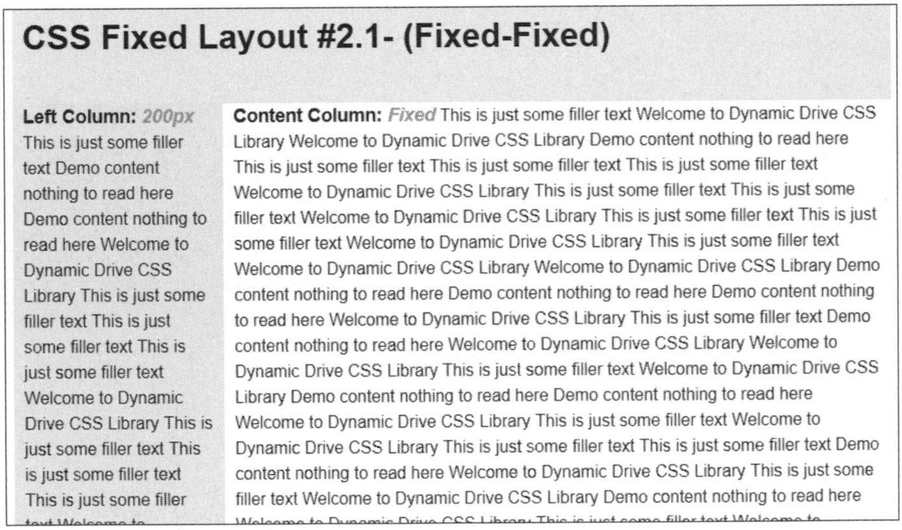

Figure 7-2: The upper half of a layout page contains a presentation of the layout.

CSS Fixed Layout #2.1- (Fixed-Fixed)

Left Column: *200px* This is just some filler text Demo content nothing to read here Demo content nothing to read here Welcome to Dynamic Drive CSS Library This is just some filler text This is just some filler text This is just some filler text Welcome to Dynamic Drive CSS Library This is just some filler text This is just some filler text This is just some filler text Welcome to...

Content Column: *Fixed* This is just some filler text Welcome to Dynamic Drive CSS Library Welcome to Dynamic Drive CSS Library Demo content nothing to read here This is just some filler text This is just some filler text Welcome to Dynamic Drive CSS Library This is just some filler text This is just some filler text Welcome to Dynamic Drive CSS Library This is just some filler text This is just some filler text Welcome to Dynamic Drive CSS Library This is just some filler text Welcome to Dynamic Drive CSS Library Welcome to Dynamic Drive CSS Library Demo content nothing to read here Demo content nothing to read here Demo content nothing to read here Welcome to Dynamic Drive CSS Library This is just some filler text Demo content nothing to read here Welcome to Dynamic Drive CSS Library Welcome to Dynamic Drive CSS Library This is just some filler text Welcome to Dynamic Drive CSS Library Demo content nothing to read here Demo content nothing to read here Welcome to Dynamic Drive CSS Library This is just some filler text Welcome to Dynamic Drive CSS Library This is just some filler text This is just some filler text Demo content nothing to read here Welcome to Dynamic Drive CSS Library Demo content nothing to read here Welcome to Dynamic Drive CSS Library Demo content nothing to read here

At the bottom of the same page, you see the CSS used to create the page's appearance as shown in Figure 7-3. The code appears in an internal CSS `<style>` tag, but you can easily move it to an external CSS file if desired.

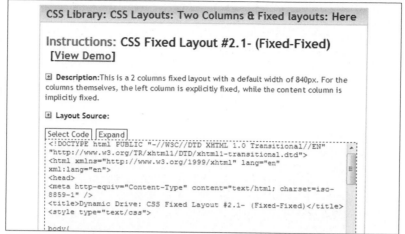

Figure 7-3:
The lower
half of a
layout page
contains the
code used
to create
the layout.

The code provides an entire page you can use for testing. The following steps tell how to access the code.

1. **Click Expand.**

    You see the code area of the page expand to show all of the code used to create the layout.

2. **Click Select Code.**

    The page selects all of the code in the code area for you.

3. **Right click the highlighted code and choose Copy from the context menu.**

    The precise technique you use varies by browser and platform. For example, you can press Ctrl+C on Windows systems or Command+C on Mac systems to perform the same task. The idea is to get the code placed on the Clipboard.

4. **Open your editor and paste the contents of the clipboard into a new file.**

    You see the same example that appeared on the Dynamic Drive site.

5. **Save the new file.**

    Use a filename that represents the layout you selected.

6. **Load the file into your browser.**

    You see the complete Dynamic Drive example for the layout.

To use the layout on your own page, simply copy the content of the `<style>` tag to the page you're creating. It's safe to ignore the script at the end of the `<head>` section — its only purpose is to fill the page with sample data.

However, you should make note of the styles used with elements in the page layout. These styles and their associated `<div>` tags provide the actual layout you see onscreen.

Modifying the layouts

It pays to try a few of the layouts to see what you want to do with them before you begin creating a production project. Copy the source code from the example on the Dynamic Drive site and place it into files as you expect to use it. For the purposes of this example, you create an HTML5 file with the following content obtained from the HTML code shown with the example. (You can find complete code for this example in the `\Chapter 07` folder of the downloadable code as `TwoColumnLayout.HTML`.)

```html
<!DOCTYPE html>

<html>
<head>
    <title>CSS Fixed Layout #2.1- (Fixed-Fixed)</title>
    <link rel="stylesheet" href="TwoColumnLayout.CSS" />
</head>

<body>
    <div id="maincontainer">
        <div id="topsection">
            <div class="innertube">
                <h1>CSS Fixed Layout #2.1- (Fixed-Fixed)</h1>
                <p><em>840px</em></p>
            </div>
        </div>
        <div id="contentwrapper">
            <div id="contentcolumn">
                <div class="innertube">
                    <p><b>Content Column:
                        <em>640px</em></b></p>
                </div>
            </div>
        </div>
        <div id="leftcolumn">
            <div class="innertube">
                <p><b>Left Column: <em>200px</em></b></p>
            </div>
        </div>
        <div id="footer">
            <p>Footer</p>
        </div>
    </div>
</body>
</html>
```

The example adds white space to the code provided on the Dynamic Drive site for the purposes of making it easier to read and also to show how the structure is created using the `<div>` tags. It's a good idea to do the same thing with any code you obtain from the site. You want to be sure that you understand how the layout works before you begin performing any required modifications.

The example removes the Dynamic Drive scripts because you don't need them to fill the sections with random content. However, it does add notes showing the number of pixels used by default for each of the sections (the Dynamic Drive example only notes the size of the fixed left column). If you modify the CSS for this site, you should also change the notes you create about the fixed column sizes.

The example also uses an external CSS file. Notice the addition of a `<link>` tag in the `<head>`. The CSS for the external file is unchanged from the `<style>` tag for the example page as shown here.

```css
body{
margin:0;
padding:0;
line-height: 1.5em;
}

b{font-size: 110%;}
em{color: red;}

#maincontainer{
width: 840px; /*Width of main container*/
margin: 0 auto; /*Center container on page*/
}

#topsection{
background: #EAEAEA;
height: 90px; /*Height of top section*/
}

#topsection h1{
margin: 0;
padding-top: 15px;
}

#contentwrapper{
float: left;
width: 100%;
}

#contentcolumn{
margin-left: 200px; /*Set left margin to LeftColumnWidth*/
}

#leftcolumn{
```

```
float: left;
width: 200px; /*Width of left column*/
margin-left: -840px; /*Set left margin to -(MainContainerWidth)*/
background: #C8FC98;
}

#footer{
clear: left;
width: 100%;
background: black;
color: #FFF;
text-align: center;
padding: 4px 0;
}

#footer a{
color: #FFFF80;
}

.innertube{
margin: 10px; /*Margins for inner DIV inside each column (to provide padding)*/
margin-top: 0;
}
```

At this point, you can load the page to start thinking about what you'd like to modify. Figure 7-4 shows the page as it appears without modification after copying it from the site and separating the HTML from the CSS.

Figure 7-4:
The two-column layout used to create an example page.

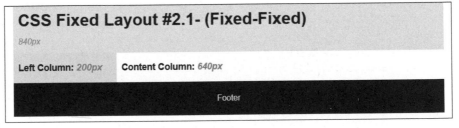

The first option you'll want to change is the colors used for the various objects. Of course, the colors need to match the color scheme for your site. The templates use hexadecimal color representations. You should modify them to match those used by other templates on your site (if necessary).

Templates that rely on fixed column widths may require tweaking to work with the rest of your site. To change the overall width of the page, you modify the `width` property of the `#maincontainer` style. The left pane width is controlled by the `width` property of the `#leftcolumn` style. The content pane size is the difference between the `#maincontainer` style width and the

#leftcolumn style width. Dynamic Drive tends to use consistent naming, so a layout that uses the right column for links would have a #rightcolumn style that you modify to change the width of that column. If you change the size of the #leftcolumn or #rightcolumn styles, then you also need to change the margin-left property of the #contentcolumn style to match.

The height of the top section is only 90px. This could cause a problem when working with a larger header. Change the height property of the #topsection style to make it compatible with other headers on your site. Likewise, the footer lacks an actual height, so you may need to modify it by adding a height property to the #footer style to ensure each page of your site looks the same.

These templates also rely on both the <b> (bold) and <em> (emphasis) tags. Although both tags are still supported by HTML5, there's a strong warning with the <b> tag to use it only as a last resort. If you plan long term use of these templates, it would be a good idea to replace the <b> tag entries with the <strong> or <mark> tags, or better yet, just avoid using the <b> and <em> tags completely in favor of CSS formatting. These tags are leftovers from the days before CSS made it possible to add various forms of emphasis and bolding using the font-style and font-weight properties. The example shows the tags intact, but the recommendation is to remove them and use other kinds of formatting instead.

Using three column layouts

Three-column layouts are commonly used on sites that provide a list of generic links on one side of the page, content in the middle, and advertising or page-specific links on the other side. The Dynamic Drive layout pages show one use of this layout where you see a list of offerings in the left pane, the actual layouts in the content pane, and a list of sponsors in the right pane. There are variations on this theme. One example appears on the Electronic Frontier Foundation site at www.eff.org/about where you see site links in the left pane, information about EFF in the content pane, and news links in the right pane. You can see a list of the three column layouts at www.dynamicdrive.com/style/layouts/category/C10/. As with the two-column layouts, you find a mix of fixed and fluid layouts when working with the three-column layouts.

Of course, there are more types of three-column layouts than there are of two-column layouts because more permutations are possible. In some of the layouts, one of the side columns is fluid, as is the content column. There's even a layout where all three columns are fluid, which means that the entire layout will resize itself to match the current browser window size.

The one type of three-column layout missing from this site is one in which the two columns are aligned, one over the top of the other. This form is commonly used for online documentation, such as the Java 7 API at http://docs.oracle.com/javase/7/docs/api/ as shown in Figure 7-5.

One way around this problem is to use another product, such as the UI Layout plug-in for jQuery described in the "Defining the Basic Page Layout" section of Chapter 6. Another alternative is to modify the CSS Fixed Layout #3.3- (Fixed-Fixed-Fixed) layout shown in Figure 7-6.

Java™ Platform Standard Ed. 7
All Classes
Packages
java.applet
java.awt
java.awt.color
java.awt.datatransf
All Classes
AbstractAction
AbstractAnnotation
AbstractAnnotation
AbstractBorder
AbstractButton
AbstractCellEditor
AbstractCollection
AbstractColorChoo
Overview Package Class Use Tree Deprecated Index Help
Java™ Platform
Prev Next Frames No Frames
Java™ Platform, Standard Edition 7
API Specification
This document is the API specification for the Java™ Platform, Standard Edition.
See: Description
Packages
Package
Description
java.applet
Provides the classes necessary tc an applet and the classes an appl communicate with its applet conte
java.awt
Contains all of the classes for cre: interfaces and for painting graphic

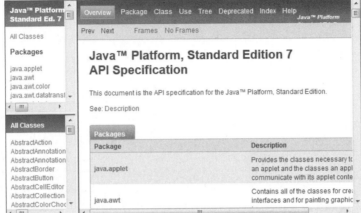

Figure 7-5: A three-column layout used for documentation purposes.

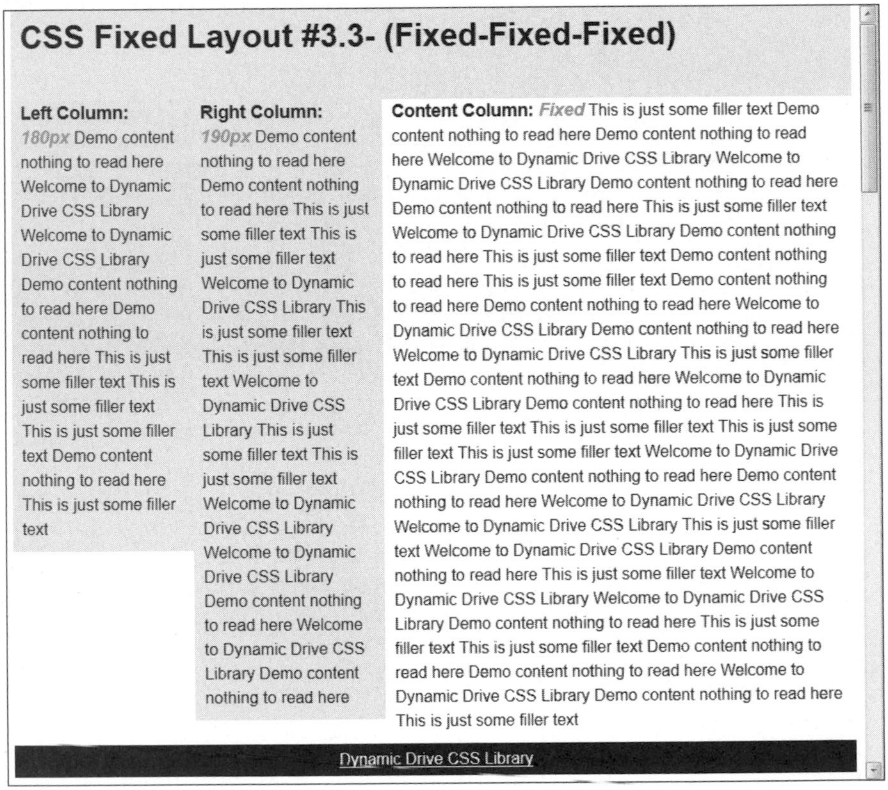

CSS Fixed Layout #3.3- (Fixed-Fixed-Fixed)
Left Column: 180px Demo content nothing to read here Welcome to Dynamic Drive CSS Library Welcome to Dynamic Drive CSS Library Demo content nothing to read here Demo content nothing to read here This is just some filler text This is just some filler text This is just some filler text Demo content nothing to read here This is just some filler text
Right Column: 190px Demo content nothing to read here Demo content nothing to read here This is just some filler text This is just some filler text Welcome to Dynamic Drive CSS Library This is just some filler text This is just some filler text Welcome to Dynamic Drive CSS Library This is just some filler text This is just some filler text Welcome to Dynamic Drive CSS Library Welcome to Dynamic Drive CSS Library Demo content nothing to read here Welcome to Dynamic Drive CSS Library Demo content nothing to read here
Content Column: Fixed This is just some filler text Demo content nothing to read here Demo content nothing to read here Welcome to Dynamic Drive CSS Library Welcome to Dynamic Drive CSS Library Demo content nothing to read here Demo content nothing to read here This is just some filler text Welcome to Dynamic Drive CSS Library Demo content nothing to read here This is just some filler text Demo content nothing to read here This is just some filler text Demo content nothing to read here Demo content nothing to read here Welcome to Dynamic Drive CSS Library Demo content nothing to read here Welcome to Dynamic Drive CSS Library This is just some filler text Demo content nothing to read here Welcome to Dynamic Drive CSS Library Demo content nothing to read here This is just some filler text This is just some filler text This is just some filler text This is just some filler text Welcome to Dynamic Drive CSS Library Demo content nothing to read here Demo content nothing to read here Welcome to Dynamic Drive CSS Library Welcome to Dynamic Drive CSS Library This is just some filler text Welcome to Dynamic Drive CSS Library Demo content nothing to read here This is just some filler text Welcome to Dynamic Drive CSS Library Welcome to Dynamic Drive CSS Library Demo content nothing to read here This is just some filler text This is just some filler text Demo content nothing to read here Demo content nothing to read here Welcome to Dynamic Drive CSS Library Demo content nothing to read here This is just some filler text
Dynamic Drive CSS Library

Figure 7-6: The three-column layout provides three fixed columns.

You don't need to make any changes to the HTML part of this example. The HTML5 version of the layout looks like this. (You can find complete code for this example in the \Chapter 07 folder of the downloadable code as ThreeColumnHelpLayout.HTML.)

```html
<!DOCTYPE html>

<html>
<head>
    <title>
        CSS Fixed Layout #3.3- (Fixed-Fixed-Fixed)
    </title>
    <link rel="stylesheet"
        href="ThreeColumnHelpLayout.CSS" />
</head>

<body>
    <div id="maincontainer">
        <div id="topsection">
            <div class="innertube">
                <h1>
                    CSS Fixed Layout #3.3- (Fixed-Fixed-Fixed)
                </h1>
            </div>
        </div>
        <div id="contentwrapper">
            <div id="contentcolumn">
                <div class="innertube">
                    <p>
                        <b>Content Column: <em>Fixed</em></b>
                    </p>
                </div>
            </div>
        </div>
        <div id="leftcolumn">
            <div class="innertube">
                <p><b>Left Column: <em>180px</em></b></p>
            </div>
        </div>
        <div id="rightcolumn">
            <div class="innertube">
                <p><b>Right Column: <em>190px</em></b></p>
            </div>
        </div>
        <div id="footer">
            <p>Footer</p>
        </div>
    </div>
</body>
</html>
```

The CSS starts with the code supplied by the site. In order to modify this code to provide the format required for help documentation, you need to make a few small changes. The following procedure tells you how.

1. **Change the margin-left property for the** `#rightcolumn` **style to** -840px.

   This change makes the right and left columns even.

2. **Change the** `width` **property for the** `#rightcolumn` **style to** 180px.

   This change makes the right and left columns equal widths.

3. **Add a** `height` **property value of** 250px **to both the** `#leftcolumn` **and** `#rightcolumn` **styles.**

   This change allows both columns to use half the available space for content.

4. **Add a** `margin-top` **property value of** 250px **to the** `#rightcolumn` **style.**

   This change positions the right column below the left column.

5. **Load the resulting page into your browser.**

   You see a three-column layout like the one shown in Figure 7-7.

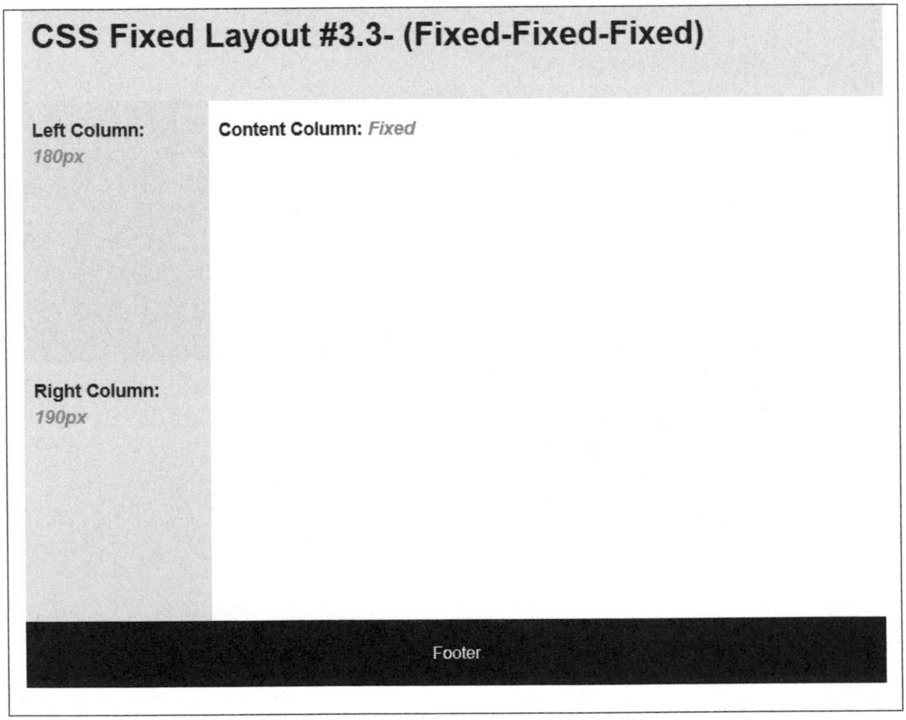

Figure 7-7:
The modified three-column layout will serve well for a documentation site.

CSS Fixed Layout #3.3- (Fixed-Fixed-Fixed)

Left Column:
180px

Content Column: *Fixed*

Right Column:
190px

Footer

The Dynamic Drive templates are flexible and can often serve other purposes with a few small changes. The important thing is to start with a layout that looks close to what you want to use.

Employing CSS frames

Frame layouts are typically quite simple and are often provided for compatibility with mobile devices. A *frame layout* consists of one or more static (fixed) content areas that could contain controls and a fluid content area used to present information.

The main differentiation between a frame layout and a standard layout is that the frame layouts contain no header or footer. As a consequence, you can mash various frames together to create a composite page.

Developers also use frame layouts to hold other content. The frame becomes a container used to hold content from various sources. The Dynamic Drive frame layouts appear at www.dynamicdrive.com/style/layouts/ category/C11/. You can find frames with one, two, three, or four static areas depending on the requirements of your site.

Unlike the other types of layout, frame layouts don't show you how they appear in the browser. You must copy the source and create the page locally to see them. However, you use the same technique as usual to copy and use the layout. Separating the CSS from the HTML will make working with the template easier. Figure 7-8 shows the appearance of a sample template. (You can find complete code for this example in the \Chapter 07 folder of the downloadable code as CSSFrameLayout.HTML.)

Figure 7-8:
CSS frame layouts are incredibly simple and work well with mobile devices.

CSS Left Frame Layout

Sample text here

Dynamic Drive CSS Library

Sample content here.

The CSS frame layouts are configured to hide the scrollbars. As a result, any content that doesn't fit in the frame is inaccessible. You can change this behavior by setting the overflow property of the #framecontent style to scroll. However, changing this setting could also reduce the usability of the layout with some types of smaller mobile devices.

Creating Menus

Most sites use a menu system of some kind. In at least some cases, the menu system uses image maps or some other technique that isn't supported by Dynamic Drive. However, most sites rely on horizontal, vertical, or combination menus. Over the years, users have gotten used to working with menus, so using them on a site simply makes sense. A user understands how to use a menu intuitively, so there's no learning curve. Of course, poorly defined or complex menu entries can still confuse users, but the mechanics of the menu itself are well understood.

Developing horizontal menus

Horizontal menus have selections that appear in a horizontal line. Normally these menus appear across the top of a content area, but menus can also appear at the bottom of the content area or any place between. The point is that a horizontal menu has a particular orientation. For most sites, the horizontal menu represents main site selections, such as going to a list of products or seeing the about page. Dynamic Drive provides seven pages of horizontal menu offerings (as of this writing) that provide various special effects. Figure 7-9 shows just part of the first page (which contains seven entries).

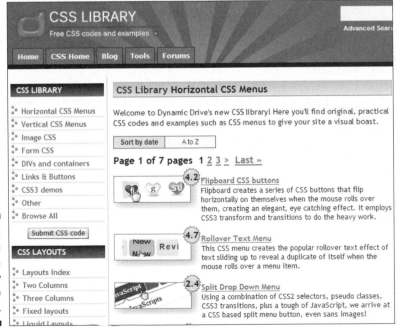

Figure 7-9: Horizontal menus are commonly used for site selections.

The menus all have a special effect. When you click a particular menu selection, you see a page with a demonstration such as the one shown in Figure 7-10. In order to see the special effect, you normally have to hover the mouse pointer over the characters or graphics supplied as part of the menu. For example, with the example menu, hovering the mouse pointer over one of the hearts makes the heart spin around to indicate that the heart has been selected as a menu option.

Notice that the top of the page also includes a description of the menu, along with a listing of compatible browsers. The description usually contains some technical notes as well. It's important to read the technical notes after reviewing the code to ensure you understand how to implement the menu.

The bottom half of the page contains the code for the example. Unlike the layouts, the CSS and HTML are placed in separate windows as shown in Figure 7-11, which means you don't have to separate them manually. In addition, the HTML part doesn't provide a complete page — it's a fragment that you'll need to embed in your own page to test. (You can find this particular example as a full page in the \Chapter 07 folder of the downloadable code as HorizontalMenu.HTML.) However, you use the same technique as you do with the layouts to expand and copy the code when desired.

Notice the link after the code. The example provides one menu that relies on heart icons. You can click this link to download the icons if desired.

Figure 7-10:
Most menus have some special effect that activates during a mouseover event.

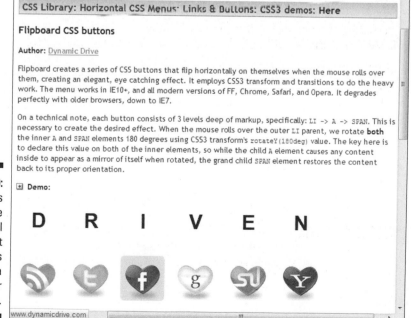

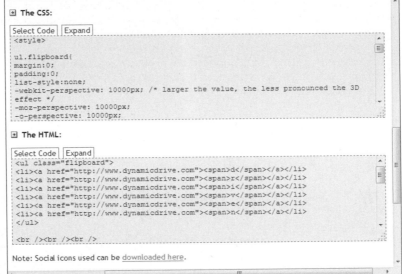

In some cases, these icons are provided by other sites. The other site may have made the icons inaccessible and you'll find that you won't be able to download them after all (such as the heart-shaped social media icons used for this example). A way around this problem is to download the icon directly from the Dynamic Drive site. For example, the RSS icon shown in the example appears at www.dynamicdrive.com/cssexamples/media/rss-heart.png.

Not all of the menus are a single layer. The Split Drop Down Menu (www.dynamicdrive.com/style/csslibrary/item/split_drop_down_menu/) provides two levels of selections A few of these menus rely on third-party products, such as jQuery. The jQuery Drop Line Menu example (www.dynamicdrive.com/style/csslibrary/item/jquery_drop_line_menu/) provides multiple menu levels (up to four levels are shown in the example). Because this isn't a pure CSS solution, however, you need to ensure that the users who access the site will have JavaScript support enabled in their browsers.

Developing vertical menus

Vertical menus can be used for site redirection. However, many sites use them for page-specific or topic-specific links. You find the vertical menu options at www.dynamicdrive.com/style/csslibrary/category/C2/. There aren't as many vertical menu options as there are horizontal menus (only three pages' worth). In addition, you might have a hard time finding compatible horizontal and vertical menu pairs (the CSS3 shadow menus come in both horizontal and vertical formats).

The vertical menus work the same as the horizontal menus do. The only difference is their orientation. The example pages contain the same types of content and you must insert the HTML code into an existing page, just as you do with the horizontal menus. The site doesn't currently provide any multi-level vertical menus, so if you need more than one menu level, you must use a horizontal menu or locate a menu on another site.

Performing Image Magic

Graphic effects help sell site content and attract user attention to elements you want to emphasize. They add pizzazz and help keep the user from clicking the link for the next site on a list of similar sites. When used effectively, graphic effects can help you produce teaching aids and convey information in a way that text or a static image couldn't convey. However, implementing image magic in the form of graphic effects is well within the purview of graphic designers and many developers feel ill-equipped to add it to their sites. That's why the CSS image library that Dynamic Drive provides at www. dynamicdrive.com/style/csslibrary/category/C4/ is so important. None of these effects are earth-shattering, but some are quite dramatic.

As with spices used on food, a few graphics go a long way. Filling your site with special effects may sound like a great idea — the thinking goes that if a few effects double traffic, then more would be even better — but the reality is that too many graphic effects are a turnoff, and the images lose their magic. It's best to go for a few well-defined graphics effects that make a specific point than to clutter your site with effects that boggle the user's mind and draw attention away from areas of interest.

The graphic effects pages work just like the pages used for layouts and menus. The top of a selected effect shows the effect and provides both a description and some explanatory notes about it. The bottom half of the page contains the code required to implement the special effect. As with menus, the graphics effects provide separate CSS and HTML sections and the HTML code is provided as a snippet, rather than a full page.

There are currently two pages of graphic effects on the Dynamic Drive site. Many of these effects help users see selections. For example, when you use image bubbles (www.dynamicdrive.com/style/csslibrary/item/ image_bubbles_using_css3_transform_and_transitions/) the image that the user points to with the mouse appears bigger than the other images — making it possible for the user to be sure of making the right selection. This type of graphic effect can be useful when implemented correctly — and when you take the needs of those with accessibility concerns into account.

One of the more interesting special effects is the Before and After (Peel Back) Image (www.dynamicdrive.com/style/csslibrary/item/before_ and_after_peel_back_image/).You could easily use this particular effect for more than simply showing an interesting graphic effect. In this case, image magic could include a teaching aid. It's possible to provide a problem scenario. After coming up with an answer, the user hovers the mouse pointer over the problem to reveal the answer underneath. It would make for an interesting way to present answers during a teaching session.

Dressing Up Forms

Business runs on forms and it's likely that your business will require some forms on its site. The form content is determined by business need, of course, and most developers can come up with a functional form for just about any need. After all, developers spend a good deal of time creating forms for just about every other application need. However, the forms that Dynamic Drive provides at www.dynamicdrive.com/style/csslibrary/ category/C6/ offer a bit more pizzazz.

There are only three formats provided, along with a few stylish Submit buttons you can use in place of the defaults. The form with the most pizzazz is the Responsive 2 Column Form (www.dynamicdrive.com/style/ csslibrary/item/responsive_2_column_form/) as shown in Figure 7-12. It features shading and rounded corners to give the form that special look. The Submit button appears at the bottom of the page — it's relatively large and red, making it a lot easier for the user to see.

All of these samples focus on design and not on functionality. You need to consider accessibility requirements and security as part of creating a functional form. For example, it's essential to define a method for checking user input to ensure the server receives usable data. These samples are a good starting point for a completed form, not the entire solution.

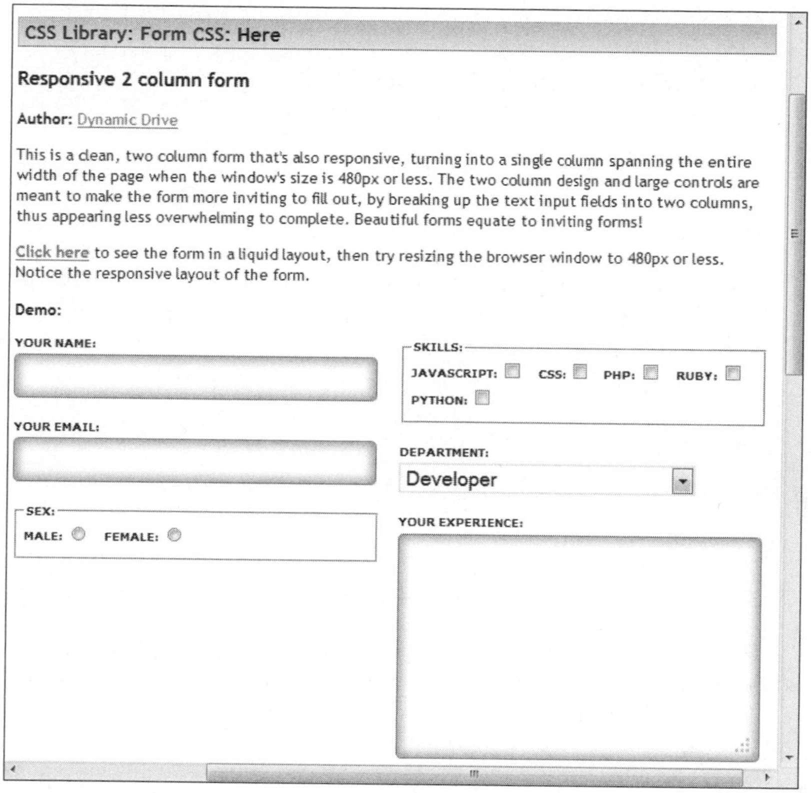

CSS Library: Form CSS: Here

Responsive 2 column form

Author: Dynamic Drive

This is a clean, two column form that's also responsive, turning into a single column spanning the entire width of the page when the window's size is 480px or less. The two column design and large controls are meant to make the form more inviting to fill out, by breaking up the text input fields into two columns, thus appearing less overwhelming to complete. Beautiful forms equate to inviting forms!

Click here to see the form in a liquid layout, then try resizing the browser window to 480px or less. Notice the responsive layout of the form.

Demo:

YOUR NAME:

SKILLS:
JAVASCRIPT: □ CSS: □ PHP: □ RUBY: □
PYTHON: □

YOUR EMAIL:

DEPARTMENT:
Developer

SEX:
MALE: ◉ FEMALE: ◉

YOUR EXPERIENCE:

Figure 7-12:
Use this two-column format to dress up your forms.

Using the Free Icons

Although most developers aren't very good artists, they want their sites to look nice. To do this, hiring a graphic artist is the best solution for truly custom art. However, most sites need only two — or possibly three — pieces of custom art (normally a logo and some sort of heading art to uniquely identify the site). The rest of the art usually consists of screenshots, clipart, line art, and photographs. The screenshots are easy to grab and most developers have used products such as Visio to create line art. Even if the developer isn't a good photographer, someone at the organization usually does possess the required skills, which leaves the clipart.

If you do some research, finding the clipart you need for your site can be relatively easy. For example, some of the example applications on Dynamic Drive include downloads for the graphics you see used with them. The "Developing horizontal menus" section, earlier in this chapter, discusses one such scenario. In this case, you see an array of heart-shaped social media icons. There are many other examples and you need to look for them as you try the examples.

Dynamic Drive isn't the only site that provides free graphics, but it does provide an interesting array of buttons and icons you can use for your site. You can view these graphics at www.dynamicdrive.com/style/graphics/. Figure 7-13 shows an example of the 48 × 48 large icons you can download (it's relatively easy to resize icons to make them smaller, but the results aren't always perfect).

Figure 7-13: The Dynamic Drive site provides access to some commonly used graphics you need.

Chapter 8

Using the Google API

In This Chapter

▶ Discovering why using Google API makes your job easier

▶ Working with the Google APIs Explorer

▶ Using multiple libraries in a single project

*Y*ou've already seen the considerable array of programming-like tasks that CSS can perform for you. However, you've also seen situations where CSS needs a little help — in the form of JavaScript — to provide a complete solution to a problem. This chapter further explores the combination of CSS and JavaScript commonly used to create complete solutions through the use of various Application Programming Interfaces (APIs). The use of APIs has become incredibly popular because they make developers more productive, reduce the requirement to maintain massive amounts of software in-house, and solve a huge array of support issues (not to mention forcing someone else to foot the bill).

So far, you've only looked at two APIs (jQuery and jQuery UI in Chapter 6) and a library of pre-defined CSS aids (Dynamic Drive in Chapter 7), but a problem should be apparent: Creating links for each of these APIs individually can become cumbersome. The Google Content Distribution Network (CDN) (which includes the Google API described later in this chapter) doesn't completely solve this problem, but it does make it possible to obtain access to a number of these APIs from one location. Instead of wandering all over the Internet looking for code, then, the Google CDN allows you to go to one central location and have a selection of APIs to use. That's the purpose of this chapter — to help you understand the benefits of using a centralized code source and then to explore that source.

Of course, part of the difficulty of using multiple APIs is learning how to manage them, so this chapter also discusses that requirement. You also find a discussion of the techniques you can use to help manage your access to the Google CDN and how to determine which APIs to use on a given occasion. The interesting part of using multiple APIs is that you get to pick the pieces you want and reject everything else. Even though you're using the same code as many other people, your distinctive combination of coding elements produces a unique site that everyone can identify as particular to your organization.

Most APIs target five browsers: Internet Explorer, Firefox, Chrome, Safari, and Opera. Of course, some of your users may rely on other browsers. These APIs, however, are never guaranteed to work on anything other than the five browsers mentioned — unless the vendor specifically mentions another browser (such as the one used with the Android). In addition, the APIs are normally tested on desktop platforms with the Mac, Windows, and Linux operating systems being the main targets. When you need to support other browser types or other platforms, the best strategy is to avoid the use of APIs completely — and instead rely on standards-based approaches such as pure CSS (ensuring that the target platform has a CSS-compliant browser).

Understanding Why Developers Like the Google API

The Google API actually has two components. The first component provides access to a number of third-party APIs and it's the part of the API you discover in the sections that follow. The second component provides access to a number of Google services. You discover that component in the "Using the Google APIs Explorer" section, later in this chapter. For now, it's important to focus on the third-party APIs and see what they have to offer you. Of course, you've already worked with two of these APIs in this book — the jQuery and jQuery UI APIs.

Many developers use multiple libraries when creating an application because each library has something special to offer. Using the API that best matches an application requirement makes sense. The more code you can get someone else to write, the less code you write yourself — and the more time you save. However, linking your code to all sorts of sites creates speed problems because each request to a different domain incurs a delay. You can improve application speed by using a single domain to request access to all the APIs you use.

Most developers also come to the conclusion that making requests from multiple domains also produces a reliability problem. All it takes is a loss of contact with one of those domains and your application won't run. The more APIs you use, the greater the number of domains — and the higher the probability of incurring this problem. Using one central domain places your application in an all-or-nothing condition that actually reduces the threat of some other support issues (such as an application that works just well enough to cause data damage because requests are started, but not completed due to a lack of library availability).

However, there are other issues to consider — such as security. Each reference to a source outside the current page can trigger a security message. This is a helpful feature of many browsers today, often supported through a plug-in. Knowing where a page looks for resources can help keep a user's machine safe. However, when a lot of messages begin cropping up about sites unknown to your users, they may throw up their hands and refuse to allow these external sites access to the page. Consequently, your application fails because it lacks access to the libraries it needs to work. The answer is to use a single source to access the libraries you need — a source that the user is likely to recognize and permit to access the browser page.

The Google CDN found at `https://developers.google.com/speed/libraries/devguide` is a series of libraries that you can use to create better applications. Google maintains all of these libraries on a common domain, `http://ajax.googleapis.com`, which means that users don't have to think so hard about each library you use in an application. All the user needs to do is approve use of a single domain. Many developers rely on the Google APIs site to gain access to libraries such as jQuery. You see it all the time when working with pages online. The libraries typically found on the Google CDN include

AngularJS	MooTools
Chrome Frame	Prototype
Dojo	Script_aculo_us
Ext Core	SWFObject
jQuery	Web Font Loader
jQuery UI	

When you want to use a particular library on the list, click its link, and Google displays a script for accessing it. For example, if you want to use jQuery, click its link to see a snippet similar to this (even though the URL wraps in the book, it should appear on a single line in your code):

```
<script
  src="http://ajax.googleapis.com/ajax/libs/jquery/1.10.1/jquery.min.js">
</script>
```

Each library entry includes the link you use to access it from the Google CDN, a link to the vendor site, and a list of stable versions as shown in Figure 8-1. Some entries contain a list of unstable versions that you shouldn't use. Other entries include notes about the versions so you know about any oddities you'll encounter in using them. When the list of supported or unstable versions is long, you can hover the mouse pointer over an entry to see a full-version list.

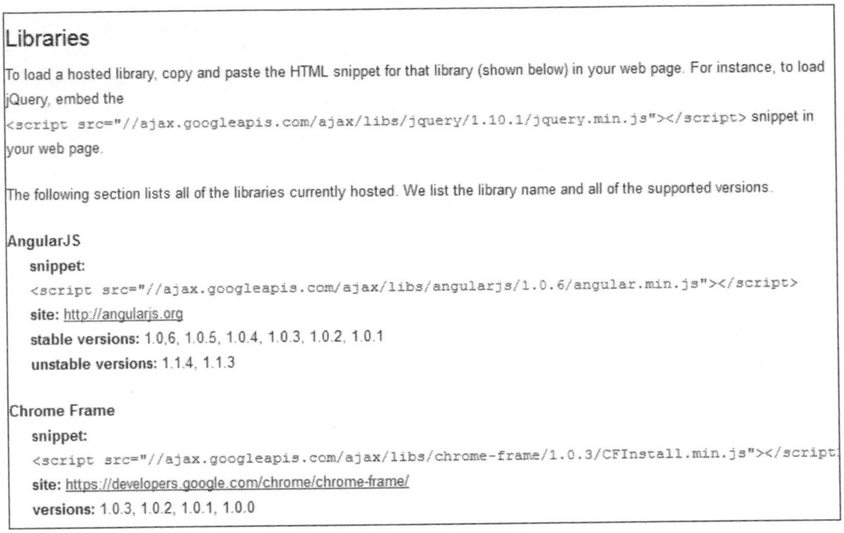

Libraries

To load a hosted library, copy and paste the HTML snippet for that library (shown below) in your web page. For instance, to load jQuery, embed the

`<script src="//ajax.googleapis.com/ajax/libs/jquery/1.10.1/jquery.min.js"></script>` snippet in your web page.

The following section lists all of the libraries currently hosted. We list the library name and all of the supported versions.

AngularJS

    snippet:

    `<script src="//ajax.googleapis.com/ajax/libs/angularjs/1.0.6/angular.min.js"></script>`

    site: http://angularjs.org

    stable versions: 1.0.6, 1.0.5, 1.0.4, 1.0.3, 1.0.2, 1.0.1

    unstable versions: 1.1.4, 1.1.3

Chrome Frame

    snippet:

    `<script src="//ajax.googleapis.com/ajax/libs/chrome-frame/1.0.3/CFInstall.min.js"></script>`

    site: https://developers.google.com/chrome/chrome-frame/

    versions: 1.0.3, 1.0.2, 1.0.1, 1.0.0

Figure 8-1: Each entry provides a modicum of information about the library.

None of the third-party libraries that Google supports requires any special access to Google on your part. Anyone can use these hosted libraries without any sort of special permission. However, when you work with some of the Google-specific services, you do need a Google account — and may require a license in order to implement a solution. It's important to take note of the differences between the free services described in this section and the monitored or paid services that Google provides. Developers who confuse the two may implement solutions that end up costing their organizations money to place the solution on a public site. (In this book I have tried to separate the coverage of the two forms of Google's API support for just this reason.)

Working with AngularJS

AngularJS (`http://angularjs.org/`) is actually a Google solution, but one that's offered freely to the public in the same way that other APIs, such as jQuery, are offered. This particular library has a lot to offer. View the various videos on the site (`www.youtube.com/user/angularjs`) to see how AngularJS compares to other third-party products, such as jQuery. The important thing to remember is that AngularJS tends to hide the coding details from view, which means you really don't know how the application code works. In addition, you're using a model-based approach to writing your applications, which means that you're essentially doing things the way AngularJS wants to do them. This approach is just fine as long as AngularJS meets your application needs — you'll have to perform testing to figure out whether the approach works.

AngularJS can be part of your solution even if the model-based approach isn't exactly for you. The various videos point out this aspect of the product, so watching them is important. You can combine approaches: You could use AngularJS in places where the model-based approach works well, and then rely on something like jQuery where you need extra flexibility or access to visual elements. Combinations like this can work as long as they allow you to maintain your ability to write functional code quickly and still achieve a desirable result. Among AngularJS's limitations: AngularJS doesn't allow you to make modifications to the way the code works through the use of simple plug-ins; plus, it doesn't enjoy the support of the development community (as jQuery does).

Unlike some desktop languages, such as C#, that use a Model-View-Controller (MVC) approach (see `http://msdn.microsoft.com/library/ ff649643.aspx` for details) AngularJS uses a Model-View-Whatever approach. Unfortunately, none of the AngularJS documentation explains this approach even a little. The best source of information about the MVW approach to modeling applications is at `http://code.google.com/p/dark-matter-data/ wiki/MVWOverview`. You don't have to read this really complicated explanation of how things work in the background to use AngularJS, but it can help to answer questions about what AngularJS actually does for you.

After viewing the AngularJS videos, the best way to work with the product is to download it to your system and experiment a little. Start with the simple example shown on the AngularJS site and work your way up.

Working with Chrome Frame

Chrome Frame (`https://developers.google.com/chrome/chrome- frame/`) is not an API. It's simply a plug-in that gives older versions of Internet Explorer some of the same capabilities of Chrome, including access to open web technologies and a faster JavaScript engine. The plug-in continues to solve problems for people who are using old versions of Internet Explorer — but as more and more users upgrade, the need for the plug-in diminishes. As a result, this particular feature will be retired in January 2014 (unless Google gives it an extension). You can read more about this particular feature and its retirement at `http://blog.chromium.org/2013/06/retiring-chrome-frame.html`. The bottom line is that this plug-in is still available if you have a site that's still experiencing problems with users who have older versions of Internet Explorer.

Working with Dojo

Dojo is a full-fledged library with features akin to those described for jQuery in Chapter 6. It includes a whole array of selectors, special effects, behaviors, and language helpers. It also provides good support for Asynchronous JavaScript and XML (AJAX).

Which product is better — jQuery or Dojo? That depends on who you talk to: Each has its adherents, and a considerable number of books, articles, and documentation exists for both. You can find a simple (mostly unbiased) comparison of the two products at `http://tech.yes-co.nl/2009/08/25/jquery-versus-dojo-versus-yui/`. A somewhat more biased coding comparison is at `http://moresoda.co.uk/blog/article/dojo-and-jquery-side-by-side-dom-basics/`. What may surprise you about the coding comparison is how much alike the two products are. From a CSS development perspective, you need to be aware that Dojo doesn't support the rich functionality of the widgets found in jQuery UI; however, it does offer some unique offerings not found in jQuery or jQuery UI, including some nice special effects that could be hard to implement using jQuery.

As with jQuery, you access Dojo by using a simple `<script>` string. You set the `src` attribute as shown here.

```
<script
    src="http://ajax.googleapis.com/ajax/libs/dojo/1.9.0/dojo/dojo.js">
</script>
```

Like jQuery, Dojo comes in a number of versions. Your application may rely on a specific version. To change the version used with the application, simply change the 1.9.0 part of the URL to another version. The Google API currently supports versions 1.1.1 to 1.9.0 (the latest version listed on the Dojo site as of this writing).

The best way to begin learning Dojo is to use the tutorials presented on the documentation page at `http://dojotoolkit.org/documentation/`. A number of authors have also written books about Dojo — most of which are listed in the Bookshelf section of the documentation page (with direct links to Amazon when you click the book's picture).

Even though Dojo and jQuery look quite a bit alike — and you use them in the same manner, for the most part — Dojo is actually a framework and jQuery is a library. A *library* is code. You call functions directly and the source for those functions is sometimes available so that you can change the function behavior. *Frameworks* provide a means of interacting with a behavior, which means that some tasks aren't visible to the developer — the developer requests that the framework perform the task, and the framework determines how to accomplish it. Some people define a framework as a packaged form of library that provides structure as well as code. For the most part, you don't need to worry about whether a product is a framework or a library — the main concern is discovering how to use the product to create better applications.

Working with Ext Core

The first thing to note is that the following link is to the core product, not to the full product. You do see an impressive list of features when you view the Sencha Ext JS site at www.sencha.com/products/extjs/. However, most of these features are for paying customers — you don't get them with the core product. You can find a listing of the core features at http://docs.sencha.com/core/ and an overview of them at www.sencha.com/blog/ext-core-30-beta-released/. The list of functions includes access to AJAX support, animations, and some data connectivity options. Unless you have a special need to provide a public version of your Ext JS applications, you'll get a lot more out of a framework such as Dojo or MooTools — or from a library such as jQuery.

Accessing jQuery

A discussion of jQuery appears in Chapter 6 (and you'll see this library discussed later in the book, too). With a simple replacement of the src attribute, you can use the Google CDN version of the library. Here's an example of the jQuery link (even though the URL wraps in the book, it should appear on a single line in your code).

```
<script
   src="http://ajax.googleapis.com/ajax/libs/jquery/1.10.1/jquery.min.js">
</script>
```

Your application may depend on a specific version of the jQuery library. If this is the case, you can access the version you want from the Google CDN. Simply replace the 1.10.1 part of the URL with the version you want. The Google CDN hosts all versions of jQuery (including the newer 2.x versions) — except versions 1.2.4 and 1.2.5, because these two versions weren't available for very long.

Accessing jQuery UI

As with jQuery, a discussion of jQuery UI appears in Chapter 6. You also find this library discussed in other chapters. To use this library with the Google CDN, you replace the src attribute with the appropriate link. Here's an example of the link you use to gain access to this library from the host (even though the URL wraps in the book, it should appear on a single line in your code).

```
<script
   src="http://ajax.googleapis.com/ajax/libs/jqueryui/1.10.3/jquery-ui.min.js">
</script>
```

When working with jQuery UI, make sure you work with a compatible version of jQuery. For example, don't try to use a 1.2.6 version of jQuery with a 1.10.3 version of jQuery UI — you won't get very satisfying results. In general, you want to use matching minor versions. To ensure that your application will work, you want to use a 1.10 version of jQuery with a 1.10 version of jQuery UI.

The functionality provided with each version of jQuery UI can vary quite a bit. Make sure you note which version of jQuery UI you used to develop a particular application — and then stick with that version unless you verify that there are no breaking changes in a newer version (always a good idea). Fortunately, the Google CDN hosts versions of jQuery UI from 1.5.2 to 1.10.3. If you request the 1.8.3 version, you actually receive the 1.8.4 version because of the short lifespan of the 1.8.3 version. To use a specific version, simply replace the 1.10.3 part of the URL with the version you want.

Working with MooTools

The opening page for MooTools (`http://mootools.net/`) says that it's targeted at intermediate to advanced developers. This powerful framework of functions helps you perform all sorts of tasks, including some appealing special effects and transitions. In addition to the standard core framework, there's also a standard server-only framework you can download from `http://mootools.net/download` when client functionality isn't required. You can see an overview of the functionality this product provides at `http://mootools.net/docs/core`.

One of the more important things to know about this particular tool is that it provides a lot less hand-holding than do other tools mentioned in this chapter. However, it also provides some superior functionality (provided you can figure out how to use it). For example, detecting a browser's name and functionality is probably easier using MooTools than any other framework or library available. It also comes with built-in support for Adobe Flash that's simple to use (see `http://mootools.net/docs/core/Utilities/Swiff` for details). You have to use a plug-in to get the required support with jQuery and Dojo's method of working with Flash seems convoluted at best. One of the more interesting classes is Chain (`http://mootools.net/docs/core/Class/Class.Extras`), which lets you execute a series of commands one after another as a single entity.

The Google CDN supports versions 1.1.1 through 1.4.5 of MooTools. As with other libraries, you can change the link for MooTools to request a specific version. Here's an example of the link used to access this framework (even though the URL wraps in the book, it should appear on a single line in your code).

```
<script
   src="http://ajax.googleapis.com/ajax/libs/mootools/1.4.5/mootools-yui-
           compressed.js">
</script>
```

Working with Prototype

The Prototype framework (`http://prototypejs.org/`) focuses on help-ing you create and maintain dynamic content on a site. As such, the docu-mentation places an emphasis on AJAX and Document Object Model (DOM) support (`http://api.prototypejs.org/`). You also find functionality for checking browser features, but not specifics such as the browser name. This means you won't be able to make tweaks to adjust the application output to compensate for specific browser bugs.

Prototype provides a nice selection of tutorials at `http://prototypejs.org/learn/`. There's no basic Hello World-type example, but the examples provided should be enough to help any moderately experienced developer get started quickly. Each tutorial focuses on a different area of Prototype, such as the creation of new classes or using Prototype with AJAX.

Some Ruby on Rails developers choose Prototype over jQuery and other products like it because Prototype is easier for them to understand due to the way in which it is written. In addition, Prototype tends to provide even treatment of all of the functionality it provides — fit and finish issues such as function naming are more consistent. The developers of Prototype have also taken great care to ensure that API calls are consistent and there is definitely some inconsistency in the jQuery calling syntax (which means you have to look at the reference to ensure you make the call correctly). You can find a somewhat biased view of the differences between jQuery and Prototype at `http://thinkrelevance.com/blog/2009/01/12/why-i-still-prefer-prototype-to-jquery`.

The Google CDN supports versions 1.6.0.2 through 1.7.1.0 of Prototype. As with other libraries, you can change the link for Prototype to request a spe-cific version. Here's an example of the link used to access this framework (even though the URL wraps in the book, it should appear on a single line in your code):

```
<script
   src="http://ajax.googleapis.com/ajax/libs/prototype/1.7.1.0/prototype.js">
</script>
```

Working with script_aculo_us

If you like Prototype, but you find it a bit limited in the user interface arena, then you need to look at script.aculo.us (`http://script.aculo.us/`). You use this Prototype add-on to create an amazing array of special effects, drag-and-drop functionality, and AJAX controls. It also provides some additional support for DOM.

However, the most interesting feature of all is that this add-on provides unit testing functionality that you won't find in many other products. Unit testing of any kind is sorely lacking with most web development products, so this is a really nice addition that may make Prototype a framework of choice for your next development project — especially when working in a large team environment where unit testing takes on added significance.

The thing you'll like most about script.aculo.us is that the site contains lots of demos and example code. Some of the demos provide a bit of fun. For example, check out the puzzle demo at `http://madrobby.github.io/scriptaculous/puzzle-demo/`. The main API reference is at `http://madrobby.github.io/scriptaculous/`. This main page provides you with an overview of the API (with clickable links to all the details) and tells you how to perform tasks such as getting script.aculo.us downloaded to your system.

The Google CDN supports versions 1.8.1 through 1.9.0 of script.aculo.us. The vendor doesn't list any particular problems with matching your version of script.aculo.us to the version of Prototype, but testing is always a good idea. As with other libraries, you can change the link for script.aculo.us to request a specific version. Here's an example of the link used to access this framework (even though the URL wraps in the book, it should appear on a single line in your code).

```
<script
    src="http://ajax.googleapis.com/ajax/libs/scriptaculous/1.9.0/scriptaculous.
            js">
</script>
```

Working with SWFObject

SWFObject (`http://code.google.com/p/swfobject/`) is a single function product designed to make working with Flash files exceptionally easy (or at least easier). It includes functionality for creating and using Flash objects. You can even choose between static and dynamic publishing methods. The documentation at `http://code.google.com/p/swfobject/wiki/documentation` provides all the details you need for using this small, but handy, add-on. This utility works with any browser that supports Flash.

Working with WebFont Loader

WebFont Loader (`https://github.com/typekit/webfontloader`) is a utility-type add-on designed to make it easier to work with fonts. For example, it provides a method for dealing with situations where a font won't download due to an Internet error. A set of events makes it possible to monitor font-download progress and success. You can use it to load and access Google Fonts, Typekit, Ascender, Fonts.com, Fontdeck, and self-hosted web fonts. In fact, there are separate modules for interacting with each font type.

As discussed in Chapter 3, obtaining access to just the right font is essential in conveying your message in some cases. Using an add-on like WebFont Loader makes it easier to manage the font selection and ensure the page appears as you expect it to appear to the end user. Even if you're using another library or framework to perform the bulk of the work on your site, using this library is quite helpful when appearance is critical.

The documentation for this add-on is a bit sparse. You do get a number of programming snippets, but no complete example applications. There are also no demos of how the product looks in use. One of the more important sections to look at in the documentation that does exist is Browser Support (`https://github.com/typekit/webfontloader#browser-support`). This section helps you understand what will happen if the host browser doesn't support loaded fonts — especially mobile devices with a desktop mode.

Using the Google APIs Explorer

Google offers a wealth of APIs that cover everything from working with Ad Exchange to presenting driving instructions with Google Maps. In fact, there are so many APIs that most developers have no idea of just how many of them exist. That's why the Google APIs Explorer (`https://developers.google.com/apis-explorer/#p/`) is important. It helps you find and access all the APIs that Google supports.

It isn't possible to cover all the APIs that Google provides. In fact, there are entire books on some APIs, such as Google Maps. With this in mind, the following sections provide a scant overview of the Google APIs environment.

Getting a Google account

You can access many Google API features without a Google account. However, many of the features do require an account and it's usually easier to sign up for one at the outset. For example, when using Google Maps, you must obtain a token to make requests from the web service.

To start the process, all you need to do is go to Google Accounts (`https://accounts.google.com`) and click Sign Up. You go to the page shown in Figure 8-2.

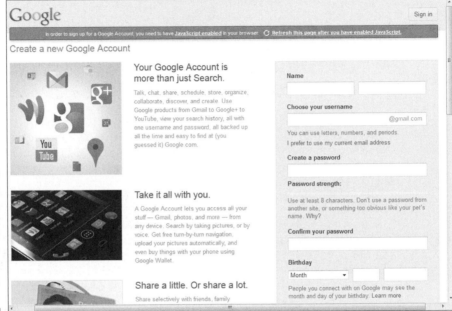

Figure 8-2: The Google account Sign Up page contains fields that ask you questions.

After you answer a number of questions, you click Next Step and follow the remaining directions. It doesn't take long to obtain the account and verify it through your e-mail account. Even if you don't use the account for other items, you'll need it for development purposes.

In some cases, the documentation for a particular API will recommend that you obtain two accounts: one for development and another for testing. The reason for this suggestion is that you could possibly lose data by working with the API. If you use data in your test account, it's usually not a problem. However, losing data in your development account could set back your application development efforts. Creating two accounts when necessary is always a good idea.

Obtaining a developer key

To work with many of the APIs, you must obtain a developer key. Google provides two kinds of keys: paid and free. You need only the free key for experimentation purposes. The paid key does provide considerably more flexibility, and you'll likely need it for any full-fledged application you create. However, for experimentation purposes, the free key works just fine. The Google API you're using will tell you about the developer key requirement as part of the documentation. (Even if it doesn't tell you, you'll discover the requirement the first time you try to make a request). For example, you obtain a developer key for Google Maps at `https://developers.google.com/maps/licensing`. Make sure you understand the terms of service fully before you begin working with the Google API.

Working with the Google APIs Explorer

Whenever you go to the main Google API Explorer page, you see a listing of the APIs (as shown in Figure 8-3). In addition, you obtain a short description of the API, the API version, and whether you'll have full access to it. Some APIs have paid support for full access or have some other requirement for their use. Unfortunately, this page won't tell you which features are missing or why the support is limited.

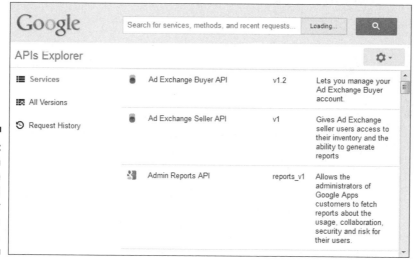

Figure 8-3:
The main page for the Google API Explorer provides a list of APIs.

When you click a link for a particular API, you see a page that provides a short description of the API, a link to the documentation, and a listing of the calls for that API (as shown in Figure 8-4). The call listing includes a short description of each API call. The listing is there to help jog your memory when you've forgotten a call.

Make sure you read the documentation for an API thoroughly before you try to do anything with it.

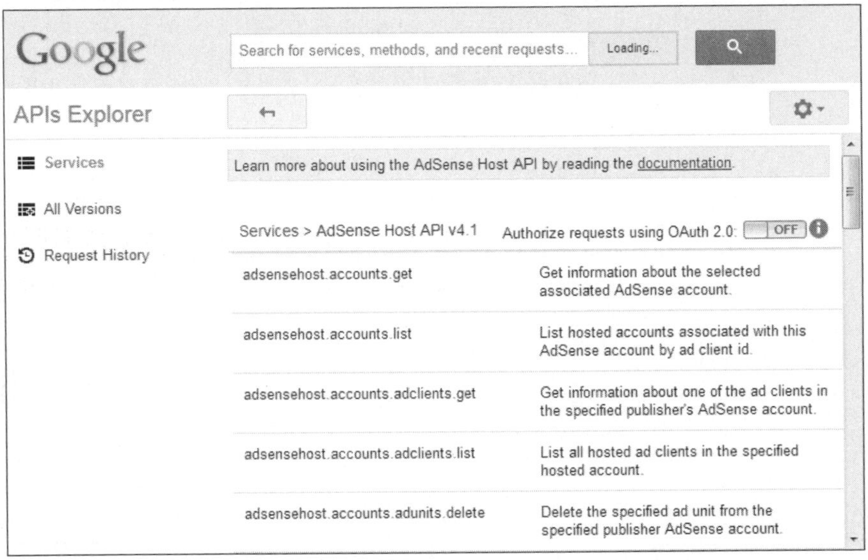

Figure 8-4:
Each API provides a listing of the calls it supports, plus a short description.

Clicking on a particular API call displays a page containing additional information about that call. In addition, you see a test page for actually executing the call to see what it does (as shown in Figure 8-5). All you need to do is fill out the fields and click Execute.

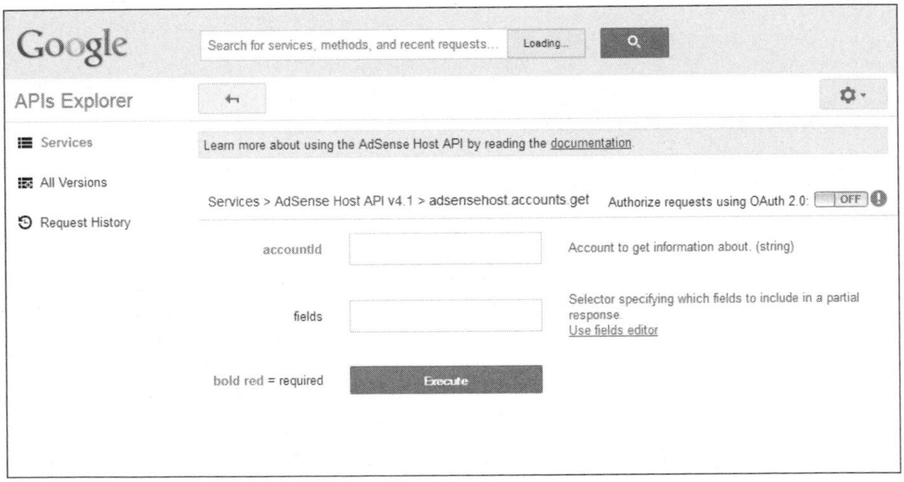

Figure 8-5:
Test each of the API calls using the test page.

The documentation page provides access to a wealth of resources for working with the API you've selected (as shown in Figure 8-6). Each API starts with an introduction that tells you all about the API. You find links for getting started, working with client libraries, and interacting with the community that uses the API. In addition, each API provides access to a guide describing how to use the API, a reference containing API specifics, and a connection to any resources that the API supports.

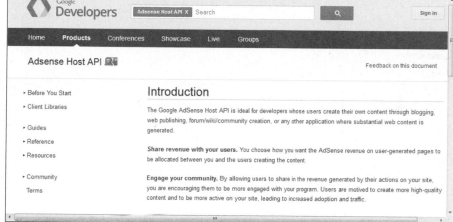

Figure 8-6:
Gain full
access to all
information
concerning
an API on its
documenta-
tion page.

One of the most important (and probably overlooked) links on the documentation page, however, is the Terms link. Make sure you understand the terms for using the API. Unfortunately, some developers run afoul of the legal requirements and find themselves with a nonworking application as a result.

Creating a Site that Uses Multiple Libraries

It's important to create robust applications for your site — applications that provide fast access to data, consistent output, reliable operation, and still ensures that the data remains secure. Even at the desktop, creating such an environment remains elusive. Part of the problem with using multiple libraries or a combination of libraries and frameworks is that you don't really know how the APIs work. As a result, you can't be sure that the libraries will even work together until you try them out as a combination. Obviously, you want to perform a significant amount of testing. In many cases, you can research the combination of products online to see how other people have fared when using them.

In many cases, it's far better to use an add-on product with the main library or framework you want to use. For example, if you work with Prototype, but find the lack of graphical features problematic, you can use an add-on such as script.aculo.us. Both of these products are available on the Google CDN. It's the need to maintain a viable work environment that keeps developers creating new *plug-ins* (pieces of software designed to be injected directly into the host library and become part of it) and *add-ons* (pieces of software that extend the host library and work as additions to it) for products such as jQuery as well.

Library makers tend not to talk with each other about code compatibility or breaking changes. Because of this lack of communication, there is always a risk that libraries that work together fine today will fail to work together tomorrow. Always research a compatible solution before you resort to using multiple products together.

When you do decide that you must use two products together, make every attempt to use each product's strengths to improve your application's functionality. In fact, it usually pays to make a checklist of which features you want to use from each product to ensure your entire team remembers how you want the application to work. Otherwise you end up with an odd mix of calls to both libraries for the same type of service. Consistent development is essential when using multiple products together.

As part of your testing setup, consider how the libraries work together (if they work together at all). Using multiple libraries will increase code bloat and possibly cause speed problems. Even if your application works perfectly, no one will want to use it if it works too slowly (or consumes too many resources on the user's machine).

One strategy for using multiple libraries on one site is to place each library on a separate page. You can dedicate pages to specific tasks and then use the library that fits best for that task. A number of developers use this approach quite successfully. If you decide to mash the pages together into a single page later, remember to check for compatibility issues. Generally, when you place the pages in frames and then display multiple frames together, there's less chance of a collision, but it pays to be sure.

Using multiple libraries together can greatly increase the flexibility of your programming environment and improve the usability of your site. You can gain access to functionality you might not otherwise have. However, always exercise care in using multiple libraries together to ensure that the tactic doesn't backfire on you.

Part III
Working with CSS3 Generators

Using the Accordion Widget

▾	Foreground Color

- ⦿ Red
- ● Orange
- ● Green
- ● Blue

▸	Background Color

▸	Options

Change Configuration

See an example of how you can use Komodo Edit to create CSS files at
www.dummies.com/extras/css3.

In this part . . .

- ✔ Add amazing color combinations to your applications using ColorZilla

- ✔ Reduce the work required to create interesting, yet usable themes using ThemeRoller

- ✔ Discover how to create animate GIFs simply using the Dynamic Drive tools

- ✔ Embellish your site using gradient images created with Gradient Image Maker

- ✔ Create your own custom micro-buttons using Button Maker Online

Chapter 9

Managing Colors Using ColorZilla

Color is an essential element in creating all sorts of sites. By using color wisely, you can add pizzazz without expending too much effort on graphics. Color is also valuable for its ability to communicate ideas to your site's visitors. For example, displaying a success message in green better conveys the idea of success than would displaying the message in another color; and a red error message easily draws attention to the fact that something has gone wrong. However, the successful management of color can sometimes be difficult — which is where ColorZilla (www.colorzilla.com/) comes into play. This tool makes it easier for developers to create useful color patterns on a page without making the page look absurd or reducing the user's ability to see details clearly.

Unfortunately, it's nearly impossible to find a color management tool that works with every browser. These tools usually work as plugins, rather than as strict browser applications written in JavaScript. Most ColorZilla features currently work only with Firefox and Chrome. Both of those browsers work in a large number of platforms, so you won't have any problem using this tool. The Ultimate Gradient Generator tool, discussed later in this chapter, will work with other browsers such as Internet Explorer, Safari, and Opera. You can use the Ultimate Gradient Generator to create gradients online and then simply copy the code to your application.

Dealing with colorblindness

When you're using color, it's important to remember that 8 percent of your male viewers and ½ percent of your female viewers will have some sort of colorblindness issue (see the colorblindness FAQ at `www.vischeck.com/faq/` for details). The term *colorblindness* is actually a misnomer. A more appropriate term would be *color-shifted*. The viewer sees a shifted version of the colors on the page, making some colors appear to look like others. For example, red and green might both appear to be a shade of brown (see examples at `www.vischeck.com/examples/`). To make dealing with colorblindness even more difficult, there are actually three main types of colorblindness — and not all colorblind people are colorblind to the same degree. Bottom line: You need to ensure that your site will be viewable by the widest possible range of users.

A number of sites provide useful tips on making your pages work better with those who have colorblindness. Two of the more useful sites are `http://msdn.microsoft.com/library/bb263953.aspx` and `www.firelily.com/opinions/color.html`. In both cases, you get helpful tips on color selections that will work for everyone. One of the best pieces of advice you can follow is to make sure that every color indication used to describe an event or condition is also followed by some other indication. For example, street signs use different shapes to indicate conditions in addition to color (red octagon for stop and yellow triangles for caution).

Just selecting what you might think are the right colors may not be enough. Sometimes you actually have to see what the other person is seeing to do a good job selecting colors. Fortunately, you can find a number of free colorblindness simulators online. Two of the better simulators are at `www.etre.com/tools/colourblindsimulator/` and `www.vischeck.com/vischeck/`. The Vischeck site also offers downloadable plugins you can use to examine pictures on your hard drive before you include them as part of your page.

You do get a number of helpful tools with ColorZilla, including an Eyedropper to grab colors from sites you like, a Color Picker to choose useful color combinations, and a Color Analyzer to check your color combinations. There's also a special tool for creating gradients, which transition from one color to another and give your site a nice appeal. There's even a tool for turning your images into a CSS form so you can create special effects with them.

Obtaining the Plugin

In order to use most ColorZilla features, you must install the plugin. (The Ultimate Gradient Generator, discussed later in this chapter, doesn't require the plugin.) The plugins used for this chapter are version 2.8 for Firefox and version 0.5 for Chrome. If you use a newer or different version of the plugin (say, for another browser), you may see some differences in the appearance of the screenshots. A little variation is normal and you shouldn't worry about it. Use the following procedure to install the plugin.

1. **Go to the ColorZilla site at** `www.colorzilla.com/.`

   You see the ColorZilla main page shown in Figure 9-1.

Figure 9-1:
The
ColorZilla
main page
provides
access to
the plugin
and the
Ultimate
Gradient
Generator.

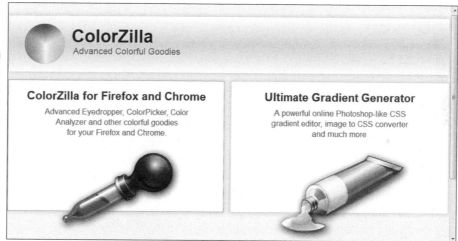

2. **Click ColorZilla for Firefox and Chrome.**

   You see options for selecting the browser type (as shown in Figure 9-2). Even though Figure 9-2 shows the Firefox page, the options for working with Chrome are the same.

3. **Click Firefox if you use the Firefox browser or Chrome if you use the Chrome browser.**

   The installation button that appears below the browser buttons changes to match the browser you selected.

4. **Click Install ColorZilla 2.8 if you use the Firefox browser or Install ColorZilla 0.5 if you use the Chrome browser.**

   You see a dialog box similar to the one shown in Figure 9-3 for Firefox that asks your permission to install the plugin. It may also tell you what the plugin will do. If you don't see the dialog box, your browser may be asking for permission to display it.

Figure 9-2:
ColorZilla
currently
supports
Firefox and
Chrome.

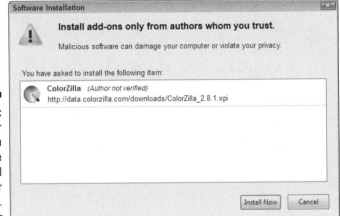

Figure 9-3:
The installer
will tell you
what the
plugin will
do after
installation.

5. **Click Install Now (or Add if you're using Chrome).**

   The installation will proceed. Firefox users may have to restart the browser (a dialog box will tell you whether this step is necessary) After a few seconds, you see a ColorZilla Installed page that describes all the features of the plugin in a little more detail, as shown in Figure 9-4.

The ColorZilla plugin provides more functionality than you see described in this chapter. The chapter does provide an overview of the most useful features, but you should also review the full list of features at `www.colorzilla.com/firefox/features.html`. For example, you can use ColorZilla to display element information such as the tag name, class, ID, size, and relative mouse-pointer position so you know how a particular page is put together. It's also possible to use ColorZilla to launch Firebug (`http://getfirebug.com/javascript`) when you need to debug the page setup.

After you get the plugin installed, you see a new eyedropper icon in the toolbar of your browser. Next to this eyedropper is a drop-down list (menu) of ColorZilla features you can use (as shown in Figure 9-5). This menu provides access to all of the ColorZilla features discussed in this chapter.

Figure 9-4: The ColorZilla Installed page is confirmation that everything went as expected.

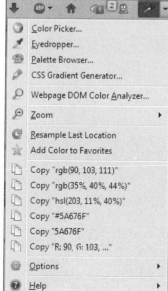

Figure 9-5: Use the drop-down list associated with the ColorZilla icon to access features.

The effects of device type and calibration on color

The color you see on your computer screen might not be the one that everyone else sees. Of course, there are differences in how each person perceives color. In addition, someone with colorblindness will never see the same colors that you see. However, these physical differences aside, you must consider two other factors in the color equation: device type and calibration.

Different device types present colors differently because they generate it differently. For example, LCD monitors come in a variety of types and each type uses a different technology to create color. In addition, backlighting affects the presentation of color on a display. If you want to know about the different monitor types, check out the presentations at `http://lifehacker.com/5992723/know-the-difference-between-types-of-computer-monitors-and-pick-the-best-one` and `http://lifehacker.com/5994223/the-difference-between-lcd-led-plasma-and-oled-tvs-explained-as-fast-as-possible`.

No matter what kind of monitor you have, it requires calibration before you can see color on it accurately. People assume that the monitor is calibrated at the factory (and it is), but the lighting and other factors that affect color perception are different in the factory than where you work. In addition, the color output will change as the monitor ages. You can invest in a really fancy color calibration application, but there are a number of free methods you can use to ensure that the color you see is as close as possible to what everyone else sees. The first (if you're using Windows) is to use the Calibrate Display Color utility as described at `http://windows.microsoft.com/en-us/windows7/calibrate-your-display`. If you want to ensure that the color on the screen also matches what people will see when they print your page, use the technique described at `www.wikihow.com/Calibrate-Your-Monitor`.

Choosing Colors with the Color Picker

The Color Picker is actually a two-function tool. The way in which you interact with it depends on how involved you want to get with color selections. You can create a completely customized view or you can let ColorZilla help you make a selection based on predefined palettes. The first option, creating a custom color, is described in the next section. The second option, using a predefined palette, is discussed in the second section that follows.

Using the Color Picker

The first item on the ColorZilla menu is the Color Picker. When you select this option, you see a dialog box (like the one shown in Figure 9-6) where you can work through color selections in a number of different ways. In many respects, the initial view of the Color Picker looks just like any other color picker you've used in the past.

Using the Color Picker saves you time. With it, you can enter colors directly by using the characteristics described at these links:

- ✔ Hue, saturation, and value (see `www.greatreality.com/color/ColorHVC.htm` for details)

- ✔ Red, green, blue (see `http://dba.med.sc.edu/price/irf/Adobe_tg/models/rgbcmy.html` for details)

- ✔ Hexadecimal color value (see `www.w3schools.com/html/html_colors.asp` for details)

- ✔ Lab color space (see `www.hidefcolor.com/color-management/lab-color-space/` for details)

- ✔ Cyan, magenta, yellow, key (see `http://searchcio-midmarket.techtarget.com/definition/CMYK` for details)

From this dialog box, you receive two different versions of CSS-specific output (both the `rgb()` function and the `hsl()` function). In addition, you also get a color name. When there's no precise color name for the color you've created, the Name field is left blank.

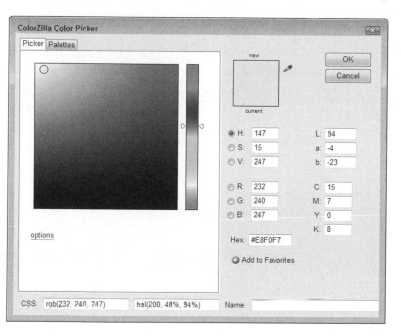

Figure 9-6:
The Color Picker makes it easy to choose colors based on a number of criteria.

Of course, some of the best features are hidden from view. Click Options and you see a single option named Color Picker Type. The Color Picker defaults to what is called a *smooth* color picker type. This setup lets you choose any color available, making it hard to choose a specific color at times. To gain more control over your color choice, select the Discrete option. The display will change as shown in Figure 9-7. Each color is now in a distinct block — making it a lot easier to choose a specific color every time you use Color Picker.

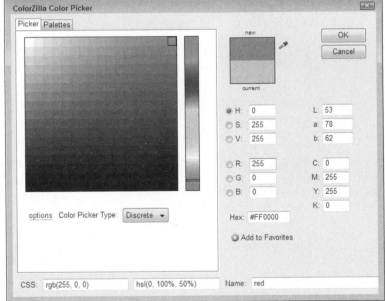

Figure 9-7:
Use the Discrete option to make choosing colors easier.

You may also see a color that you like on a page somewhere. In this case, click Sample Color from Document (the icon that looks like an eye dropper) and then click on the color you want to use from the page. The Color Picker will automatically display the values used to create that color.

Using the Palette Browser

Using the Picker tab will be too much work for many people. It's a lot easier if the tool helps you choose a specific color. That's where the Palettes tab (shown in Figure 9-8) comes into play. The Palettes tab provides several methods for organizing and categorizing colors to make them a lot easier to work with. (You can also access this tab immediately by selecting the Palette Browser option on the menu.)

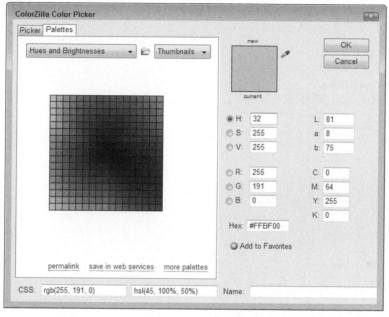

Figure 9-8:
The Palettes
tab helps
you orga-
nize and
categorize
colors.

The two drop-down lists help you make good color choices. The first drop-down list contains methods for organizing the color selections. By default, you can choose colors based on

✔ Favorites

✔ History

✔ Hues and Brightness

✔ Hues and Saturations

✔ System CSS Colors

✔ W3C Named Colors

✔ Colors by Hue

✔ Web Named Colors

✔ Web Safe Colors

✔ X Named Colors

The .GPL files that hold the palette selections are actually written using a text editor. You can create your own palettes if you want to, using any of the existing .GPL files as a template. Click the Palettes Folder icon (the folder between the two drop-down lists) to gain access to the .GPL files on your system. You can also create a list of personal favorites by clicking Add to Favorites whenever you see a color you like.

The default display shows the colors as thumbnails. Selecting the List option shows the colors as a list that includes a larger color sample, hexadecimal value, and named value (when available). Figure 9-9 shows a typical view of this display option.

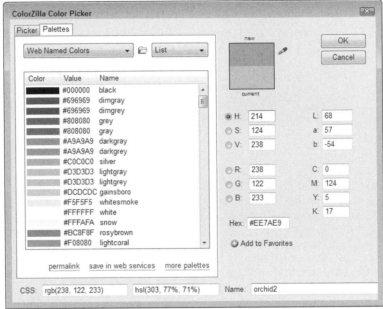

Figure 9-9: Some developers prefer the list view because it provides additional information.

There are three links at the bottom of the selection area that you should know about as well. Clicking any of these links will open a page in your browser. However, the browser window doesn't gain focus automatically, so it may appear that nothing has happened. Check your browser for the new page. Here's a list of what these links do:

- **permalink:** Shows the permanent link for the palette option you've selected.

- **save in web services:** Provides a method for sending the selected palette to your account or to someone else's account online. You can choose from one of the following services:

  - del.icio.us

  - digg

  - facebook

  - netscape

- technorati
- blinklist
- blogmarks
- live
- google bookmarks
- stumbleupon
- furl
- yahoo! myweb
- newsvine
- reddit
- ma.gnolia
- tailrank

✔ **more palettes:** Displays a wealth of other palettes you can download to your system and use.

Grabbing Colors Using the Eyedropper

The Eyedropper menu option displays a plus-sign mouse cursor. As you move the mouse cursor around a page, a bar at the top of the page displays the current color value and other information, as shown in Figure 9-10. (The additional information includes the mouse cursor's position and the CSS style name.)

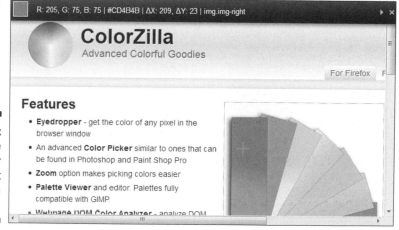

Figure 9-10: Use the Eyedropper to select colors from the page.

When you click a particular color, the Eyedropper copies the information you see to the Clipboard. The bar will display the message "Copied to Clipboard" for a few seconds, and then the bar will disappear. The output sent to the Clipboard is the hexadecimal color value. (Choose a different copy option on the Options⇨Auto Copy menu if you want to receive something other than a hexadecimal color value.) You don't see all of the other information that appears on the bar when you paste the value into an editor.

The default ColorZilla option is to display the Eyedropper. You don't have to choose a menu option to activate this particular feature — just click the Eyedropper icon in your browser instead.

The Eyedropper doesn't work with linked images or icons in many cases. When you see the Eyedropper mouse icon change to some other icon, such as a pointing hand, then you know that color isn't accessible by Eyedropper. This problem occurs most often with images used to depict items you would click for additional information. The best option is to hover the mouse cursor over the item you want to interact with and see whether the cursor changes. If the cursor remains the same (as shown in Figure 9-10), then you can probably access that color value.

Working with the Color Analyzer

You might see a page that has great color combinations and not want to spend hours figuring those colors out one at a time. The Color Analyzer makes it possible to full list all the colors used on a site.

This utility works with the CSS colors, not the colors used for images. As a result, you see the colors used for a menu, but not the colors used for a logo. If you want to obtain the colors used in the logo, employ the Eyedropper instead.

Performing the analysis

To perform an analysis, choose the Webpage DOM Color Analyzer option from the menu. The bottom half of the browser window will open with a new pane that contains the color analysis from the current page (as shown in Figure 9-11).

However, you don't just get the color analysis. Hover the mouse cursor over a particular color and you see where that color is used on the page (as shown in Figure 9-12). In this case, black is used to outline just about every object on-screen. Even though the screenshot doesn't show it, you also see a tooltip containing the color information for the color you selected.

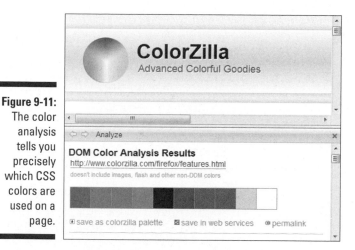

Figure 9-11:
The color
analysis
tells you
precisely
which CSS
colors are
used on a
page.

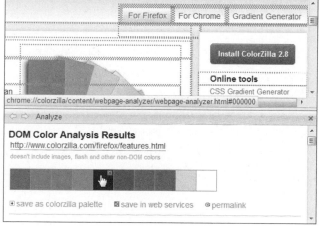

Figure 9-12:
Selecting
a color
automati-
cally shows
you where
the color is
used.

Notice the little X in the upper-right corner of the black square in Figure 9-12. Clicking this X will hide the color from view. The reason you might want to do this is to keep the color from being part of the palette you eventually use for your own site. You might choose to work with another color as a replacement, but still want to use the majority of the color selections.

Seeing the details

Scroll the analysis page down and you find details of the color usage (as shown in Figure 9-13). Each color has its own entry in the list, so you can see specifically where each color is used.

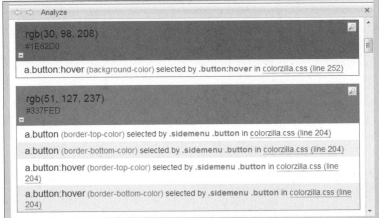

Figure 9-13:
The analysis
includes
specific
details
about each
color's use.

The color entries provide quite a bit of information. The entry begins with the CSS style name, followed by the property that the color affects. The output tells you how the color is selected and you even see where the color appears in the `.CSS` file.

Each of the file entries is actually a link. When you click on this link, ColorZilla displays the precise location of the color usage in the `.CSS` file, in the upper pane of the browser, by opening a new tab (as shown in Figure 9-14).

Note: Any link marked `inline attribute` won't open a corresponding location in the original HTML file — this feature only works on `.CSS` files.

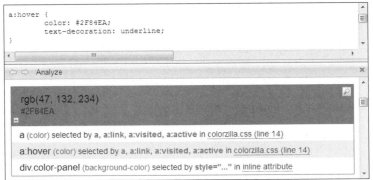

Figure 9-14:
You can
check the
CSS by
clicking the
appropriate
color link
to it.

Saving the output

After you're satisfied with the results of your analysis and selections, you can save the choices you've made. There are three methods for accomplishing this task:

✔ **save as colorzilla palette:** Displays a Palette Name dialog box where you type the name of the palette as you want to save it on your hard drive. Click OK and you see a Palette Saved dialog box that you can clear by clicking OK. The palette will now appear as one of the selections on the Palettes tab of the ColorZilla Color Picker dialog box, as discussed in the "Using the Palette Browser" section, earlier in this chapter.

✔ **permalink:** Shows the permanent link for the palette option you've selected. The URL for this link contains the hexadecimal values for each of the colors; here's an example:

```
http://colorzilla.com/colors/1E62D0+337FED+2F84EA+3D94F6+000000+5555
        55+666666+6A6A6A+DDDDDD+FFFFFF?source-url=www.colorzilla.
        com%2Ffirefox%2Ffeatures.html&post=1
```

The formatting of the URL in this manner means you can send it to anyone and your recipient can reconstitute the color selections based on the URL alone.

✔ **save in web services:** Provides a method for sending the selected palette to your account or to someone else's account online. This option provides the same functionality as the feature described in the "Using the Palette Browser" section, earlier in this chapter.

Creating a Gradient

Gradients are commonly used for presenting special effects on pages because they have a lot of pizzazz and don't require code to accomplish their task. Any browser that supports CSS3 can display dazzling gradients without much effort — and the user isn't exposed to any sort of potential virus or other hacking trick (so far). You can find a discussion of gradients in Chapter 4, which shows you how to create your first gradient by hand. In that chapter I show you what other people have done to create interesting displays. This section takes a middle road between creating the gradient by hand and relying on others to do all the work.

The Ultimate Gradient Generator (`www.colorzilla.com/gradient-editor/`) can create some truly interesting effects for you and it's more flexible than many of the other generators you find online. However, it still won't produce the amazing results found on sites such as `http://lea.verou.me/css3patterns/`. These sorts of patterns are the work of dedicated artists who are willing to hand-code the gradients. Even so, you might be surprised at the sorts of gradients you can create, given a little time to play around with the settings on this site. The following sections will get you started.

Developing a basic gradient

Many online tools provide little help with getting a gradient together — but that's not the case with Ultimate Gradient Generator. As shown in Figure 9-15, this tool begins with a series of presets. Just select one of the blocks in the Preset list and you already have a gradient that works. It may not work perfectly for your needs, but it will give you a good start.

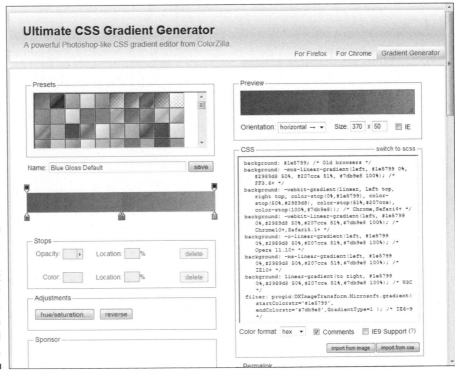

Figure 9-15: The Ultimate Gradient Generator comes with all sorts of useful presets.

Two basic ways of tweaking the resulting gradient are (1) to modify its size and (2) to change its orientation. For example, you can start with the Blue Gloss Default present, modify the size, and change to a radial format to create the gradient shown in Figure 9-16. The result is quite a bit different — despite not having changed the colors at all.

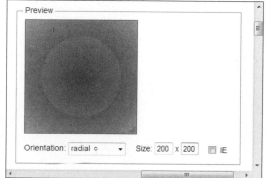

Figure 9-16: Little changes can make a big difference.

When you're finally satisfied with the changes you make, you can copy the resulting CSS directly to a project. Adding comments so that you know what the CSS is doing is always a good idea, so make sure you check the Comments option (as shown in Figure 9-17). If you plan to support Internet Explorer 9 users, make sure you check the IE9 Support option. Choose a color format option as well. (When your gradient includes transparent areas, you must choose one of the options that allow transparency.) When you've finished selecting options, hover the mouse cursor over the code and a Copy button appears. Click this button to copy the CSS to the Clipboard. At this point, you can copy it to your project for testing.

When using specific kinds of effects, such as radial gradients, the Ultimate Gradient Generator will also supply you with a script or other requirements to make the gradient work in older browsers. This is especially true when working with Internet Explorer 9. If you don't add this special support, users of older browsers will see a less spectacular, but equally nice, gradient. For example, the radial gradient will default to a kind of linear gradient as required.

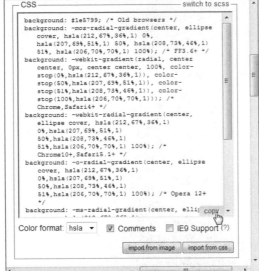

Figure 9-17:
Use the
Copy fea-
ture to copy
the CSS to
your project.

Adding special effects

You have access to a number of special effects when creating gradients using Ultimate Gradient Generator. The first is to change colors and add color stops. A *color stop* signifies a change in color. Notice the color bar in Figure 9-15 has four tabs on the bottom. These tabs control the colors used and where each color starts and ends.

When you click one of the tabs, you see the little triangle above the square tab turn from white to black. In addition, the settings in the Stops area change, as shown in Figure 9-18.

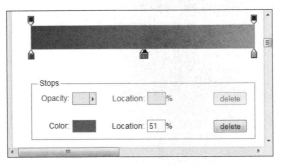

Figure 9-18:
Change indi-
vidual stop
settings
using the
Stops area's
features.

To change a color, click inside the Color field. You see a color picker (similar to the one shown in Figure 9-6) that you can use to select a new color. Set the color you want and click OK to change the color of the selected stop.

To change the stop position, either type a new value in the Location field or slide the stop along the bar. As you change the setting, you see modifications to the output of the gradient.

You can also click Delete to remove a color stop you don't want. To add a new color stop, hover the mouse near the bottom of the color bar. You see the cursor change to a pointing hand with a plus sign. Click wherever you want to add the new stop along the color bar and then configure the stop as needed.

The second special effect is the use of transparency. Look again at Figure 9-15 and you see two tabs at the top of the bar. These tabs control transparency. When you click one of these tabs, its triangle turns black, just as the color tabs do. However, in this case, the upper settings of the Stops area become active, as shown in Figure 9-19.

Figure 9-19: Opacity modifies the appearance of your gradient by making the background visible.

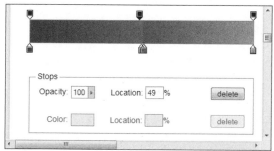

The default setting makes the gradient *opaque*, which means that the user can't see through it. However, you can adjust the opacity to allow some of the background to show through — or make the gradient transparent so the user can only see the background in a particular area onscreen. As with color stops, you can add or delete transparency stops as needed to produce a particular effect.

Saving the result

It's important to save the gradients you want to use again. To save a gradient locally, you can type a name in the Name field (located under the Presets) and click Save. The new gradient appears in the Presets list.

You can also click the unique link entry in the Permalink area of the page. This creates a new tab that shows your gradient. The URL will provide details about the custom gradient you created so someone else can reproduce it.

Converting an image to CSS

A special feature of the Ultimate Gradient Generator is the capability to turn your existing image into a CSS gradient that you can use on your site. This is an interesting way to define some complex gradients with little effort; note, however, that this feature works best with images like the one in Figure 9-20. Even if you provide a complex graphic, the resulting gradient will use only the colors on the left side of the image. Anything after the first color is ignored. (You can find the image for this example in the \Chapter 09 folder of the downloadable code as MyGradient.JPG.)

Figure 9-20: Use an image that will translate well into a gradient.

Refer to the bottom of Figure 9-17 to find the Import from Image button. Click this button and you see the bottom of the CSS area expand to include the form shown in Figure 9-21. You can obtain images from a location online or from your local hard drive. When you want to use your hard drive as a resource, click Browse to display a File Upload dialog box, locate the file, and then click Open.

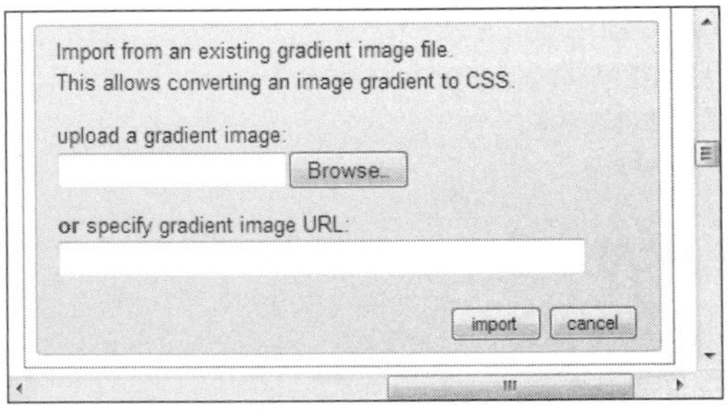

Figure 9-21: Fill in this form to use an image to generate CSS.

Import from an existing gradient image file.
This allows converting an image gradient to CSS.

upload a gradient image:

[   ] [Browse..]

or specify gradient image URL:

[   ]

[import] [cancel]

After you provide a source for the image, click Import. The Ultimate Gradient Generator imports the file and creates the CSS required to mimic the image and its applied gradient. You can then make tweaks and changes as needed to produce the desired result. After you're done, you can save the CSS as usual and include the gradient in your application.

After you provide a source for the image, click Import. The Ultimate Gradient Generator imports the file and creates the CSS required to mimic the image and its applied gradient as shown in Figure 9-22. You can then make tweaks and changes as needed to produce the desired result. After you're done, you can save the CSS as usual and include the gradient in your application.

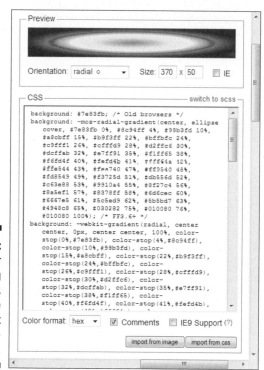

Figure 9-22: After importing the image, you can see the gradient and associated CSS.

Chapter 10

Creating Themes Using ThemeRoller

ThemeRoller (http://jqueryui.com/themeroller/) is a special kind of tool and plugin for jQuery that makes it possible to create a theme for your site. A *theme* is a mixture of fonts, color, and graphic styles that gives your site a particular feel. You can use ThemeRoller to perform tasks such as defining the appearance of buttons when a user hovers the mouse cursor over them. The output of ThemeRoller is a custom version of jQuery and jQuery UI that meets requirements that you specify. So you get the same combination of CSS and JavaScript that you'd get when using these two libraries, but the result meets your specific needs far better.

Of course, you may not want to take the time to create a theme entirely by hand, even if the process is automated using various screens on the ThemeRoller site. The ThemeRoller site also includes a number of predefined themes you can use. These themes are designed to meet most people's needs and to provide a balanced and aesthetically pleasing appearance. As a consequence, you may want to check out ThemeRoller even if you have no desire to create a custom theme.

Understanding ThemeRoller

jQuery and jQuery UI are relatively complex libraries that provide a substantial amount of customization. The problem is that many developers have no idea how to perform the required customization and probably wouldn't have time to do it if they did. The overall purpose of ThemeRoller is to simplify the task of customizing the appearance of the effects and widgets provided by these two libraries so that you can achieve a distinct appearance without a lot of work. In fact, there are methods of using these libraries so you don't have to do any work at all.

However, using ThemeRoller has other, less obvious benefits. For example, by using ThemeRoller you can give your users access to multiple themes without much additional work at all. All you really need to do is provide a means of selecting a different link site for the required theme — the one that the user wants. Providing access to multiple themes makes it possible to address all sorts of user needs, such as making it possible for colorblind users to see the page with greater ease.

Using ThemeRoller also helps you better understand jQuery and jQuery UI. The themes you create include demonstrations of all major features so that you can see them at work. It helps to see the features using the theme that you've chosen so that it's easier to make tweaks. One of the handier features is a listing of the framework icons, as shown in Figure 10-1. You can hover your mouse cursor over an icon to see what it is called as part of jQuery UI.

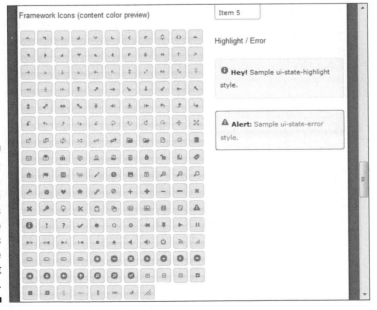

Figure 10-1: The framework icon listing is a way to see what's available and what it's called.

jQuery and jQuery UI become even more powerful when you add other plugins to them. These libraries are popular enough that you can probably find a plugin for every need. Check out the list of plugins at `http://plugins.jquery.com/`. The themes you create with ThemeRoller will work with all of the available plugins unless the plugin implements some special (breaking) functionality.

Using the ThemeRoller Interface

The ThemeRoller interface consists of the main page and a number of configuration pages, as shown in the examples in this chapter. The main page contains links to other jQuery UI functionality along the top, a ThemeRoller-specific menu along the left side, and examples of the various jQuery UI widgets in two columns on the right (as shown in Figure 10-2).

Figure 10-2: The main page provides access to the various configuration features.

The ThemeRoller menu shown in Figure 10-3 contains general options across the top (such as creating custom themes using the Roll Your Own option). The menu content changes depending on the tab you select. Figure 10-3 shows the content of the Roll Your Own tab, which I explain in the "Creating Custom Themes" section, later in this chapter. I discuss the Gallery options in the "Working with Predefined Themes" section, also later in this chapter.

Figure 10-3:
The
ThemeRoller
menu
content
changes
depending
on the tab
selected.

The Help tab provides an overview of the purpose of ThemeRoller. It also provides links to the two main ways you can use ThemeRoller: to create custom themes or to use predefined themes. Later in the help section, you see information regarding plugin usage and the recommendation to read the CSS-specific information about jQuery UI before creating a new plugin. All plugin developers are supposed to test any of their applications that use themes to ensure that they work with ThemeRoller.

It's important to read the Help tab because otherwise you might end up spending hours attempting to fix an unfixable problem. For example, the Help tab tells you that the rounded corners won't work in Internet Explorer versions 6 and 7 because these versions don't provide the required support. The corners will still appear, but they'll be square instead of round. Without checking the Help tab, you might spend all day trying to correct this problem.

Working with Predefined Themes

The folks at jQuery UI realize that not everyone is an artist. For that matter, not everyone has a good sense of which colors go together. Most developers don't have the schooling required to know which rules to follow when creating a theme. With this in mind, ThemeRoller provides a wealth of predefined themes. You can use these themes knowing that they provide you with a reasonably well-balanced page appearance and that the results will be aesthetically pleasing to your users. The following section describes predefined themes in more detail.

Viewing the predefined themes

To see the list of predefined themes, select the Gallery tab of the ThemeRoller menu shown in Figure 10-3. You see a listing of the themes by name as shown in Figure 10-4. Notice that each theme entry includes a snapshot of the theme, the theme name, and two buttons for downloading or editing the theme as needed. There are currently 24 predefined themes from which to choose (although the screenshot shows only two of the 24 possibilities).

Figure 10-4:
Each pre-defined theme provides a quick view of how the theme appears onscreen.

The iconic view of the theme only gives you a taste of how it will appear onscreen. If you really want to see the theme fully, select it by clicking its entry in the list. When you do so, the page changes so that you can see how the theme affects the overall appearance of the page.

In some cases, you find that the iconic view of a theme is misleading. For example, look at the Le Frog (green) theme in the Gallery list. The icon would lead you to believe that everything about this theme is green. However, only the widgets are affected by this choice as shown in Figure 10-5.

Figure 10-5:
Some theme icons are misleading, so it pays to view each theme fully.

Accessing the predefined themes directly

After you find the predefined theme that best matches your requirements, you can add it to your application. The easiest way to perform this task is to use the quick access URLs. You see a sample of them at the bottom of the ThemeRoller page as shown in Figure 10-6.

Figure 10-6:
Use the quick access URLs to add a predefined theme to your application.

The only problem is that the URL for the themes doesn't change — it always shows the URL for the Smoothness theme. In order to use a theme in your application, you must have the correct URL for it, and the URL isn't available on the ThemeRoller website. The following list presents the theme names followed by the requisite URL for that theme when using jQuery UI 1.10 — you add this URL to your code in order to use that theme in your application.

- **UI lightness:** `http://code.jquery.com/ui/1.10.3/themes/ui-lightness/jquery-ui.css`

- **UI darkness:** `http://code.jquery.com/ui/1.10.3/themes/ui-darkness/jquery-ui.css`

- **Smoothness:** `http://code.jquery.com/ui/1.10.3/themes/smoothness/jquery-ui.css`

- **Start:** `http://code.jquery.com/ui/1.10.3/themes/start/jquery-ui.css`

- **Redmond:** `http://code.jquery.com/ui/1.10.3/themes/redmond/jquery-ui.css`

- **Sunny:** `http://code.jquery.com/ui/1.10.3/themes/sunny/jquery-ui.css`

- **Overcast:** `http://code.jquery.com/ui/1.10.3/themes/overcast/jquery-ui.css`

- **Le Frog:** `http://code.jquery.com/ui/1.10.3/themes/le-frog/jquery-ui.css`

- **Flick:** `http://code.jquery.com/ui/1.10.3/themes/flick/jquery-ui.css`

- **Pepper Grinder:** `http://code.jquery.com/ui/1.10.3/themes/pepper-grinder/jquery-ui.css`

- **Eggplant:** `http://code.jquery.com/ui/1.10.3/themes/eggplant/jquery-ui.css`

- **Dark Hive:** `http://code.jquery.com/ui/1.10.3/themes/dark-hive/jquery-ui.css`

- **Cupertino:** `http://code.jquery.com/ui/1.10.3/themes/cupertino/jquery-ui.css`

- **South Street:** `http://code.jquery.com/ui/1.10.3/themes/south-street/jquery-ui.css`

- **Blitzer:** `http://code.jquery.com/ui/1.10.3/themes/blitzer/jquery-ui.css`

- **Humanity:** `http://code.jquery.com/ui/1.10.3/themes/humanity/jquery-ui.css`

- ✔ **Hot Sneaks:** `http://code.jquery.com/ui/1.10.3/themes/hot-sneaks/jquery-ui.css`

- ✔ **Excite Bike:** `http://code.jquery.com/ui/1.10.3/themes/excite-bike/jquery-ui.css`

- ✔ **Vader:** `http://code.jquery.com/ui/1.10.3/themes/vader/jquery-ui.css`

- ✔ **Dot Luv:** `http://code.jquery.com/ui/1.10.3/themes/dot-luv/jquery-ui.css`

- ✔ **Mint Choc:** `http://code.jquery.com/ui/1.10.3/themes/mint-choc/jquery-ui.css`

- ✔ **Black Tie:** `http://code.jquery.com/ui/1.10.3/themes/black-tie/jquery-ui.css`

- ✔ **Trontastic:** `http://code.jquery.com/ui/1.10.3/themes/trontastic/jquery-ui.css`

- ✔ **Swanky Purse:** `http://code.jquery.com/ui/1.10.3/themes/swanky-purse/jquery-ui.css`

The basic way for declaring a theme in your application works for every predefined theme that ThemeRoller provides. All you need to do is add the following code to your style sheet. Just replace the theme URL in the following code with URL for the theme you want to use.

```
<link
   rel="stylesheet"
   href="http://code.jquery.com/ui/1.10.3/themes/ui-lightness/jquery-ui.css" />
```

Creating Custom Themes

The 24 predefined themes provide a broad range of color, text, and other choices. However, it's possible to create a significantly greater number of themes by using the custom approach. You could start with the default theme setup and work from there, but the best approach is to find a predefined theme that looks close to what you want and modify it instead. Not only will you do less work this way, but you may find that there aren't that many features to change once you have a predefined theme in mind. The following sections help you create a custom theme using ThemeRoller.

Choosing a predefined theme as a starting point

Select any of the predefined themes located on the Gallery tab. When you find the theme you want to modify, click Edit. (Refer to Figure 10-4 to see the Edit button on the right side of each theme entry.) ThemeRoller automatically takes you to the Roll Your Own tab. However, the tab's settings will contain the values required to create whatever theme you've selected.

Performing the configuration

Each theme consists of a number of settings. (Refer to Figure 10-3.) By changing a particular setting, you control the appearance of all the jQuery UI features, including all of the widgets. Each of these settings has a number of subsettings you can use to control the overall appearance of your theme. The following list provides an overview of these settings.

✔ **Font Settings:** Determines the overall appearance of text in the theme. You can choose the font family, weight, and size of the font.

✔ **Corner Radius:** Determines the size of the rounded corners used for the various elements. This setting won't affect a browser that doesn't support rounded corners, such as Internet Explorer 7.

✔ **Header/Toolbar:** Specifies the settings for the background and border used for all headers and toolbars.

When working with the background, you can choose the background color, texture, and percentage of coverage. A *texture* specifies how the background is patterned, such as the use of diagonals or diamonds. Clicking the texture field automatically displays a pictorial list of acceptable textures (as shown in Figure 10-7) — just choose the texture you want to try. Selecting the right texture can add pizzazz to your site.

The border settings control the border, text, and icon colors. When you click one of these fields, you see a color selection dialog box (as shown in Figure 10-8). However, you can also type a specific color value, using hexadecimal notation.

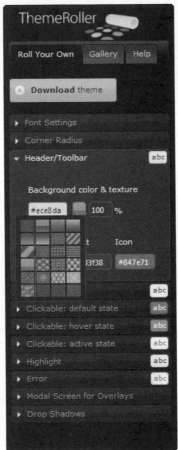

Figure 10-7:
Select the
texture you
want to use
from the
pictorial list.

✔ **Content:** Provides the same background and border selections as those provided by the Header/Toolbar settings. The difference is that these settings affect the page content, rather than headings and toolbars.

✔ **Clickable: default state:** Provides the same background and border selections as those provided by the Header/Toolbar settings. The difference is that these settings affect controls that are in the default state, rather than headings and toolbars.

✔ **Clickable: hover state:** Provides the same background and border selections as those provided by the Header/Toolbar settings. The difference is that these settings affect controls that are in the hover state (when the mouse cursor is placed over the top of the control), rather than headings and toolbars.

Figure 10-8:
Choose the colors you want to use with your page.

✔ **Clickable: active state:** Provides the same background and border selections as those provided by the Header/Toolbar settings. The difference is that these settings affect controls that are in the active (selected) state, rather than headings and toolbars.

✔ **Highlight:** Provides the same background and border selections as those provided by the Header/Toolbar settings. The difference is that these settings affect anything the user has highlighted onscreen, rather than headings and toolbars.

✔ **Error:** Provides the same background and border selections as those provided by the Header/Toolbar settings. The difference is that these settings affect error messages (including content), rather than headings and toolbars.

✔ **Modal Screen for Overlays:** Defines the way in which overlays appear on screen. An *overlay* is information that is presented over the top of existing content in much the way a dialog box displays over the top of an application. The settings control the background and overlay appearance.

The background settings set the color, texture, and percentage of coverage of the background. The textures used for an overlay are completely different from those used for other elements, so you need to check them carefully. In every other respect, the background settings work the same as those used for the Header/Toolbar settings.

The Overlay Opacity setting controls how well you can see the underlying content. In most cases, ThemeRoller provides a modicum of show-through to give the page a glasslike appearance (found in some operating systems today). However, you can change this setting to provide various special effects. Setting this value too low tends to prove distracting for the reader because the original content is seen too easily.

✔ **Drop Shadows:** Modifies the appearance of drop shadows, which tend to give some page elements a 3D effect. You can control the background and the overall appearance of the drop shadow. The background controls are precisely the same as those used with Modal Screen Overlays.

The overall appearance of the drop shadow is defined by the shadow opacity, thickness, and offset from the shadowed element, as shown in Figure 10-9. You can also control the rounding of the shadow corners (when the feature is supported by the browser).

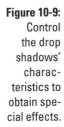

Figure 10-9:
Control
the drop
shadows'
charac-
teristics to
obtain spe-
cial effects.

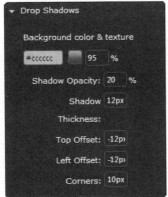

After you modify all of the settings you want to change, you can save the page's URL for later use. In fact, it's always a good idea to save the URL so you can create multiple versions of your custom theme (such as development and production versions). However, the URL won't let you use the theme within an application. In order to use a custom theme that you create, you must download the theme and use it with the application locally.

Downloading Themes to Your System

It's possible to use predefined themes directly from the ThemeRoller site. Downloading a predefined theme to your site will improve the speed of your application because the server won't have to fetch the required files each time a user makes a request. However, if you want to use a custom theme, you must create and then download it for use on your site. In both cases, using a downloaded copy of the theme reduces potential security risks because everything needed for the application is downloaded from a single domain. The use of a single domain makes it possible for the administrator to lock down the browser better and reduce the risk of cross-site scripting problems.

Downloading a predefined theme

In order to obtain some additional speed from your application and to reduce the potential for security issues, you might decide to download the predefined theme to your system. The following steps help you perform this task. (Even though the steps show the UI lightness theme, the same steps work for any theme you want to download.)

1. **Click Download under the theme you want to use.**

   Figure 10-4 shows predefined theme entries. You can see the Download button on the left side of each theme entry. ThemeRoller displays the Download Builder page shown in Figure 10-10.

2. **Select the version of the theme you want to use.**

   The default version is the best option in most cases. However, you may need to download an older version to support older applications.

3. **Select the features you want to use from the library.**

   In most cases, you want to leave all the feature options checked when downloading a development version of the theme — because you don't know, at the outset, which features you really need. When you complete the development process, you can create a smaller version of the theme by selecting only those features that your application actually uses. The smaller version will download faster so that the user sees results quicker.

4. **(Optional) Type a value in the CSS Scope field.**

   The scope makes it possible to override internal CSS styles using an external .CSS file. You can read more about the use of scope at `http://css-tricks.com/saving-the-day-with-scoped-css/` and `http://updates.html5rocks.com/2013/03/What-s-the-CSS-scope-pseudo-class-for`.

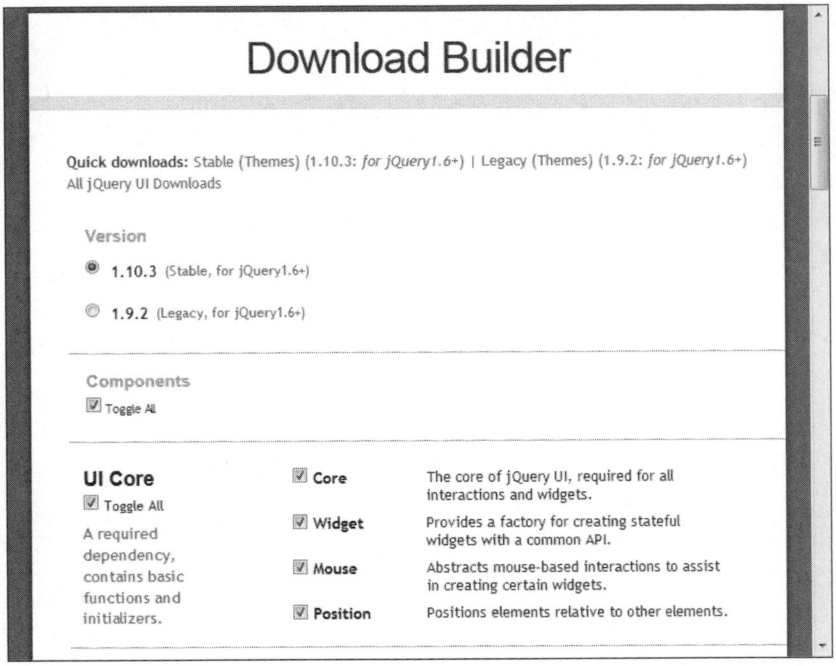

Download Builder

Quick downloads: Stable (Themes) (1.10.3: *for jQuery1.6+*) | Legacy (Themes) (1.9.2: *for jQuery1.6+*)
All jQuery UI Downloads

Version

◉ **1.10.3** (Stable, for jQuery1.6+)

◯ **1.9.2** (Legacy, for jQuery1.6+)

Components
☑ Toggle All

UI Core
☑ Toggle All

A required
dependency,
contains basic
functions and
initializers.

☑ **Core** — The core of jQuery UI, required for all interactions and widgets.

☑ **Widget** — Provides a factory for creating stateful widgets with a common API.

☑ **Mouse** — Abstracts mouse-based interactions to assist in creating certain widgets.

☑ **Position** — Positions elements relative to other elements.

Figure 10-10:
The
Download
Builder
helps you
customize
the kind of
download
you want.

Some developers have complained that the scoping feature doesn't work completely in ThemeRoller. You can see one such example at `http://bugs.jqueryui.com/ticket/8095`.

5. Click Download.

You see a download dialog box for your browser and platform. The file you receive is an archive that contains all the special features you requested during the configuration process.

Downloading a custom theme

In order to use a custom theme with your application, you must download it. There aren't any URLs you can use to access the theme from the ThemeRoller site. The following procedure helps you download a custom theme.

1. Click Download Theme in the ThemeRoller menu.

ThemeRoller displays the Download Builder page shown in Figure 10-10.

2. Select the version of the theme you want to use.

The default version is the best option in most cases. However, you may need to download an older version to support older applications.

3. Select the features you want to use from the library.

Because this is a custom theme, you need to download all of the features for development purposes to ensure you have a complete setup. Unlike a predefined theme, a custom theme makes it harder to go back later and obtain items that at first you thought you wouldn't need but ended up requiring. Yes, you can use the URL you saved during the creation process to reproduce the theme, but this means keeping the URL in a location that you can remember. When you come up with versions of the theme that you want to keep, saving them at the outset is always a better idea.

4. Type a name for your theme in the Theme Folder Name field.

Select a unique name for your theme that reflects the design or purpose of the theme. Otherwise you may end up with a number of custom themes that are hard to identify later.

5. (Optional) Type a value in the CSS Scope field.

The scope makes it possible to override internal CSS styles using an external .CSS file. You can read more about the use of scope at `http://css-tricks.com/saving-the-day-with-scoped-css/` and `http://updates.html5rocks.com/2013/03/What-s-the-CSS-scope-pseudo-class-for`.

Some developers have complained that the scoping feature doesn't work completely in ThemeRoller. You can see one such example at `http://bugs.jqueryui.com/ticket/8095`.

6. Click Download.

You see a download dialog for your browser and platform. The file you receive is an archive that contains all of the special features you requested during the configuration process.

Adding Custom Themes to Your Projects

A custom theme isn't much good unless you use it in an application. However, before you use it in a custom application, it pays to become familiar with the appearance and functionality of the theme. The archive you download contains a customized version of jQuery, jQuery UI, and the CSS used to implement the theme. It also includes an overview of the theme you created, as well as individual examples of the various widgets. The following sections provide an overview of the contents of your archive and also show how to add the resulting theme to an application.

Viewing the index.html file

The topmost file in the archive is `index.html`. It provides you with an overview of the theme, along with some additional information about it. The first thing you should do after downloading the theme is to open this file to see how it looks on your local system. Figure 10-11 shows how the Le Frog theme looks as a custom download.

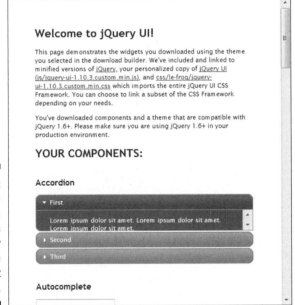

Figure 10-11:
Review the theme you created as an overview before looking at specifics.

The top of the page contains instructions for working with the custom theme. In addition, it contains links to the locations of the various files you need. You can also find these links at the top of index.html. In fact, it's a great idea to simply copy the links from index.html to your own project.

After the introductory material, you see a quick example of each of the widgets that the theme supports. The widgets are only there for show — you can't actually do anything with them. However, viewing the widgets will tell you whether you have everything at least started correctly. If not, you can always make additional changes.

Viewing the interactive demos

The `development-bundle` folder contains a lot of useful material. One of the first pieces you should look at is the contents of the `development-bundle\demos` folder, which contains examples of how to use the various jQuery UI features with your theme. Unfortunately, none of these examples actually use the theme you created unless you modify them to do so. For example, the `custom-icons.html` example in the `development-bundle\demos\accordion` folder shows how to perform this task, but doesn't use your theme by default as shown in Figure 10-12.

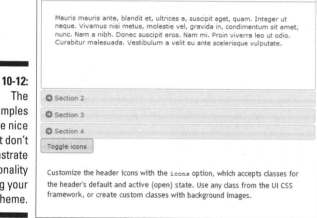

Figure 10-12: The examples are nice but don't demonstrate functionality using your theme.

Fortunately, it's easy to modify the example so that it does appear with your theme in place. The following procedure tells you how to modify the `custom-icons.html` example — other examples follow the same pattern.

1. **Remove the existing jQuery, jQuery UI, and style tags.**

   You need to remove the general tags shown here for this example.

```
<link rel="stylesheet"
      href="../../themes/base/jquery.ui.all.css">
<script src="../../jquery-1.9.1.js"></script>
<script src="../../ui/jquery.ui.core.js"></script>
<script src="../../ui/jquery.ui.widget.js"></script>
<script src="../../ui/jquery.ui.accordion.js">
</script>
<script src="../../ui/jquery.ui.button.js"></script>
<link rel="stylesheet" href="../demos.css">
```

2. **Add the updated jQuery, jQuery UI, and style tags shown here.**

   Make sure you use the links provided in `index.html`. Because this example is several layers deep in the hierarchy, you must add `../` for each folder level that the example is below the main level (normally three levels, as shown here).

```
<script
    src="../../../js/jquery-1.9.1.js">
</script>
<script
    src="../../../js/jquery-ui-1.10.3.custom.js">
</script>
<link
    rel="stylesheet"
    href="../../../css/le-frog/jquery-ui-1.10.3.custom.css" />
```

3. **Reload the page.**

   You see the themed output. Figure 10-13 shows a typical example of what themed output might look like.

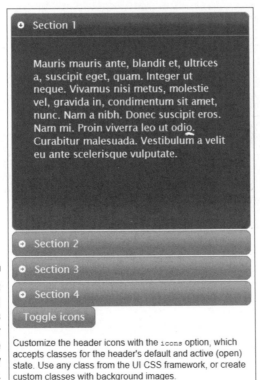

Figure 10-13:
Seeing examples using your theme is really helpful.

Looking at the documentation

It's helpful to have documentation for your theme. You can find basic jQuery and jQuery UI documentation in the `development-bundle\docs` folder of the theme. Each of the files contains information about a particular widget, effect, or other library feature. For example, when you open `accordion.html`, you see information about the accordion widget (as shown in Figure 10-14).

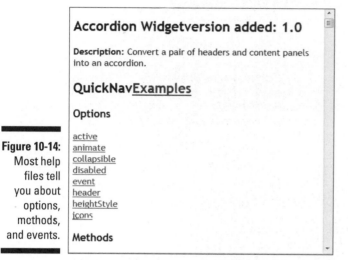

Accordion Widgetversion added: 1.0

Description: Convert a pair of headers and content panels into an accordion.

QuickNav<u>Examples</u>

Options

<u>active</u>
<u>animate</u>
<u>collapsible</u>
<u>disabled</u>
<u>event</u>
<u>header</u>
<u>heightStyle</u>
<u>icons</u>

Methods

Figure 10-14: Most help files tell you about options, methods, and events.

The top half of the page contains links to specifics about a particular topic. For example, if you want to find out more about the `active` option, you click its link on the page. (Figure 10-15 shows typical content.) You see a short description of the feature, any required type information, and a coding example.

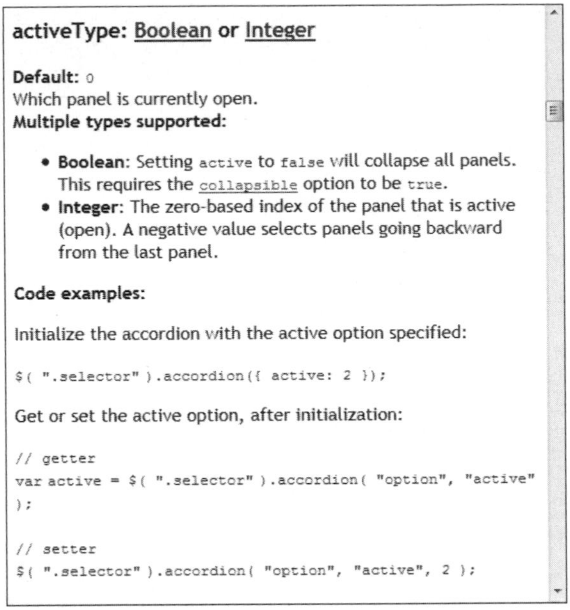

activeType: <u>Boolean</u> or <u>Integer</u>

Default: 0
Which panel is currently open.
Multiple types supported:

- **Boolean:** Setting `active` to `false` will collapse all panels. This requires the <u>collapsible</u> option to be `true`.
- **Integer:** The zero-based index of the panel that is active (open). A negative value selects panels going backward from the last panel.

Code examples:

Initialize the accordion with the active option specified:

```
$( ".selector" ).accordion({ active: 2 });
```

Get or set the active option, after initialization:

```
// getter
var active = $( ".selector" ).accordion( "option", "active"
);

// setter
$( ".selector" ).accordion( "option", "active", 2 );
```

Figure 10-15:
The documentation provides enough details for most developers to work with the option, method, or event.

Adding a custom theme to your own project

Seeing the vendor samples and working through the documentation are helpful, but most developers want to see a theme in action. Part IV of this book contains a number of jQuery and jQuery UI examples you can work with. In every case, the only thing you really need to modify is the `<style>` link. However, to ensure that the example works completely and reliably, you need to modify the jQuery and jQuery UI links as well. Copy the Accordion. HTML example to the same folder you've used for your theme. The following code shows the tags you should use to replace those used in Part IV when using the Le Frog theme (make sure you include the appropriate changes for your theme).

```
<script
    src="js/jquery-1.9.1.js">
</script>
<script
    src="js/jquery-ui-1.10.3.custom.js">
</script>
<link
    rel="stylesheet"
    href="css/le-frog/jquery-ui-1.10.3.custom.css" />
```

Load the example in your browser to see if the changes have worked. In most cases, you'll see something like the example shown in Figure 10-16.

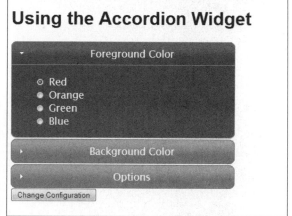

Figure 10-16: The updated example: Something's not quite right.

The first thing you should notice is that the jQuery UI control does indeed use the new theme. However, the submission button doesn't use the style. This is because the example used a standard `<input>` button to perform the task. When working with themes, you need to use the full assortment of jQuery UI controls. You can fix this problem by adding a jQuery UI button to the script, as shown here in bold:

```
<script language="JavaScript">
   $(function()
     {
         $("#Configuration").accordion();
         $("input[type=submit]").button();
     });
</script>
```

The page will now present the correct appearance. Because you haven't attached any jQuery UI behaviors to the button, it will continue to work as it did before.

Chapter 11

Using the Dynamic Drive Tools

Dynamic Drive (www.dynamicdrive.com/) is a JavaScript library that provides a wealth of tools to make your job easier, while also enhancing overall site appearance, speed, reliability, and security. The focus of this site is on appearance. However, some features, like the Image Optimizer, also make it possible to create a better experience for the user — which translates into better reliability. Any time you can create a better experience, you make it less likely that your user will click away from your site and go somewhere else. In the competitive Internet environment, the user experience is what matters most.

Unlike jQuery and many of the other libraries described in the book, Dynamic Drive focuses mainly on graphics, which is an area where many developers lack skills. You can use features such as Image Optimizer to improve the apparent speed of your site. In some respects the graphics will download faster, but in other ways, the focus is on making the image *appear* to download faster by providing incremental feedback the user can see. *Incremental display* means displaying the graphic a piece at a time so the user gets constant feedback and knows the site is making progress toward loading everything to make it functional.

Graphics are an important part of most sites today because they provide aesthetic appeal and convey information that's hard to convey by using text. However, too many graphics can actually become distracting and cause your message to disappear. In addition, some special-needs users won't be able to appreciate the graphics. For them, you need to provide text alternatives — or even a method for eliminating the graphics in some cases. The point is, don't become so entranced with graphics that they *become* the message. Instead, make sure your graphics accent the site as a whole, so that you present the message you want to convey.

Dynamic Drive can also help you create more interesting tools. For example, this chapter discusses techniques for creating more interesting buttons and also shows how to add a ribbon to your application. Ribbon rules provide separation between page elements and make the page easier to use. Both features provide an interesting way to use graphics in an unusual way.

The remainder of this chapter provides a quick overview of some other tools that Dynamic Drive has to offer. There's a wealth of them and a single chapter can't discuss them all. One of the more interesting tools discussed here is the Email Riddler — used to make it a lot harder for spam harvesters to gain access to your e-mail address.

You can access all of the Dynamic Drive tools from the main page shown in Figure 11-1.

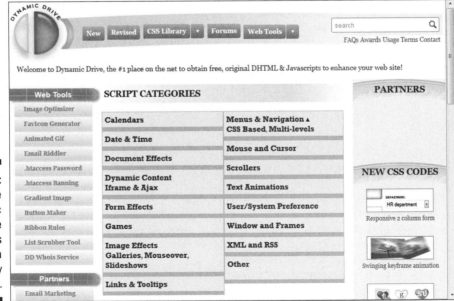

Figure 11-1: The Dynamic Drive site provides access to a wide variety of tools.

Managing Images with Image Optimizer

The Image Optimizer makes it possible to create images that load quickly and efficiently. A user is less likely to click away from your site when it's speedy, so optimizing the images is always a good idea. Even small changes in perceived speed (if not actual speed) can make a difference. To access the Image Optimizer, click Image Optimizer on the Web Tools menu of the main page. You see a page similar to the one shown in Figure 11-2.

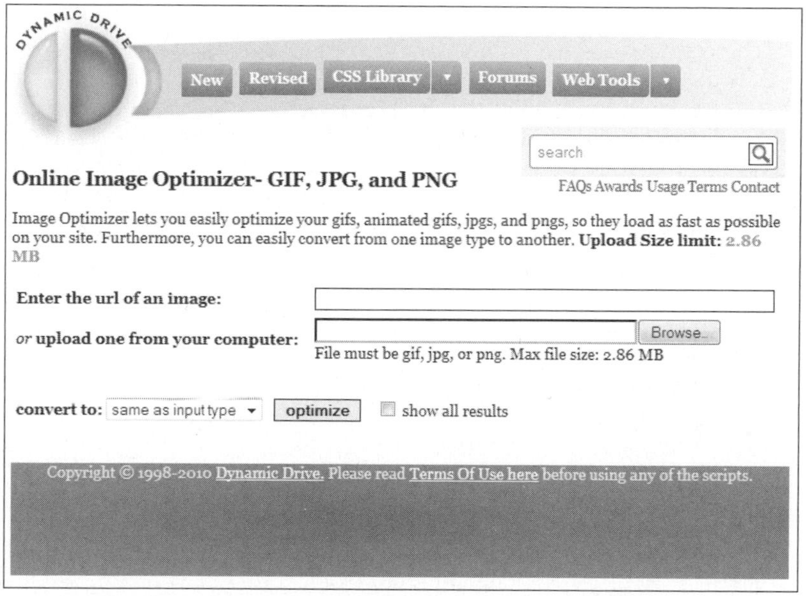

DYNAMIC DRIVE
New
Revised
CSS Library
Forums
Web Tools
search
Online Image Optimizer- GIF, JPG, and PNG
FAQs Awards Usage Terms Contact
Image Optimizer lets you easily optimize your gifs, animated gifs, jpgs, and pngs, so they load as fast as possible on your site. Furthermore, you can easily convert from one image type to another. Upload Size limit: 2.86 MB
Enter the url of an image:
or upload one from your computer:
Browse...
File must be gif, jpg, or png. Max file size: 2.86 MB
convert to: same as input type
optimize
show all results
Copyright © 1998-2010 Dynamic Drive. Please read Terms Of Use here before using any of the scripts.

Figure 11-2: Use the Image Optimizer to make your site faster.

You can provide the URL of an image online or the location of an image on your hard drive as your input (using the correct field). Click the Browse button to make it easier to find an image on the hard drive. You'll see a File Upload dialog box you can use to locate the file on your hard drive. The maximum file size that Image Optimizer will accept is 2.86 MB. If your file is larger than this size, you need to crop or resize it before uploading it.

- Cropping removes part of the image without affecting image quality.
- Resizing maintains the entire image, but reduces image quality as a result.

REMEMBER

With the Image Optimizer you can convert an image to another type. The image type you use determines just how much optimization that the Image Optimizer can provide. However, when working with a lossy file format, such as Joint Photographic Experts Group (.JPG), it also determines the quality of

the image the user sees. A *lossy* file format is one that sacrifices some content in order to make the file smaller. When image quality suffers too much, the user becomes frustrated and leaves your site despite the improvement in page download speed. The example begins with a 1.05MB .JPG image. The following list shows the optimized sizes for each output file type. (You can find the image for this example in the \Chapter 11\Image Optimizer folder of the downloadable code as FallWoods.JPG along with all of the variations shown in the list so you can compare quality.)

- ✔ **.GIF (8 color):** 794 KB
- ✔ **.GIF (4 color):** 530 KB
- ✔ **.GIF (2 color):** 284 KB
- ✔ **.JPG (quality 80):** 1.03 MB
- ✔ **.JPG (quality 70):** 943 KB
- ✔ **.JPG (quality 60):** 783 KB
- ✔ **.JPG (quality 50):** 633 KB
- ✔ **.JPG (quality 40):** 589 KB
- ✔ **.JPG (quality 30):** 486 KB
- ✔ **.JPG (quality 20):** 380 KB
- ✔ **.JPG (quality 10):** 239 KB
- ✔ **.PNG (8 color):** 975 KB
- ✔ **.PNG (4 color):** 634 KB

To perform the image optimization, choose an image type from the Convert To field, optionally check Show All Results, and click Optimize (as shown in Figure 11-3). The optimization process can require a few minutes to complete. What you see as output is the original image and some suggested alternative images. In this case, you see Graphic Interchange Format (.GIF) output, which saves size by reducing the color depth. The Portable Network Graphics (.PNG) also saves space by changing the color depth; .JPG saves space by reducing image quality. Each of the image entries will tell you how much smaller the converted image is and what you can expect to save in download size.

To save a particular version of the optimized image to disk, right-click the image and choose Save Image As from the context menu. Provide a filename for the image and click Save to complete the process.

Some image conversions can produce special effects that look quite nice on a site. For example, changing an input image to a two-color .GIF file can create a nice abstract look that works well for a background image. Try various conversions to determine whether any of the effects will be useful on your site (in addition to saving download time).

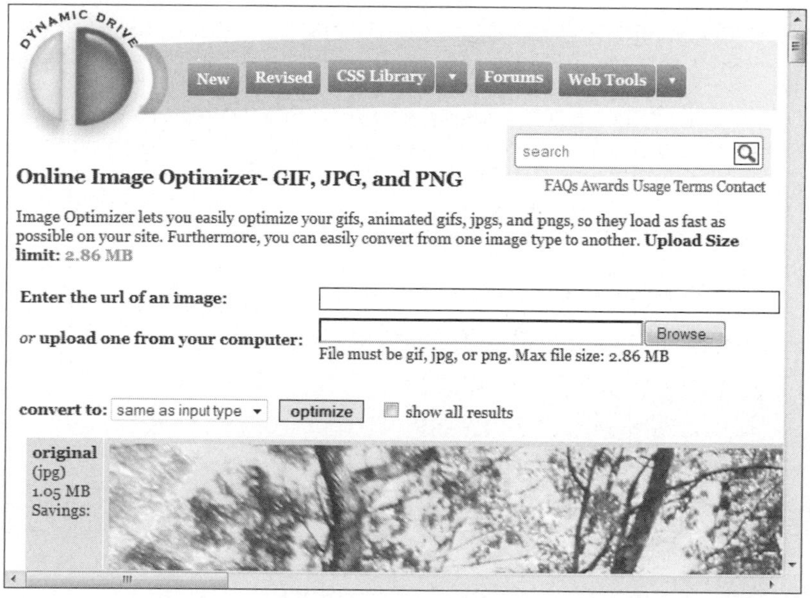

Figure 11-3:
Image
Optimizer
outputs
sample
images
using the
file format
you request.

Creating Icons Using FavIcon Generator

A *favorites icon* is one that appears in the browser's address field when people access your site. The icon can also appear on tabs and also in the user's favorites list. Using a favorites icon can help people remember your site and make it easier to find in a list of sites. Of course, site branding is an essential part of giving a site a special feel. The FavIcon Generator takes any .BMP, .GIF, .JPG, or .PNG file you own and turns it into an icon you can associate with your site. When working with .BMP or .PNG files, you can also create transparent areas so that the icon can have something other than a square shape.

To access the FavIcon Generator, you click FavIcon Generator on the Web Tools menu of the main page. Figure 11-4 shows how the page appears when you access it.

Provide the name of a compatible graphics file on your hard drive to use for the favorites icon. You can use any file up to 150 KB in size. As an option, you can also choose to include both a desktop icon and a large icon with the resulting favorites icon. After you make your selections, you see the output. Figure 11-5 shows typical output for the example in this section. (You can find the image for this example in the \Chapter 11\FavIcon Generator folder of the downloadable code as TestImage.GIF.)

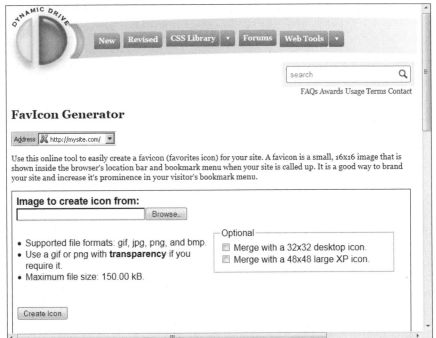

Figure 11-4: Create a Favorites icon to brand your site and make it easier to remember.

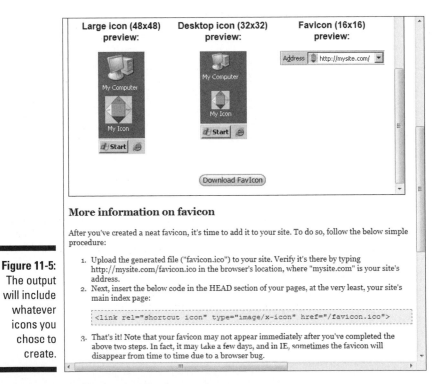

Figure 11-5: The output will include whatever icons you chose to create.

Click Download FavIcon to obtain a copy of the result in icon (. ICO) format. When you select other icon sizes, all three icons appear in the single file. The browser or operating system will select the correct size for a particular need.

The More Information on FavIcon section of the page tells you how to use your icon to brand your page. All you need to do is add a tag to your page so that the browser knows which icon to display. The change isn't immediate and it does take time for many browsers to recognize the icon.

Creating Animations with Animated Gif

Many sites use animation to good effect. Text conveys an abstract level of meaning, graphics can make the meaning more concrete, but the use of good animation can communicate in ways that text and standard graphics can't. The addition of motion has a huge impact on how the viewer sees the information. The Animated Gif tool helps developers create simple animations. You access it by clicking Animated Gif on the Web Tools menu of the main page. Figure 11-6 shows how the tool appears when you first access it.

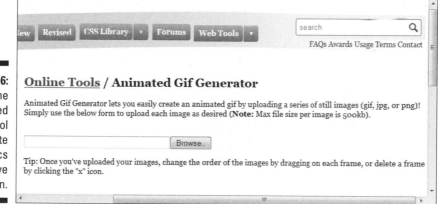

Figure 11-6: Use the Animated Gif tool to create graphics that have motion.

Of course, animated GIFs can also be a lot of fun. There are people out there who create animated GIFs to entertain, generate a laugh, or to dress up just about anything having to do with the Internet. For example, you can find a wide range of free animated GIFs at www.gifs.net/gif/, http://heathersanimations.com/, http://gifgifs.com/, and www.amazing-animations.com/ (amongst many others). The point of using this tool is to create an animated GIF for special circumstances that the free libraries don't support.

Animations are actually a series of still pictures that are presented one at a time at a specific speed. There are complex applications that can perform all sorts of special effects, vary the time between transitions, and do other things that would make your hair stand on end. Complex applications are for professional developers. All you need is a series of images to use this tool, which makes it simple enough for developers.

You can create the images using any tool you want, such as Paint. In fact, the images need not be drawn at all. An animated GIF could actually consist of a series of screenshots showing the transition from a starting point to a final result. The point is that you display a series of images, in a specific order, to produce a result that appears to have some type of motion. The example, shown in Figure 11-7 is a simple box with circles in it. The animation occurs when each of these circles turns red in turn. You could use it as part of a progress indication. (You can find the series of images for this example in the \Chapter 11\Animated Gif folder of the downloadable code as Progress01.PNG through Progress06.PNG.)

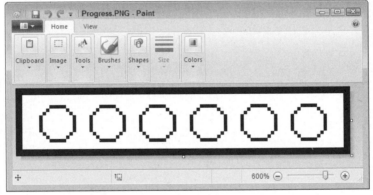

Figure 11-7:
The example animates this simple drawing.

To create an animated GIF, click Browse, select the first image in the series in the File Upload dialog box, and then click Open. You perform this task for each image in the series until you've uploaded all the images. Figure 11-8 shows how the example appears at this point. (If you make a mistake and upload an image in the wrong place, simply click the X for that image's square to remove it from the sequence.)

You need to decide how large to make your GIF and how fast the animation should run. These settings usually require a little trial and error. Try the settings you think will work and then click MakeGif. What you'll see is a sample of the GIF on screen. When you're happy with the result, click the Download Image link that appears next to the GIF.

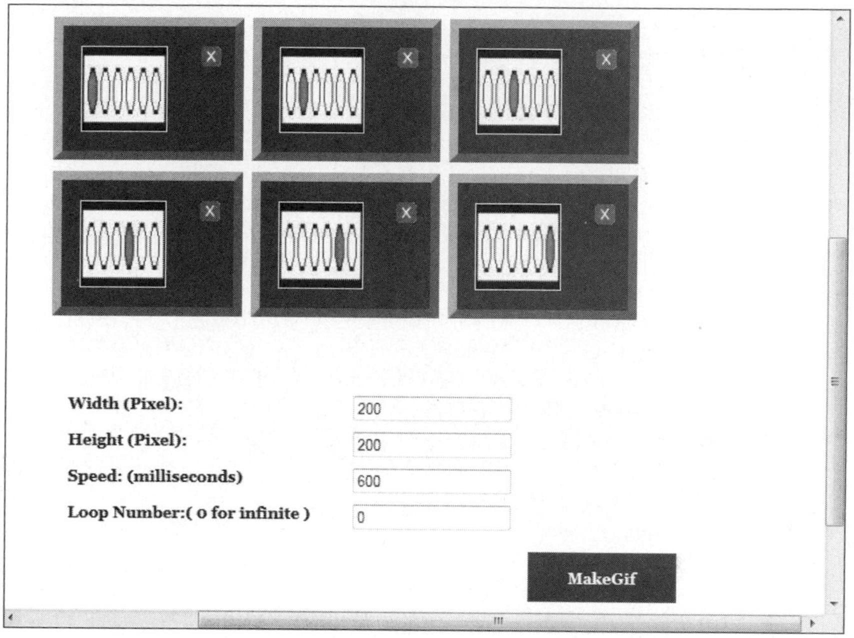

Figure 11-8:
Add all of
the images
you want to
use to the
page.

Of course, now that you have an animated GIF, you'll want to see it on a
page. All you need to provide is the standard `<img>` tag — the animation is
built into the file you downloaded. The following code shows how to create
a test page for this example. (You can find complete code for this example
in the `\Chapter 11\Animated Gif` folder of the downloadable code as
`TestAnimation.HTML`.)

```
<!DOCTYPE html>

<html>
<head>
    <title>Test an Animated GIF</title>
</head>

<body>
    <h1>Test an Animated GIF</h1>
    <img src="Test.GIF" />
</body>
</html>
```

Generating Images Using Gradient Image Maker

You've already seen a number of other programs described that create gradient images. It seems as if every site provides one. The Dynamic Drive Gradient Image Maker is different, though: It actually creates an image file, rather than creating CSS that eventually creates an image on screen. The difference is important. Using an image means that the browser only needs to support images — something that every browser out today can do — but when using CSS, you need to know that the host browser actually supports the required level of CSS. You access Gradient Image Maker by clicking Gradient Image on the Web Tools menu of the main page. Figure 11-9 shows how the tool appears when you first access it.

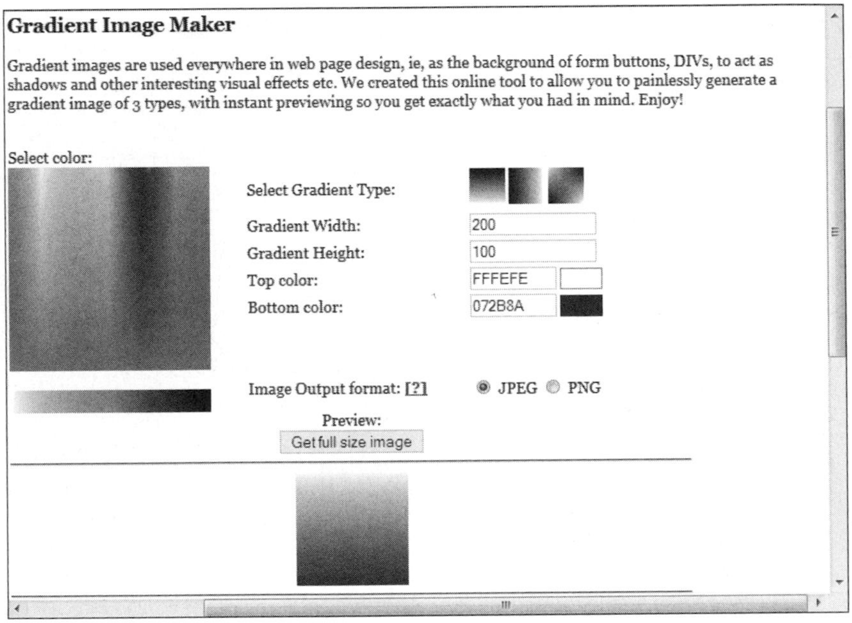

Figure 11-9: Gradient Image Maker sports a simple interface and outputs actual images.

The Gradient Image Maker sports a simplified interface. All you do is select the kind of gradient you want to create (horizontal, vertical, or diagonal), define the gradient size, and choose the colors you want to use. When choosing a color, you can either click in an area in the color selector or you can type the hexadecimal code for the color you want to use. There's little flexibility in using this tool. It's specifically designed to provide a simple, quick means of creating a gradient.

When you're satisfied with the gradient, choose an image output format. The JPEG format will generally produce smaller files, while the PNG format will generally produce higher-quality files. Click Get Full Size Image and you see another tab open with the gradient image you requested. Right-click the image and choose Save Image As from the context menu to save the image to your hard drive.

There's a trick to using the image as a background. HTML supports a `background` attribute for the `<body>` tag. Supposedly this attribute is deprecated and you shouldn't rely on it being available forever. However, it still works in every browser targeted by this book (and on all platforms). The following code uses the `background` attribute, and will display a page with the gradient as a background image in the size requested. (You can find complete code for this example in the `\Chapter 11\Gradient Image Maker` folder of the downloadable code as `TestGradient.HTML`.)

```
<!DOCTYPE html>

<html>
<head>
    <title>Testing a Gradient Image</title>
</head>

<body background="Gradient.JPG">
    <h1>Testing a Gradient Image</h1>
    <p>Some Sample Text</p>
</body>
</html>
```

This technique does have the advantage of not using any form of CSS to display the image, but it's somewhat risky as future changes are made to how HTML works in browsers. For now, however, it appears that every browser on the planet still supports this particular method of displaying a background image (when some won't use the CSS method). Figure 11-10 shows how the gradient looks in action.

Testing a Gradient Image

Some Sample Text

The current way to use the image is to apply it using CSS. In this case, you apply it using the `background` property for the body style, as shown here. (You can find complete code for this example in the `\Chapter 11\Gradient Image Maker` folder of the downloadable code as `TestGradient2.HTML`.)

```html
<!DOCTYPE html>

<html>
<head>
    <title>Testing a Gradient Image</title>
    <style type="text/css">
        body
        {
            background: url("Gradient.JPG");
            background-size: 80px 80px;
        }
    </style>
</head>

<body>
    <h1>Testing a Gradient Image</h1>
    <p>Some Sample Text</p>
</body>
</html>
```

The advantage of this approach is that you can control the background size, origin, and other features. Using CSS, whenever possible, greatly increases the flexibility of using a gradient image. However, if you're going to use CSS anyway, it often pays to apply the gradient itself by using CSS. The main advantage of using an image over pure CSS is that you can quickly swap one image for another, using any of a number of techniques to change the page appearance, without writing any new code.

Generating Controls Using Button Maker Online

Many sites use micro buttons to make it possible to perform tasks such as creating a Really Simple Syndication (RSS) feed for the site. These buttons pop up all over the place — you see them mainly on informational sites, but they appear other places as well. A *micro button* is either 80 × 15 pixels or 88 × 31 pixels in size. It normally contains two pieces of text in a bicolored button; it can use several color combinations, but the text itself is a single color.

The Button Maker Online tool makes it possible to generate these micro buttons quickly and efficiently. You access Button Maker Online by clicking Button Maker on the Web Tools menu of the main page. Figure 11-11 shows how the tool appears when you first access it.

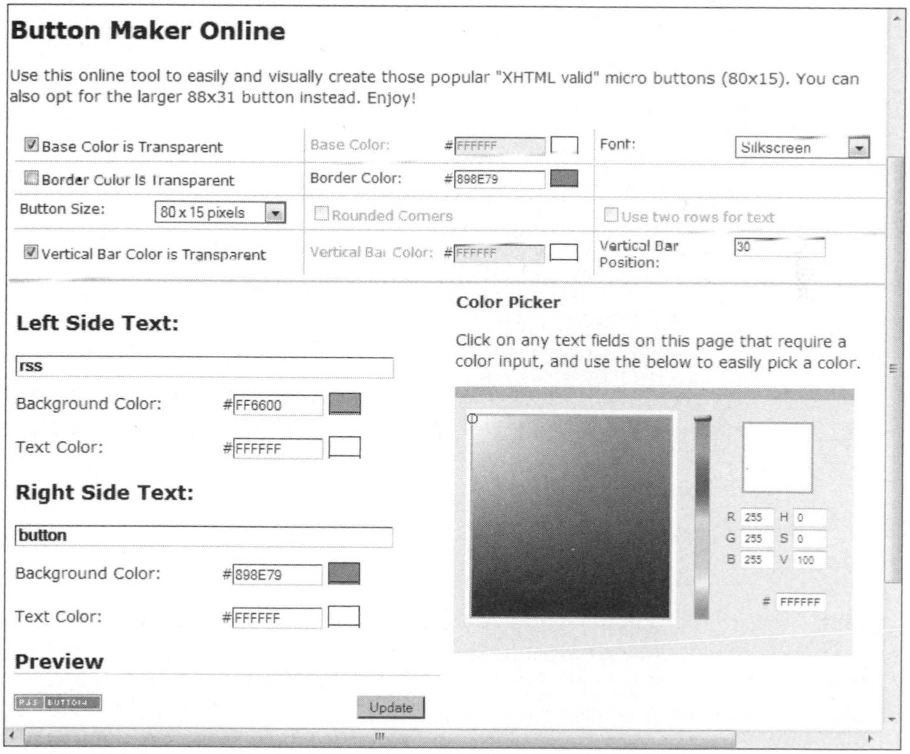

Figure 11-11: Use Button Maker Online to create micro buttons for your site.

Creating the button

Even though the form looks quite complicated, you can create a micro button relatively fast. The following procedure leads you through the task of creating a micro button. (You can find the image for this example in the `\Chapter 11\Button Maker Online` folder of the downloadable code as `MyButton.GIF`.)

1. **Choose a size for the button in the Button Size field.**

   The button size determines how much text can appear in the micro button. You should set the size before changing anything else because the size of the button also modifies how the other changes appear onscreen.

2. **(Optional) Check the Rounded Corners option when desired (and available).**

   The Rounded Corners option is only available when working with an 88×31 button.

3. **(Optional) Check the Use Two Rows for Text option when desired (and available).**

   The Two Rows for Text option is only available when working with an 88×31 button.

4. **Choose a base color or check Base Color is Transparent.**

   The *base color* appears behind all of the other elements of the button. A transparent base will allow the background to show through. The base color always results in a square image, even if you check the Rounded Corners option.

5. **Choose a border color or check Border Color is Transparent.**

   The *border color* defines the outside of the actual button, but there's a 1-pixel border between the edge of the border and the end of the base, so that a colored base will always show through. Choosing the Rounded Corners option results in a border with rounded corners.

6. **Choose an option in the Font drop-down list box.**

   The tool provides access to two different fonts. The Sans-Serif option works best when using an 88×31 button with a vertical bar.

7. **Choose a bar color or make the bar transparent.**

   The button always uses a vertical bar for 80×15 buttons, but can use either a vertical or horizontal bar for 88×31 buttons. The name of the bar option changes to match the bar's orientation.

8. **Type a value in the Left Side Text field.**

   The button can hold about ten characters worth of text total when working with a single row of text with a vertical bar. Each row can accommodate about 19 characters worth of text (38 characters total) when using two rows of text.

9. **Set the Left Side Text field background and foreground colors.**

   You can use the Color Picker or type the hexadecimal value into the appropriate fields.

10. **Type a value in the Right Side Text field.**

11. **Set the Right Side Text field background and foreground colors.**

    You can use the Color Picker or type the hexadecimal value into the appropriate fields.

12. **(Optional) Set the Vertical Bar Position when desired (and available).**

    The Vertical Bar Position setting is only enabled when the button uses a vertical bar. Two row text uses the entire width of the button for each row.

13. **Click Update.**

    You see all the changes you made to the button.

14. **Make any required changes and click Update after each change.**

    Eventually the button will look precisely as you want it to look.

15. **Right-click the button and choose Save Image As from the context menu.**

    You see a Save Image dialog box.

16. **Type the name you want to use for the button and click Save.**

    The button is ready for use.

Using the button

At this point, you have a wonderful new micro button to try. There are a number of ways to use a micro button. For example, some people include them within an anchor (<a>) tag. However, for the purposes of this example, you'll see how to use a micro button inside a regular button. (You can find complete code for this example in the \Chapter 11\Button Maker Online folder of the downloadable code as TestButton.HTML.)

```
<!DOCTYPE html>

<html>
<head>
    <title>Testing a Micro Button</title>
    <style type="text/css">
        #MicroTest
        {
            border: none;
            background-color: transparent;
        }
    </style>
</head>

<body>
    <h1>Testing a Micro Button</h1>
    <button id="MicroTest"
            onclick="alert('Clicked!')">
        <img src="MyButton.GIF">
    </button>
</body>
</html>
```

In this case, the .GIF file containing the button image appears as part of an <img> tag within a <button> tag. The <button> tag provides access to the onclick attribute, which is used to react to a user click with an alert() function call. You see a dialog box containing the word Clicked!

Of course, you also have a problem with the button appearing onscreen. The internal style, #MicroTest, makes the button disappear by changing its border to none and setting the background-color to transparent. As a result, all you see is the micro button (as shown in Figure 11-12).

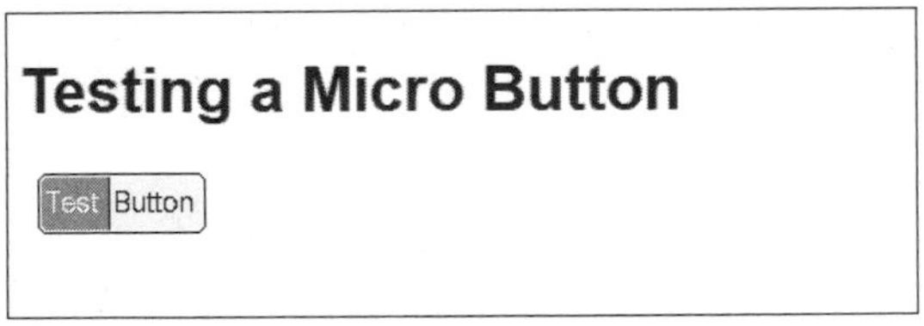

Figure 11-12:
Micro buttons add a bit of pizzazz to your site, along with a familiar appearance.

Testing a Micro Button

Adding Pizzazz Using Ribbon Rules

Ribbon rules are colorful graphic rules that have replaced the standard HTML rule on many sites. The graphic rule adds an accent to the site and makes it appear a bit more finished. You access Ribbon Rules Generator by clicking Ribbon Rules on the Web Tools menu of the main page. Figure 11-13 shows how the tool appears when you first access it.

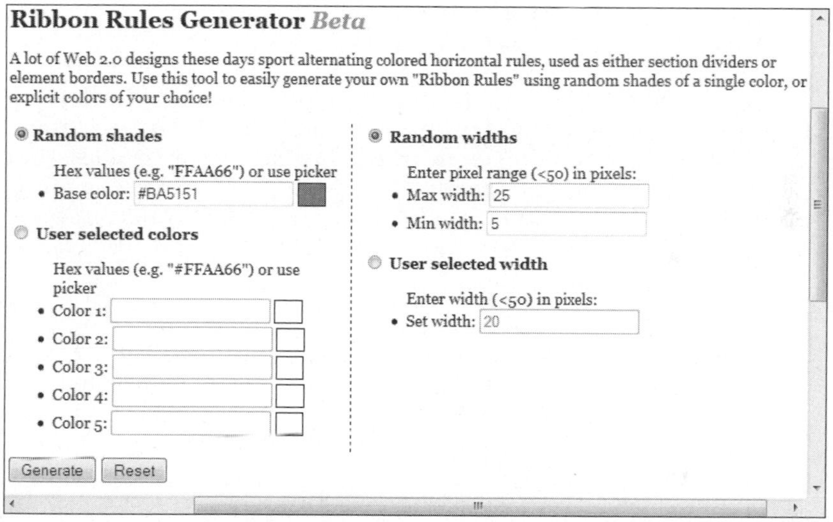

Ribbon Rules Generator *Beta*

A lot of Web 2.0 designs these days sport alternating colored horizontal rules, used as either section dividers or element borders. Use this tool to easily generate your own "Ribbon Rules" using random shades of a single color, or explicit colors of your choice!

⦿ **Random shades**

    Hex values (e.g. "FFAA66") or use picker
- Base color: #BA5151

○ **User selected colors**

    Hex values (e.g. "#FFAA66") or use picker
- Color 1:
- Color 2:
- Color 3:
- Color 4:
- Color 5:

⦿ **Random widths**

    Enter pixel range (<50) in pixels:
- Max width: 25
- Min width: 5

○ **User selected width**

    Enter width (<50) in pixels:
- Set width: 20

[Generate] [Reset]

Figure 11-13: Using ribbon rules will dress up your site and make it look more finished.

Creating the ribbon rule

Generating a ribbon requires that you specify the color and spacing to use for the ribbon element. The choice for color is to use a randomly generated sequence based on a base color, or to use specific color choices. The spacing is either random within the range you specify, or a specific size for each color choice.

The user selected colors and sequence spacing require a little extra care when you use them. First, make sure that any hexadecimal values you input are preceded by the pound sign (#) or else the ribbon will appear black when you generate it. Second, the color choices you make will appear exactly in the sequence you make them in the output ribbon. If you plan to use the ribbon in a repeating manner, create a sequence and spacing that works together. Testing shows that a spacing of 26 works great — you end up with an even repeating sequence that will look great on the page.

After you make your choices, click Generate. Ribbon Rules Generator will create a ribbon rule for you and display it under the form. You can use the ribbon as it appears, or make changes for a different look. To save the ribbon you've created, right click its entry on the page and choose Save Image As from the context menu. Provide a name for the image and click Save to complete the action. (You can find the images for this example in the \Chapter 11\Ribbon Rules Generator folder of the downloadable code as UserRule.GIF and RandomRule.GIF.)

Using the ribbon rule

You can use the image containing the ribbon rule anywhere you can use any other image. However, most people will use the ribbon rule as part of a style. The following code shows one example of how you could use the ribbon rules created by this example. (You can find complete code for this example in the \Chapter 11\Ribbon Rules Generator folder of the download-able code as TestRibbonRule.HTML.)

```
<!DOCTYPE html>

<html>
<head>
    <title>Test the Ribbon Rules</title>
    <style type="text/css">
        #Area1
        {
            margin: 5px;
            padding: 5px;
            border-style: solid;
            border-width: 6px;
            border-image:url(UserRule.GIF) 960 10 repeat;
        }

        #Area2
        {
            margin: 5px;
            padding: 5px;
            border-style: solid;
            border-width: 6px;
            border-image:url(RandomRule.GIF) 960 10 repeat;
        }
    </style>
</head>
```

```
<body>
    <h1>Test the Ribbon Rules</h1>
    <div id="Area1">
        <h2>This is Area 1</h2>
        <p>This area uses the user-selected settings.</p>
    </div>
    <div id="Area2">
        <h2>This is Area 2</h2>
        <p>This area uses the random settings.</p>
    </div>
</body>
</html>
```

You saw this same technique applied to the graphics in Chapter 4. However, this time you use them to create a rule on a page. The page contains two areas. The first displays a ribbon rule created with user-specific settings; the second displays a ribbon rule created by using random settings. Of course, there are infinite possibilities in creating ribbon rules — these examples are simply representative of what you can do. Figure 11-14 shows typical output from this example.

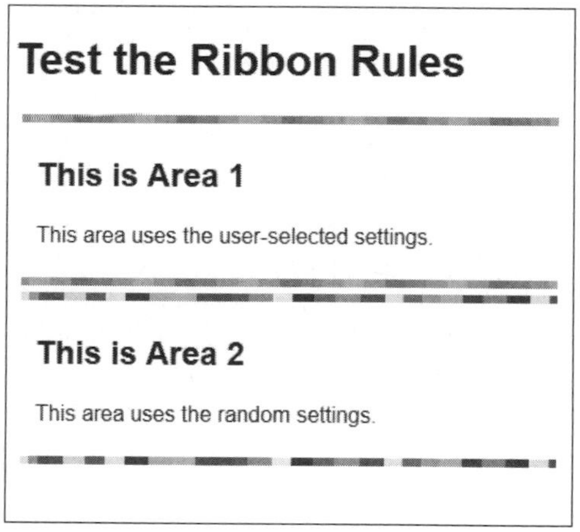

Figure 11-14: Ribbon rules can rely on any combination of random and user-specified settings.

Accessing the sample scripts

The main page of the Dynamic Drive site contains a listing of scripts categorized by type. For example, if you click Date and Time, you see an entire list of scripts that have something to do with date and time. Each of the entries in the list provides the script name, which browsers can use it, whether it was user-submitted, and a short description.

Clicking a specific entry takes you to another page that tells you more about the script. Most of the scripts include a running example so you can see how the script works. After that, you see a box containing the source code and directions for using the script in your own application. What is most important is that the majority of these scripts include a nicely written description of precisely how the script works, so you can learn more about scripting while you improve your site with the functionality that the script provides.

In most cases, the scripts you access on this site provide enough information that you can use the script even if you don't fully understand how it works. Dynamic Drive tries to make things as easy as possible so you can create a nice-looking site while you also develop new skills. Make sure you understand the terms of service for using the scripts at `www.dynamic drive.com/notice.htm`. For the most part, you're allowed to make needed changes and use the scripts as needed on your site, but you can't send the modified scripts to other people to use. The rules seem simple and fair.

Part IV

Modifying Pre-Built Content for a Unique Look

Creating a Category/Detail View

▾ Flowers

Cactus
Nanking Cherry

▸ Seasons

▸ Gardening

See examples of how you can create table-like effects using CSS3 and HTML5 tags at www.dummies.com/extras/css3.

In this part . . .

- ✔ Discover where vendors typically hide the CSS for a library or generator

- ✔ Decide which modification techniques and tools will work best for your library or generator

- ✔ Create special effects for the jQuery and jQuery UI features

- ✔ Use modified forms of the Dynamic Drive scripts to enhance your applications

Chapter 12

Understanding CSS for Libraries and Generators

- -

In This Chapter

▶ Discovering how libraries and generators use CSS

▶ Viewing the CSS used by libraries and generators

▶ Determining which elements to modify

▶ Using modification aids

- -

*T*he third-party libraries and generators in this book have had one thing in common — they all rely on CSS in some way to accomplish their work. So far, the book has demonstrated that using CSS makes it possible to format page content and perform programming-like tasks. The third-party products you've examined all make your job easier by creating an environment in which you can focus on output, rather than on the means to obtain that output.

You've also been subject to the whims of each product's developer because each product forces you to perform tasks in a specific way. This chapter helps you solve that problem, at least partially, by viewing and modifying the CSS used by these third-party products in order to see output in the way you'd prefer. For example, you might want to see rounded corners on controls, rather than square corners, and this chapter tells you how to make that sort of change. Of course, changes go beyond the visual to behavior so that you can obtain new functionality from existing libraries by augmenting the behaviors they provide.

Working with text-based programming environments makes it a lot easier for you to see how things work and then make modifications as needed. Browser-based applications are more accessible than compiled applications at the desktop (where the closed environment makes seeing how anything works nearly impossible). An open environment also makes it possible to find people (such as other developers) who will help you make modifications and even locate third party aids. The chapter helps you understand the need for community support when making changes to products — when enough people request a change, the change often gets incorporated into the product as a permanent feature.

The emphasis in this chapter is on modification and tweaking. Nudging a library or generator in a desired direction is completely different from rewriting it. When you find yourself spending a lot of time delving into third-party code, it's time to think about whether the library or generator actually does meet your needs. There's no lack of third-party products out there, so settling for a solution that doesn't really meet your needs shouldn't be an option. In addition, making too many modifications makes updating to the next version of the library cumbersome or impossible. Always work with the library or generator and make as few modifications or tweaks as needed to produce acceptable results.

Finding the CSS for a Library or Generator

There are a number of ways to find the CSS for a library or generator. The easiest way is for the developer to provide it to you directly. For example, when you work with jQuery UI, you must include a link to the CSS as part of using the library. This means you know where the CSS is located, and by viewing the URL, you can see how it works. As an example, check out the link for jQuery UI:

```
<link
    rel="stylesheet"
    href="http://code.jquery.com/ui/1.9.2/themes/base/jquery-ui.css" />
```

The `href` attribute points you to the CSS for the library. When you plug this URL into your browser, you see something like the code shown in Figure 12-1.

When a vendor doesn't provide the link to you directly, you can often find information about the product on another site. There's strong support from a variety of sources for tweaks on third-party libraries and generators. In many cases, all you really need to do is find the right support group, site, or forum (such as Stack Overflow, `http://stackoverflow.com/`)..

Your browser can also help you locate both the JavaScript and CSS used for a third-party product. Most browsers include a feature for viewing the page source. When working with Firefox, for instance, you right-click the page and choose View Page Source from the context menu. The source viewer will often turn references to external files into links that you can click and view.

```
/*! jQuery UI - v1.9.2 - 2012-11-23
* http://jqueryui.com
* Includes: jquery.ui.core.css, jquery.ui.accordion.css, jquery.ui.autoco
* Copyright 2012 jQuery Foundation and other contributors; Licensed MIT

/* Layout helpers
--------------------------------*/
.ui-helper-hidden { display: none; }
.ui-helper-hidden-accessible { border: 0; clip: rect(0 0 0 0); height: 1p
.ui-helper-reset { margin: 0; padding: 0; border: 0; outline: 0; line-he:
.ui-helper-clearfix:before, .ui-helper-clearfix:after { content: ""; disp
.ui-helper-clearfix:after { clear: both; }
.ui-helper-clearfix { zoom: 1; }
.ui-helper-zfix { width: 100%; height: 100%; top: 0; left: 0; position: a


/* Interaction Cues
--------------------------------*/
.ui-state-disabled { cursor: default !important; }


/* Icons
--------------------------------*/

/* states and images */
.ui-icon { display: block; text-indent: -99999px; overflow: hidden; backg


/* Misc visuals
--------------------------------*/
```

Figure 12-1:
Many librar-
ies provide
you with a
link to the
CSS used to
give them
a special
look.

Unfortunately, the browser's source viewer might not be up to the task of telling you everything about the page. In this case, a third-party tool can help you locate and access both JavaScript and CSS files. For example, when working with Firefox, you can obtain a copy of JSView (`http://jsview.soft pedia.com/`) — an add-on that will tell you which JavaScript and CSS files are attached to the current file (you can use this utility with Windows, Mac, and Linux systems). You can select the file you want to view from a drop-down list box, as shown in Figure 12-2. The figure shows the ExternalCSS. HTML example from Chapter 1; JSView correctly tells you that it has one CSS file attached, `ExternalCSS.CSS`.

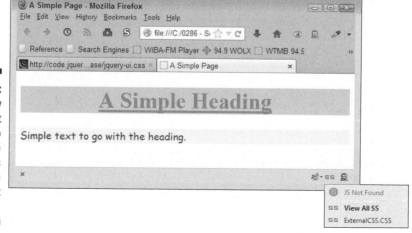

Figure 12-2:
JSView
makes it
possible to
determine
what is
attached to
the current
page.

In order to view the CSS, you select its entry from the list. The code usually opens in whatever program your browser provides for viewing source code. Using a third-party tool like this makes it possible to locate all of the external links quickly and reliably. In addition, you can open more than one of the external links at a time.

It's important to understand that real people, often individuals or small companies, create these libraries and generators. If you can't find any other source of information about the library or generator — and really do need to make modifications or tweaks for some specific purpose — try contacting the makers of the product you're using. They're obviously interested in their product and would likely want to hear your ideas (a few won't, but that's the exception, rather than the rule). The best thing to remember is to try to locate another source of information first and only then ask for help from the product's creator. However, don't be afraid to contact the product's creator — the worst that can happen is that the person will say no.

Viewing the CSS

Once you've found the CSS online, you'll want to view it. In at least some cases, the CSS will use plenty of white space and could include comments. For example, when you view the standard version of jquery-ui.css, you see a fully commented file with plenty of white space, as shown in Figure 12-3.

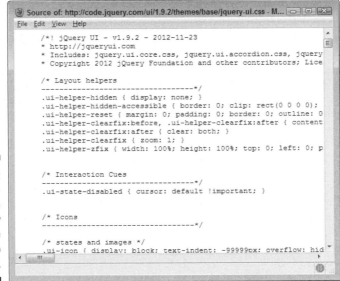

Figure 12-3:
The standard version of the jQuery UI CSS file is easy to read.

On the other hand, trying to view some JavaScript or CSS files can prove nearly impossible. For example, when viewing `jquery-1.4.2.min.js`, you see the mass of undecipherable text shown in Figure 12-4. The browser can read this text without any problem whatsoever, but any developer attempting to read it will encounter problems.

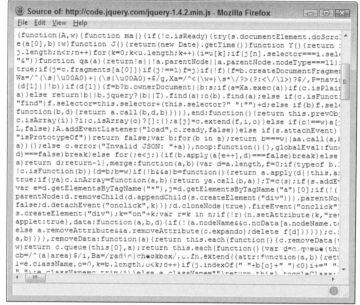

Figure 12-4: Some CSS and JavaScript files are not so easy to read.

You could handle the problem in a number of ways, but the easiest method is to use a third-party utility such as JavaScript Beautifier Online (`http://jsbeautifier.org/`). All you do is copy the code from the browser's code viewer, paste the code into the page, select the settings you want to use, and then wait a few seconds (often less) while the utility automatically adds whitespace so you can see what is happening with the code. Figure 12-5 shows the output from `jquery-1.4.2.min.js`. Even though this utility is called JavaScript Beautifier Online it works fine with all sorts of files. Just give it a try whenever you need to see packed source code.

After you make the code readable with a product such as JavaScript Beautifier Online, you can copy it out and place it on your local drive. As you work through the file you can add your own comments. The idea is to become thoroughly familiar with whatever code you're working with before you make any decisions about modifications or tweaks. In addition, you need to be able to talk with anyone who knows more about the file in an intelligible manner.

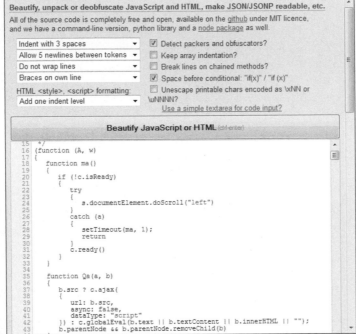

Figure 12-5:
Make the
source code
readable
using a
third-party
utility.

Deciding What to Modify or Tweak

Some libraries and generators produce perfect (or close enough) results immediately and don't require any sort of modification or tweaking, but the reality is that you don't find them often enough. In many cases, you must make some sort of major change (a modification) or at least a small change (a tweak) for the library or generator to work as expected. For most developers, the issue of what to modify (or tweak) comes down to asking two important questions:

✔ **When should I modify?** The answer to this question is based on a balance. You must decide whether the issue surrounding a particular library or generator is severe enough to cause users problems. Yes, there are fit and finish issues that you might consider, but the pressing matter is whether the problem is severe enough to cause delays in entering data or could cause the user to enter data incorrectly. The goal is to determine whether a problem will distract the user, or cause some other definable problem that could result in reduced productivity, increased security breaches, or significant down time.

✔ **How long should I modify?** Once you determine that the problem must be fixed, you also need to consider how long to spend fixing it. Developers can experience problems with letting go of a problem after investing a significant amount of time in it. The goal of using a third-party library or generator is to save time. If you're not saving time, then the library or generator simply isn't a good fit for you and you need to look elsewhere. This may seem like a simplistic way to view things, but many projects are derailed when the developer fails to realize that the library or generator isn't meeting the goals set for it by the developer.

Most developers will make certain kinds of modifications to libraries and to the output of generators because these changes are small, fast, and produce large returns in user efficiency. Here's a list of the most common changes you find described in various places (both in books and online).

✔ Graphical changes that make controls and other objects easier to use

✔ Presentation modifications that make the selections or other functionality clearer

✔ Content alterations that give the user precise selections or options

The one thing you want to avoid is making changes in how something works — making the library do something that it was never intended to do by modifying the base library code, rather than extending it or adding functionality through CSS changes. When you get to this point, you're taking over for the library or generator developer and that's a losing proposition for any developer. For one thing, you don't have access to the developer's source code. For another, you must keep the goal of working with the library or generator in mind so that you actually do save time.

Locating Modification Aids

Modification aids, tools or code that augment the base functionality of a library, come in many forms. You've already seen some of these aids in action in previous chapters. For example, Chapter 10 explores the use of ThemeRoller, which is merely a modification aid for jQuery UI in that it extends the functionality provided by jQuery UI. ThemeRoller is also a tool because it makes it possible to create something entirely new (in the form of unique themes) using a wizard-type interface. Some modifications require coding or other low-level techniques that appear in the chapters that follow this one. The following sections provide some pointers on finding and using modification aids that will meet your specific needs.

Searching for modification aids

Most of the modification aids you find are created by interested third parties who had a problem similar to the one you encountered. These third parties publish their answers to the problem so that you don't have to reinvent the wheel. Of course, you have to be willing to look for the solution. Unfortunately, this requires spending some time with your favorite search engine, locating the solutions that might fit and then reading about them one at a time.

To reduce the time spent looking for solutions; make sure you define search terms carefully. In fact, it's important to consider the order of the search terms. Developing a technique and then trying several searches with it will eventually save you time and effort. For example, when working with Google, you can use the `site:` attribute in a search line to look for entries on your favorite site. If you want to look for something on Microsoft Developer Network (MSDN), you use `search term site:msdn.microsoft.com` to limit the search (where search term is the definition of the solution you need). The advanced search page (`www.google.com/advanced_search`) also provides access to a number of filters you can use.

Using other developer solutions

Some of the solutions you find are quite refined and combine controls to create a special setup. For example, look at the Ben's Sandbox solution (`http://bseth99.github.io/projects/jquery-ui/3-jquery-ui-spinner-extensions.html`) — shown in Figure 12-6 — for enhancing a jQuery UI Spinner with a Slider to make it easier for the user to see a specific selection range. Making changes like this will reduce the number of input errors that a user makes and will also reduce the time required to make the entry. Instead of typing numbers, the user can choose a number using the slider.

Developers are also constantly creating articles that will help you create some interesting modifications or tweaks of existing libraries of generators. For example, the article entitled, "Exploring the New jQuery UI Spinner – Beyond the Basics" at `http://benknowscode.wordpress.com/2012/10/18/exploring-the-new-jquery-ui-spinner-beyond-the-basics/` describes how to define a spinner that displays letters instead of numbers, as shown in Figure 12-7.

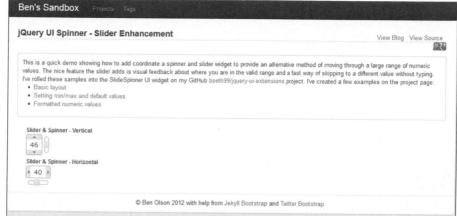

Figure 12-6: Enhancements often involve combining controls.

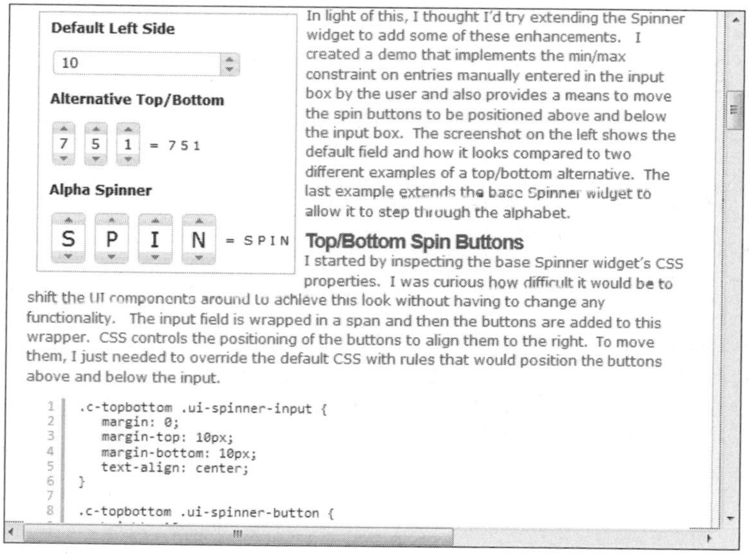

Figure 12-7: Many articles you find will contain interesting ideas that you can use.

Notice that the spinner is at the top and bottom of the control. In fact, the spinner looks nothing like the jQuery version of the spinner, yet all you're doing is modifying the CSS for the control. This particular example is so interesting that I describe it in more detail in Chapter 13 (and implement it in a different way).

It's important to realize that modification is a process. As a result, looking for articles that discuss this process is always a good idea. For example, the article entitled, "Tips for Developing jQuery UI 1.8 Widgets" (`http://www.erichynds.com/blog/tips-for-developing-jquery-ui-widgets`) helps you avoid the errors that many developers make when extending jQuery UI by creating a new widget.

Getting answers from other professionals

If you can't seem to find an answer anywhere for your question on how to perform a particular modification or tweak, there are many places where professionals go to get answers. One of the better places to ask is the Stack Overflow site (`http://stackoverflow.com/`). You generally get an answer quickly and the initial answers work quite a bit of the time (when an answer doesn't work, the forum members are usually interested enough to continue discussing your question).

Make sure you verify that the question hasn't been asked before by searching for it on the forum first. When using some of these forums, you need to define search criteria to ensure you find the answer as quickly as possible. When working on Stack Overflow, you define a set of tags at `http://stackover flow.com/tags` to locate a specific answer.

Chapter 13

Modifying the jQuery and jQuery UI CSS

*j*Query and jQuery UI are two of the most popular libraries used to enhance browser-based applications for good reason — they both provide significant functionality in small, well-documented packages. Using these two libraries alone can give you most of the functionality any developer could want. However, the wealth of available third-party tweaks, modifications, add-ons, and plugins suggests that many other developers think jQuery and jQuery UI could use something more. That's what this chapter is all about — obtaining a bit more from jQuery and jQuery UI. The simple act of modifying the CSS associated with jQuery and jQuery UI can create some amazing effects.

Of course, you don't want to simply plunge in and start making changes to any library. It's important to make measured changes that obtain the result you want with the fewest modifications to the way the library works. Otherwise you risk altering the library in a way that causes problems with future versions of the library. *Breaking changes* (those that cause the library to work incorrectly in the future) are one of the biggest problems with any change you make.

This chapter reviews a number of common modifications that people make to the jQuery and jQuery UI libraries. Of course, the most common is a specialized form of an existing control — one that uses the basic control, but augments it in some way. For example, you may decide that the control should be coupled with another control to make it easier to use (as with the spinner-and-slider combination discussed in Chapter 12). You may also want to create special application effects based on control state or output. Adding graphics is another common change. The point is that you have a number of ways to modify how jQuery and jQuery UI work so that they better fit your application's requirements.

Most of the examples in this chapter use some amount of JavaScript that's based on the jQuery (`http://api.jquery.com/`) and jQuery UI (`http://api.jqueryui.com/`) examples. Many developers simply copy and paste code they find online in order to reproduce an effect without really understanding JavaScript at a low level. This approach does work, but it's more helpful if you know how to write applications using JavaScript — at least at the novice level (to gain that knowledge, you can read my book on JavaScript entitled, *HTML5 Programming with JavaScript For Dummies*). The explanations in this chapter are complete enough that most people with at least a little coding experience should be able to follow them. However, you can use the code in your application by simply copying and pasting it as needed.

Looking at the jQuery and jQuery UI CSS

Most of the changes you make to jQuery and jQuery UI involve modifications of the CSS. You can perform this task in a number of ways. For example, you can create an internal style that modifies the behavior of the default style. When your application uses external styles, the style overrides must appear later than the jQuery and jQuery UI styles in the list of styles. The following sections discuss some essentials you must know before overriding a style.

Understanding the basic layout

The makers of jQuery and jQuery UI do a good job of documenting the internals of their library. From a CSS perspective, the material found at `http://api.jqueryui.com/theming/css-framework/` tells you about the styles used to create the output you've seen in various places in the book. Figure 13-1 gives you a good idea of how the initial page of documentation is laid out.

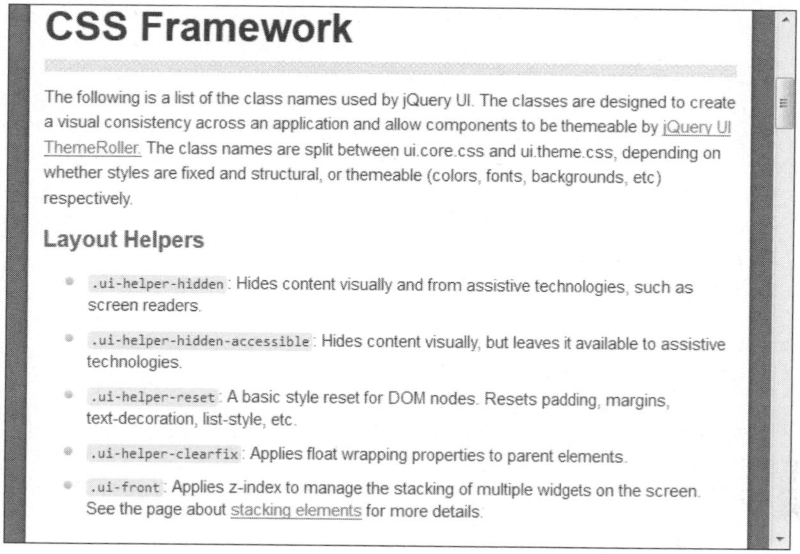

CSS Framework

The following is a list of the class names used by jQuery UI. The classes are designed to create a visual consistency across an application and allow components to be themeable by jQuery UI ThemeRoller. The class names are split between ui.core.css and ui.theme.css, depending on whether styles are fixed and structural, or themeable (colors, fonts, backgrounds, etc) respectively.

Layout Helpers

- `.ui-helper-hidden` : Hides content visually and from assistive technologies, such as screen readers.

- `.ui-helper-hidden-accessible` : Hides content visually, but leaves it available to assistive technologies.

- `.ui-helper-reset` : A basic style reset for DOM nodes. Resets padding, margins, text-decoration, list-style, etc.

- `.ui-helper-clearfix` : Applies float wrapping properties to parent elements.

- `.ui-front` : Applies z-index to manage the stacking of multiple widgets on the screen. See the page about stacking elements for more details.

Figure 13-1: Start with the CSS documentation to discover how to make modifications.

One of the first things you notice on this page is that the developers recommend you use ThemeRoller (see Chapter 10 for details) to make your changes whenever possible. However, there are many cases where ThemeRoller simply won't do the job, so you need to make the modifications in a more traditional manner. The list that follows describes each of the classes and their range of effects. I've divided the classes into two files with a number of styles within each file:

✔ **jquery.ui.core.css:** Contains all of the styles that affect structural elements in some way. These include

- **Layout helpers:** Determines the overall layout of objects onscreen; makes it possible to interact with assistive technologies; and provides a method for resetting the layout as needed.

- **Interaction cues:** Defines when an object is disabled.

- **Icons:** Specifies the icon state.

- **Overlays:** Determines the size and position of overlays.

✔ **jquery.ui.theme.css:** Defines any styles that affect thematic elements, such as color, fonts, and backgrounds. These include

- **Component containers:** Specify the appearance of content within various object containers. The containers normally include the overall object, object headers, and object data (specified as content within the styles).

- **Interaction states:** Determine the appearance of an object when specific interaction states occur. The four interaction states are: `default` (when nothing is happening with the object), `hover` (when the mouse cursor is over the object), `active` (when the user is actually performing a task with the object), and `focus` (when the user has selected the object, but isn't doing anything with it).

- **Interaction cues:** Determine the appearance of an object that's in a particular state to help the user understand the object's status. The interaction cues are: `highlight` (the object or content is selected for interaction); `error` (an error has occurred with an object); `error text` (an error has occurred with content, usually text, within an object); `disabled` (the object or content are disabled); `primary` (an object is the primary or first-level object in a hierarchy of objects); and `secondary` (an object is the secondary or second-level object in a hierarchy of objects).

- **Icons:** Define the state and positioning of the icons used with an object. The state and positioning are controlled separately. The state information determines whether the icon is part of a header or the content. In addition, it determines formatting based on the status of the icon: `default`, `hover`, `active`, `highlight`, `error`, and `error text`. Icons are positioned individually based on icon name, such as `.ui-icon-carat-1-n`.

  The icons are actually defined in block format as part of the states and images section of the `icons` portion of the file.

  You can see the widget-specific icon images at `http://code.jquery.com/ui/1.9.2/themes/base/images/ui-icons_222222_256x240.png`.

  The default icon images appear at `http://code.jquery.com/ui/1.9.2/themes/base/images/ui-icons_888888_256x240.png`.

  You can find the active icon images at `http://code.jquery.com/ui/1.9.2/themes/base/images/ui-icons_454545_256x240.png` and those used for highlighting at `http://code.jquery.com/ui/1.9.2/themes/base/images/ui-icons_2e83ff_256x240.png`.

  When an application experiences an error, you see the list of icons at `http://code.jquery.com/ui/1.9.2/themes/base/images/ui-icons_cd0a0a_256x240.png`.

- **Corner radius:** Creates rounded corners on the various objects.

- **Overlays:** Determines the formatting of content within overlays and the formatting of the overlay shadow (so that you can see there's an object behind the object in the front).

In order to better understand how things work, it's a good idea to look at the actual files. You can find the first file at a location such as `http://code.jquery.com/ui/1.9.2/themes/base/jquery.ui.core.css` where `http://code.jquery.com/ui/` is the base URL, `1.9.2` is the version of jQuery or jQuery UI in question, and `themes/base/jquery.ui.theme.css` is the specific file location. To obtain a copy of the CSS for a different version of jQuery or jQuery UI, simply change the version number part of the URL. The second file is found at a location such as `http://code.jquery.com/ui/1.9.2/themes/base/jquery.ui.theme.css`. Figure 13-2 shows what you'll see when looking at `jquery.ui.core.css`.

```
/*!
 * jQuery UI CSS Framework 1.9.2
 * http://jqueryui.com
 *
 * Copyright 2012 jQuery Foundation and other contributors
 * Released under the MIT license.
 * http://jquery.org/license
 *
 * http://docs.jquery.com/UI/Theming/API
 */

/* Layout helpers
----------------------------------*/
.ui-helper-hidden { display: none; }
.ui-helper-hidden-accessible { border: 0; clip: rect(0 0 0 0)
.ui-helper-reset { margin: 0; padding: 0; border: 0; outline:
.ui-helper-clearfix:before, .ui-helper-clearfix:after { conte
.ui-helper-clearfix:after { clear: both; }
.ui-helper-clearfix { zoom: 1; }
.ui-helper-zfix { width: 100%; height: 100%; top: 0; left: 0;


/* Interaction Cues
----------------------------------*/
.ui-state-disabled { cursor: default !important; }


/* Icons
----------------------------------*/
```

Figure 13-2: Checking the individual CSS files helps you understand how things work.

Viewing the files provides details on how the various styles are constructed, so you can make modifications safely. In addition, the files often contain notes. For example, when you look at `jquery.ui.theme.css`, you find that one of the styles is actually deprecated (no longer supported), as this note tells you:

```
/* ui-icon-seek-first is deprecated, use ui-icon-seek-start instead */
```

The style is commented out so that you can't use it. However, the note is still important because it tells you which style to use instead.

Picturing the use of jquery-ui.css

In the examples in Chapter 6, notice that none of the examples uses either `jquery.ui.core.css` or `jquery.ui.theme.css`. That's because these files are actually incorporated into `http://code.jquery.com/ui/1.9.2/themes/base/jquery-ui.css`. This single file actually contains a number of CSS files:

✔ `jquery.ui.core.css`

✔ `jquery.ui.accordion.css`

✔ `jquery.ui.autocomplete.css`

✔ `jquery.ui.button.css`

✔ `jquery.ui.datepicker.css`

✔ `jquery.ui.dialog.css`

✔ `jquery.ui.menu.css`

✔ `jquery.ui.progressbar.css`

✔ `jquery.ui.resizable.css`

✔ `jquery.ui.selectable.css`

✔ `jquery.ui.slider.css`

✔ `jquery.ui.spinner.css`

✔ `jquery.ui.tabs.css`

✔ `jquery.ui.tooltip.css`

✔ `jquery.ui.theme.css`

The use of a single file makes it easier for developers to interact with jQuery and jQuery UI. However, when working through changes you want to make to the library, it's usually easier to view the individual CSS file. Otherwise you'd have to wade through a lot of styles and wouldn't get the full picture of how these various styles interact because the structure that jQuery and jQuery UI provide is collapsed into this single file.

Defining reasonable changes

Because the jQuery and jQuery UI API is so well documented, there's a tendency to think it's possible to modify anything about these libraries. However, changing the way anyone's code works can result in unforeseen consequences. For example, a change may make sense in your mind, but actually cause the library to break and behave in an unacceptable way. In general, you need to consider the smallest amount of change that will accomplish a given purpose. For example, rather than making a coding change, try to use the programming-like functionality provided by CSS to obtain the change you want.

In some cases, you want to substitute your own art to obtain an effect. For example, you may choose to use custom icons for your application. In this case, you must create an icon file that precisely matches the one used for jQuery and jQuery UI. The number of icons, the icon size, and the icon arrangement must match precisely in order to make the change work. With this in mind, look at the icons at `http://code.jquery.com/ui/1.9.2/themes/base/images/ui-icons_222222_256x240.png`. As shown in

Figure 13-3, the icons are arranged in a specific manner — they don't follow one after the other and you can see they are grouped according to type. Yes, you can use your own art, but only as long as the art matches the mechanical specifications of the original art. (The icons are a little hard to see on the actual page, so viewing them at the bottom of the ThemeRoller page at `http://jqueryui.com/themeroller/` is helpful.)

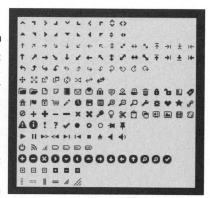

Figure 13-3: When substituting your own icons, make sure the icon size and arrangement matches.

At some point, you'll want a change that you can't provide through new art or an updated CSS. In this case, you need to create a plugin. For example, you may want to modify a behavior that you simply can't modify without adding code. Reasonable changes include adding new behaviors or allowing a widget to accept a new type of input from the user. What you want to avoid is completely rewriting the widgets, behaviors, or other jQuery and jQuery UI features so that the result becomes something completely different from what the authors originally intended. This approach will almost certainly result in failure (if not now, then with a future update to either jQuery or jQuery UI).

Avoiding potential error conditions

Ensure that you're familiar with the area of jQuery or jQuery UI that you want to modify before you make any sort of changes to it. This means acquainting yourself with the way in which the library performs tasks and uses resources. When you design an alternative resource, such as a list of icons, the resource must precisely match the mechanical attributes (size, order, and content) of the original resource. In addition, you need to test carefully to ensure the new resource behaves as you expect it to. Some changes can cause undesirable side effects. For example, making an icon one pixel too wide or too high will cause problems in using that icon with the library.

Sometimes you do need to resort to coding in order to meet your objective. However, it would be an error to modify the .JS or .CSS files directly. Always modify an external file to obtain the results you want. Fortunately, the authors of jQuery and jQuery UI provide a well-documented method for extending the functionality these libraries provide through the use of plugins. The "Working with Plug-ins" section, later in this chapter, discusses various techniques you can use to work with existing plugins. If you really do need to write new code, the "Finishing with the Coded Bits" section, at the end of this chapter, provides advice on how to create your own plugin.

Of course, the sage advice for working with someone else's code is to test heavily after you make a change. Test as many different situations as you can and look for odd quirks that tend to pop up as the result of changes you make. The library should work precisely as it did before, but with the added functionality you've provided in place.

Defining a Specialized Control

All the jQuery UI widgets lend themselves to customization. Most of the changes you make deal with using built-in features correctly. You can also work with the CSS that jQuery UI employs to format the widgets to produce special effects. Of course, if nothing else, you can always use JavaScript to modify the actual widget behavior as needed. The point is that you can change widgets (such as `Spinner`) to meet specific needs without having to reinvent the wheel. The modifications are usually short and easy to do, which means you don't have to start from scratch with an idea you have to code by hand.

Spinners are popular because you can use them to control user input in a number of ways. The idea is to provide control for data that's normally variable, so you can't use something like a drop-down list box. One of the most interesting uses of spinners is shown on the Ben Knows Code site at `http://benknowscode.wordpress.com/2012/10/18/exploring-the-new-jquery-ui-spinner-beyond-the-basics`. In this case, the author shows how to perform tasks such as moving the location of the arrows and creating an alphabetical spinner. The example in this section plays off the example on this site, but it's a bit more straightforward and easier to understand. Once you understand the example in this section, you can go to the Ben Knows Code site and understand that example right away.

Spinners normally deal with numeric input. However, you might have a need for alphabetic input instead. To create an alphabetic input, you need to give the appearance of letters without actually using letters, because the `Spinner` widget works only with numbers. The following example takes a standard jQuery UI `Spinner` widget and transforms it to use letters instead of numbers.

(You can find complete code for this example in the \Chapter 13\
Spinner folder of the downloadable code as Spinner.HTML.)

```
$(function()
  {
    var CurrentValue = 65;

    var ThisSpinner = $("#Spinner").spinner(
      {
        // Set the minimum to the code for A
        // and the maximum to the code for Z.
        min: 65,
        max: 90,

        // When the user starts to spin the spinner,
        // convert the value to a number and hide the
        // text from view.
        start: function(ui, event)
        {
          ThisSpinner.spinner("value", CurrentValue);
          $("#Spinner").css("color", "transparent");
        },

        // When the user stops spinning the spinner,
        // save the numeric value, convert it to a
        // letter and display the text onscreen.
        stop: function(ui, event)
        {
          CurrentValue =
            ThisSpinner.spinner("value");
          ThisSpinner.spinner("value",
            String.fromCharCode(CurrentValue));
          $("#Spinner").css("color", "green");
        }
      });
  });
```

When you see a section of code in a jQuery or jQuery UI application that
begins $(function(){}), it means that the application should wait until the
page is fully loaded and ready for use before doing any processing. All of the
code in this chapter (and the vast majority of examples you see online for that
matter) begins by telling jQuery or jQuery UI to wait until the page is ready for
use. The code between the curly brackets ({}) defines what you want jQuery
or jQuery UI to do after the page is ready.

The code begins by creating a variable, CurrentValue, that tracks the
numeric value of the spinner. The value, 65, is the numeric equivalent of the
letter *A*. So the spinner starts with a value of A, but it stores this value as the
number 65.

Creating the spinner, `ThisSpinner`, comes next. You must set minimum and maximum values that reflect the numeric values of *A* and *Z*. This same technique can work for any series of letters. You could just as easily use lowercase letters, if desired. For that matter, any series will work, including special characters. It's even possible to use this approach for enumerated values.

The simplest approach provides handlers for the `start` and `stop` events. When the user clicks one of the two arrows, it starts a spin event. The change occurs, and then the spin stops. For the spinner to work correctly, the `value` attribute must contain a numeric value. The code sets value to `CurrentValue`, which is the code that equates to the currently selected letter. However, at this point, you can see the numeric value as text in the spinner, which is distracting. To keep this from happening, the event handler also sets the text color to transparent, so the user can't actually see the text onscreen.

Make sure you think about how you set the colors for hidden items. There's a tendency with some developers to set the hidden item's color to the background color, but the background color can change. Even though many references don't actually state it, one of the recognized colors is transparent, which means no color at all. Always use transparent objects when you want to hide something.

The `stop` event handler stores the new spinner value in `CurrentValue`. It then converts the numeric value from a number, such as 65, to a letter, such as *A* (as shown in Figure 13-4). The code then changes the text color to green so the user can see the letter onscreen.

Figure 13-4:
The example application asks the user to enter the first letter of his or her last name.

Creating a Custom Spinner

First letter of your last name: A

This example also changes a few of the widget styles. These styles are listed as part of the jQuery UI CSS file at `http://code.jquery.com/ui/1.9.2/themes/base/jquery-ui.css`. In this case, you don't want the user to be able to type more than one character, so the width of the widget is changed to accept just one letter. In addition, the text color is changed to green, as shown here:

```
.ui-spinner
{
   width: 45px;
}


.ui-spinner-input
{
   color: green;
}
```

Using a combination of events and CSS lets you create all sorts of custom effects with any of the jQuery UI widgets. All you need to do is experiment a little to create some really interesting output.

Creating Specialized Control Effects

A specialized effect is any sort of activity that a control (widget) isn't designed to handle at the outset. For example, it's possible to use XML files (or databases) to hold just about anything related to a browser-based application. By adding XML functionality to an existing control, such as a tabbed interface, you can modify how that control works. The effect is that you can make changes to the user interface by modifying the XML, rather than working directly with the page code. There are many ways in which to generate XML, so this technique adds a significant amount of flexibility to the user interface.

In this example, you see how to create a jQuery UI tabbed interface by using data stored in an XML file. In addition, this example relies on jQuery to get the XML file rather than relying on handwritten code to perform the task. What you're doing is combining features found in jQuery UI with those found in jQuery to create a composite control. The code you create using jQuery is shorter than handwritten code; somewhat easier to understand; and, most important of all, more likely to work with browsers that you didn't originally test as part of the initial application design.

Developing the page code

The following code shows the jQuery method of creating a tabbed interface. (You can find complete code for this example in the \Chapter 13\XMLTab folder of the downloadable code as XMLTab.HTML.)

```
$(function()
  {
    // Create variables to hold temporary data.
    var TabHeads = "";
    var TabContent = "";

    // Obtain the XML data file and process it.
    $.get("XMLTabData.xml", function(data)
      {
        // Locate each Heading entry and use it to
        // create a tab heading.
        $(data).find("Heading").each(function()
          {
            TabHeads +=
              "<li><a href='" +
              $(this).attr("href") +
              "'>" + $(this).attr("caption") +
              "</a></li>";
          });

        // Append the data to the heading area.
        $("#Headings").append(TabHeads);

        // Locate each Content entry and use it to
        // create the tab content.
        $(data).find("Content").each(function()
          {
            TabContent +=
              "<div id='" + $(this).attr("id") +
              "'>" + $(this).text() + "</div>";
          });

        // Append the data to the tab content area.
        $("#Tabs").append(TabContent);

        // Complete the process by displaying the
        // tabs.
        $("#Tabs").tabs();
      });
  });
```

The code begins by creating two variables: TabHeads and TabContent, to contain the data used to fill in the tabbed interface. This information is eventually added to two HTML tags, as shown here:

```
<div id="Tabs">
   <ul id="Headings" />
</div>
```

The `get()` method obtains the XML file, `XMLTabData.XML`, and places the content in `data`. What `data` contains is a fully formed XML file that's passed to an anonymous function (one that has no name) that you define as: `function(data){}`. The function is executed when the data retrieval is complete, so it acts as a callback for an asynchronous data read.

The XML file is described in the "Creating the XML file" section later in this chapter. All you need to know for the moment is that the XML file contains `<Heading>` elements that contain the data used to create the tab entries, as well as `<Content>` elements that contain the data placed within each tab (as shown in Figure 13-5). In this case, Tab 1 would be a heading and `"This is some content for Tab 1."` would be content for that tab.

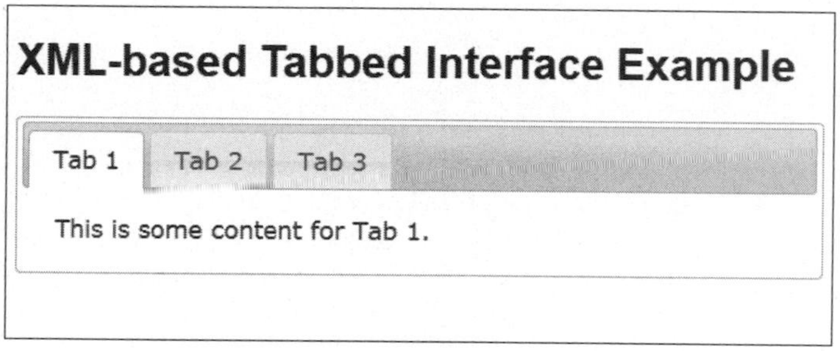

Figure 13-5:
Dynamic tab configuration is just as easy as creating dynamic menus.

XML-based Tabbed Interface Example

| Tab 1 | Tab 2 | Tab 3 |

This is some content for Tab 1.

All of the heading information appears within the `<Heading>` elements. So, the code asks jQuery to `find()` each of the `<Heading>` elements and process them one at a time using the `each()` method. The `each()` method creates a loop that automatically provides access to individual `<Heading>` elements through the `this` variable. Tab headings are stored in an unordered list (`<ul>`), `Headings`, that's already part of the HTML for the example page.

The content for each tab appears in `<div>` elements that are appended after the `<ul>` element, `Headings`. The content could be anything — including controls as used for the previous tabbed-interface example (demonstrated in the section on using the Tabs widget in Chapter 6). The most important issue to consider is how to store information in the XML file. Be sure you escape any tags so that they're not misinterpreted as XML elements.

As with the headings, the code uses `find()` to locate each of the `<Content>` elements in the XML file and convert them to the HTML required to create the tab content. The `each()` method creates the loop used to process each element one at a time.

Creating the XML file

In order to make this example work, you need an XML file named
`XMLTabData.XML`. This file has a specific format that you must follow to
make the example work properly. Here's the XML file used for this example:

```
<?xml version="1.0" encoding="UTF-8"?>
<Tabs>
    <TabData>
        <Heading id="Tab1"
                 href="#Tabs1"
                 caption="Tab 1" />
        <Heading id="Tab2"
                 href="#Tabs2"
                 caption="Tab 2" />
        <Heading id="Tab3"
                 href="#Tabs3"
                 caption="Tab 3" />
    </TabData>
    <TabContent>
        <Content id="Tabs1">
            This is some content for Tab 1.
        </Content>
        <Content id="Tabs2">
            This is some content for Tab 2.
        </Content>
        <Content id="Tabs3">
            This is some content for Tab 3.
        </Content>
    </TabContent>
</Tabs>
```

Notice that the file has a root element named `<Tabs>` that contains child elements: `<TabData>` and `<TabContent>`. These child elements contain the
`<Heading>` and `<Content>` data used to fill in the tabbed interface. There's
one `<Heading>` element for each `<Content>` element. The actual content
can be anything you want it to be, as long as it follows the structure shown in
the example.

Working with Added Graphics

On a website, graphics can take many forms. For example, you can have a
free-standing piece of static art used for a logo or some other purpose. The
chapter has already discussed using alternative art with jQuery and jQuery
UI, such as replacement icons for the various controls. This section discusses
graphics used in an interactive way, which many sites do. In this case, the

example relies on a *master/detail view* where a tab provides the mechanism to group like graphics and entries in the content section provide access to individual graphics within the category.

There are many situations where you need to provide a master/detail view. Of course, the most common use for such a view is in database applications where you present data such as the orders associated with a particular client. The view is also used in many other places; the Windows Explorer and Mac Finder applications, for example, use a master/detail view in presenting the folder hierarchy in one pane and the content of the selected folder in the other. The example application shows categorized data and the details of that data. Like every other master/detail view you've ever seen, the categories and their associated content appear in the left pane and the selected item appears in the right, as shown in Figure 13-6.

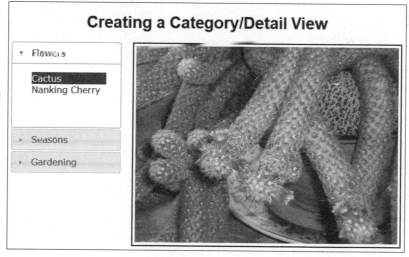

Figure 13-6: A category/ detail view provides a useful method of presenting information to the user.

What you're actually seeing here is a combination of the jQuery UI `Accordion` widget and the `Selectable` interaction — both of which are discussed in Chapter 6. The following sections break the application into pieces to make it easier to understand.

Creating the HTML

As with any other jQuery UI example, this one relies on a framework of HTML tags to support the widgets. The following code shows how to create the HTML for the application shown in Figure 13-6. (You can find complete code for this example in the `\Chapter 13\CategoryDetail` folder of the down-loadable code as `CategoryDetail.HTML`.)

```
<div id="Categories">
   <h2>Flowers</h2>
   <div>
      <ol id="FlowerSelect" class="Selections">
         <li id="Cactus">Cactus</li>
         <li id="Nanking">Nanking Cherry</li>
      </ol>
   </div>
   <h2>Seasons</h2>
   <div>
      <ol id="SeasonSelect" class="Selections">
         <li id="Nanking">Nanking Cherry</li>
         <li id="Mountain">Mountain View</li>
         <li id="Harvest">Squash Harvest</li>
         <li id="Snow">First Snow</li>
      </ol>
   </div>
   <h2>Gardening</h2>
   <div>
      <ol id="SeasonSelect" class="Selections">
         <li id="Nanking">Nanking Cherry</li>
         <li id="Harvest">Squash Harvest</li>
      </ol>
   </div>
   <div id="DrawingContainer">
      <img id="Drawing" />
   </div>
</div>
```

The left pane consists of a series of three `<h2>` and `<div>` pairs, with the `<h2>` tag defining the tab headings and the `<div>` defining the tab content. Each tab content area contains a list of potential choices as an unordered list.

The right pane consists of a `<div>` and `<img>` combination. The `<div>` has an `id` of `DrawingContainer`, whereas the `<img>` has an `id` of `Drawing`. These two tags act together to display the image that the user has selected.

Designing the CSS styles

There are a number of considerations for this application from a style per-spective. However, the most pressing need is to provide a means of display-ing the graphics in a way that the user would expect, despite the manner in which the tags are defined. Normally, these components would appear one over the other. You need to create some CSS in order to obtain the required appearance. Here's the CSS for this example:

```
<style>
   h1
   {
      text-align: center;
   }

   #Categories
   {
      width: 220px;
   }

   .Selections .ui-selected
   {
      background: blue;
      color: white;
   }

   .Selections
   {
      margin: 0;
      padding: 0;
      width: 150px;
      list-style-type: none;
   }

   #DrawingContainer
   {
      width: 533px;
      height: 400px;
      border: solid;
      position: absolute;
      left: 250px;
      top: 80px;
   }

   #Drawing
   {
      width: 523px;
      height: 390px;
      margin: 5px;
   }
</style>
```

Notice that the width of Categories is such that the DrawingContainer can appear to the right of it. The Selections are set up to fit fully in Categories. When setting the width of Selections, you must account for the indent that jQuery UI automatically provides as part of the Accordion widget. The most important part of the DrawingContainer setup is the left setting, which must be configured to accommodate the Accordion widget to the left of it. The size of Drawing is such that the application can maintain the aspect ratio of the images it will display. With some additional work, you could allow for images of multiple sizes to fit easily within the space — the example images are all the same size.

Developing the required code

The example requires surprisingly little code to perform its work. That's because jQuery UI does most of the heavy lifting for you. The act of displaying the image is surprisingly easy because of the way the <img> tag works. Here's all the code you need to make this example work:

```
$(function()
  {
    // Create an Accordion as a means to
    // organize the data.
    $("#Categories").accordion();

    // Choose a particular image based on the
    // user's selection. Display it using the
    // src attribute of the <img> tag.
    $(".Selections").selectable(
      {
        selected: function(event, ui)
        {
          switch(ui.selected.id)
          {
            case "Cactus":
              $("#Drawing").attr(
                "src", "CactusBlossom.jpg");
              break;
            case "Nanking":
              $("#Drawing").attr(
                "src", "NankingCherry.jpg");
              break;
            case "Mountain":
              $("#Drawing").attr(
                "src", "MountainView.jpg");
              break;
            case "Harvest":
              $("#Drawing").attr(
                "src", "SquashHarvest.jpg");
              break;
            case "Snow":
              $("#Drawing").attr(
                "src", "FirstSnow.jpg");
              break;
          }
        }
      });
  });
```

A production application might perform some additional work with the input handling, but testing will show you that the application is fully functional now, and there's little the user can do to cause the application to crash. The trick is in the `ui.selected.id`. Each of the selections has a unique `id` value that the `switch` statement can capture. All that you need to do then is modify the `src` attribute of the `<img>` tag to match the desired drawing.

Working with Plug-ins

Plug-ins extend libraries to perform tasks that the original author didn't consider or that require some special level of expertise to implement. You can find a vast array of plug-ins for jQuery and jQuery UI. It really does pay to search for a plug-in should you need to do something that jQuery or jQuery UI don't do natively.

In this case, the example extends one of the widgets. Users need to enter time values as well as date values. The jQuery UI library comes with a `Datepicker` widget (see `http://jqueryui.com/datepicker`), which is fine but not quite enough for modern applications where users have to modify the time independently of the date. Fortunately, there's a solution in the form of a third-party plugin on the Trent Richardson site at `http://trentrichardson.com/examples/timepicker`. To use this plugin, you add the following reference to your code. (You can find complete code for this example in the `\Chapter 13\Timepicker` folder of the downloadable code as `Timepicker.HTML`.)

```
<script
   src="http://trentrichardson.com/examples/timepicker/jquery-ui-timepicker-
            addon.js">
</script>
```

All you need to do is add a simple `<input>` tag to your code and provide an `id` value for it. This widget has a number of forms. For example, you can request both a date and time if desired. The simplest form is to request the time by using the following code:

```
$(function()
   {
      $("#TimeSet").timepicker();
   })
```

As with most widgets, you can configure the Timepicker by using various options — and they're considerable. There aren't any events to handle except those provided natively by jQuery UI. The default settings present a 24-hour clock, but you can override the presentation and use a 12 hour clock, if desired. Figure 13-7 shows typical output from this example.

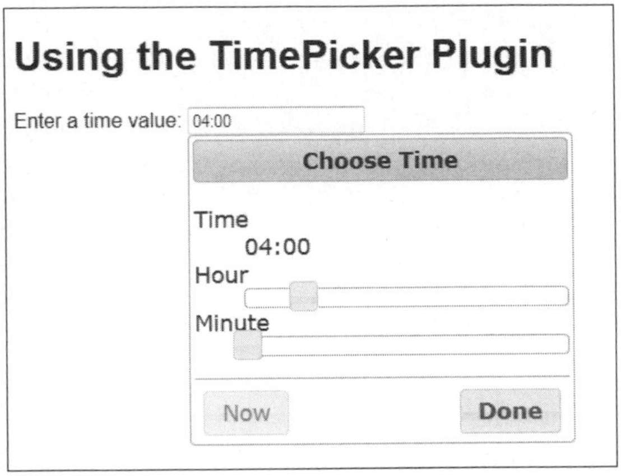

Using the TimePicker Plugin

Enter a time value: 04:00

Choose Time

Time
04:00

Hour

Minute

Now Done

Figure 13-7:
Users
now have
an easy
method for
adding time
values to
forms.

Viewing the plug-ins on Unheap

There are many locations online with one, two, or even twenty jQuery or jQuery UI plug-ins. However, few sites have the number of plug-ins supported by Unheap (`www.unheap.com/`). At the time of this writing, you can find 699 different plug-ins listed on this site, which are listed over 47 pages. You can find all sorts of interesting plug-ins, such as TextFit (`http://strml.github.io/examples/jquery.textFit.html`), a plug-in that helps you fit text into a container without doing a lot of measurement work yourself. The ScrollTo plug-in (`http://individual11.github.io/Scroll-To/`) creates a smooth scrolling setup so users don't see the usual jittery interface every time the page scrolls for some reason. There are whole categories of plug-ins devoted to just one widget, such as the `Accordion` (`www.unheap.com/section/navigation/accordion/`). If you want to include social media on your site, you can find a number of plug-ins to do that, too (`www.unheap.com/section/other/social-rss/`). The point is that if you want a single site to explore for plug-ins, this would be a good choice.

Hovering the mouse cursor over an entry tells you more about it and displays two buttons:

✔ **Demo:** Click this button to access the demo that each of the plug-ins provide so you can try it before downloading it. Many of the plug-in demo pages include coding examples so you can see how the author implemented a particular behavior. Most demos rely on JavaScript, so you must enable JavaScript support to see the demo work.

✔ **Launch:** After you decide to use a particular plug-in, click Launch to gain access to it. The browser will go to a page where you can download the plug-in and the latest documentation for it.

Trying to find what you need could be daunting on such a large site. Fortunately, the content is organized into categories, such as Interface, and subcategories, such as Layout. All you need to do is click the grouping level that makes the most sense for the kind of plug-in you need.

Finishing with the Coded Bits

There's a small chance that you'll encounter a situation where you can't modify an existing jQuery or jQuery UI feature by using either CSS or JavaScript — and can't locate a useful plug-in either. In these cases, you have to create a plug-in of your own. Creating a plug-in means writing JavaScript code that extends or overrides existing jQuery or jQuery UI functionality. You can't create one in any other way. For example, there's no automated tool you can use to define what you'd like the plug-in to do and have the tool write some or all of the code for you. Creating plug-ins is strictly a manual process.

Fortunately, you can get quite a bit of help directly from the jQuery site. There's an actual page devoted to creating plug-ins at `http://learn.jquery.com/plugins/`. However, even in this case, the first topic of discussion is techniques for finding and using existing plug-ins. The wealth of existing plug-ins really is that bountiful.

If you want to get right into creating a plug-in, you can read the "How to Create a Basic Plugin" topic at `http://learn.jquery.com/plugins/basic-plugin-creation/` as a starting point. Essentially, a plugin is nothing more than a special kind of function. Once the function is attached to a page, you can access the features it provides just as you would any normal jQuery or jQuery UI feature. The tutorial discusses all sorts of techniques you can use to create a basic plug-in. Once you complete this tutorial and have had some practice creating a basic plug-in of your own, you can move on to the advanced tutorial at `http://learn.jquery.com/plugins/advanced-plugin-concepts/`. A final tutorial at `http://learn.jquery.com/plugins/stateful-plugins-with-widget-factory/` discusses techniques for writing plug-ins that track state information.

 Experienced developers will emphasize the importance of not reinventing the wheel. When it comes to writing plug-ins, make sure you check out the code of other developers, especially for plug-ins that perform the same sorts of tasks that your plug-in will perform. Because all plug-ins are written in JavaScript, you can generally see the entire listing by accessing the .JS file used to hold the plug-in. Tracing through the plug-ins you use with a debugger will also help you understand them better and make creating your own plug-in significantly easier.

Chapter 14

Modifying the Dynamic Drive CSS

In This Chapter

▶ Defining the script categories

▶ Finding the CSS you want to change

▶ Making simple changes to Dynamic Drive

▶ Using menus to your advantage

*Y*ou first encountered Dynamic Drive (www.dynamicdrive.com/) in Chapter 11. Dynamic Drive is actually a set of tools and scripts that make it possible for you to add all sorts of special functionality to your application. Chapter 11 provides the highlights of the tools that appear on this site. This chapter focuses on the scripting examples and how you can modify them to meet your specific needs. It's important to realize that these scripting examples are designed along the same lines as extensions for APIs such as jQuery (http://jquery.com/) and jQuery UI (http://jqueryui.com/). Dynamic Drive doesn't provide a pure API environment for you to use.

This chapter doesn't discuss all of the script categories in detail. For example, Dynamic Drive provides access to a number of game scripts. These scripts are interesting and fun, but a developer is unlikely to use such a script in an application, so this chapter doesn't discuss that category in detail. Instead, you'll find some general techniques you can use for any of the Dynamic Drive scripts, which make it easier to adapt any of the scripts to a particular need.

Some script categories do require special attention. For example, Dynamic Drive provides more than a few menu scripts you can modify to meet particular needs. This chapter provides details about making modifications to these special script categories so that you have a better idea of how you can use them in an application.

In most cases, Dynamic Drive labels the source of their scripts. For example, if a script was submitted by a user, then the write-up about it tells you that it was user-submitted. When you see a script that doesn't include source information, you can normally assume that it was provided directly by Dynamic

Drive; you can verify that this is so by reviewing the source code. Always ensure that the scripts you use in an application come from a reliable source, especially when working with a script submitted by a user. Unfortunately, this often means going through user-submitted scripts line-by-line looking for potential sources of problems.

Understanding the Script Categories

The Dynamic Drive scripts appear in several categories. Each category contains a number of scripts that meet specific needs. For example, you may need a pop-up calendar, rather than one that sits statically on the page. Dynamic Drive provides the Calendars category, whose scripts address both needs.

Each of the script entries provides you with the script name, the browser name and version it was tested under, whether the script was submitted by a user, and a short description of what the script does. The browser information uses abbreviations, such as FF1+ IE5+ Opr7+, to indicate (respectively) that the script will work on Firefox 1 and above, Internet Explorer 5 and above, and Opera 7 and above. Some scripts will also have an updated icon next to them to indicate that the script has changed or a new icon to indicate that the script has been added recently. The following list describes the kind of scripts that you can expect to find in each of the categories.

- **Calendars:** All of these scripts are user submitted. They include a number of basic, dynamic, and pop-up calendars. At least one entry is designed to make it easier for the user to input a date by typing it, rather than selecting it with a mouse.

- **Date & Time:** Most of these scripts were created by Dynamic Drive. They include a number of digital and analog clock examples. A few of the digital examples also include date as part of the output, so that you can see days, hours, minutes, and seconds since a particular event occurred (as an example). At least one of the examples presents the date in text format.

- **Document Effects:** Many of these scripts were created by Dynamic Drive. Each script provides a method for interaction with document content in a special way. For example, you can find numerous ways to present documents using a tabbed or list-selectable interface. However, some of the scripts actually present a special effect, such as adding snow or autumn leaves to a page. A few scripts are quite practical, such as the magnifying-glass script that makes it easy to zoom in on page content.

A few of the scripts in this category are marked with the wizard icon. What this means is that you make selections, submit the changes, and the page generates a script to perform the required task. In short, the page offers a kind of scripted tool that you can customize.

✔ **Dynamic Content:** Most of these scripts were created by Dynamic Drive. The purpose of these scripts is to present page content in unique ways. For example, you can display longer page content as a slideshow so that the user can move from one topic to the next with ease. There are also scripts to display messages and ads of various sorts. You can even see an example of how to create a notepad application for storing textual information input by the user for later use. All of these techniques rely on some combination of Inline Frames (IFrames) and Asynchronous JavaScript and XML (AJAX) to perform their work.

Some of the examples include images that could be copyrighted. Dynamic Drive normally provides you with some level of assurance that an image is acceptable to use, but it's always better to be safe than sorry. Use your own images for page content whenever possible, or obtain an image that you're certain is acceptable to use.

✔ **Form Effects:** Most of these scripts were created by Dynamic Drive. All of the scripts deal with forms in some way. You can find controls that provide hints, display the progress of a submission, and perform various kinds of validation. There are even examples of predefined content controls, such as one that asks the user to accept the terms of using a particular feature. A few of the scripts are form-specific versions of scripts that appear in other categories, such as a pop-up calendar used to input dates into forms.

✔ **Games:** All of these scripts are user-submitted. The games are incredibly simple and do demonstrate some gaming theory (such as the use of statistics in deciding game actions), but really aren't much fun. You can choose from old favorites like tic-tac-toe or newer-style games like Cross Browser Snake.

✔ **Image Effects:** Many of these scripts were created by Dynamic Drive. You can find scripts to perform a variety of tasks, such as creating on-page effects such as flying planes. A few of the scripts perform special effects, such as displaying a reflected image of an original image. The most practical scripts perform tasks such as magnifying images so that viewers can see them with greater ease. The following subcategories provide access to additional scripts that perform special effects on images for the most part: Image Slideshows, Image Galleries and Viewers, and Mouseover Images.

✔ **Links & Tooltips:** Most of these scripts were created by Dynamic Drive. In most cases, each of these scripts enhances the presentation of information through a tooltip of some sort. For example, you can hover the mouse cursor over a link and see both a picture and a description of where that link leads. Some scripts provide special effects, such as to change the color of a link dynamically when you hover the mouse cursor over it. A few of the scripts deal with other controls, such as buttons, making them easier to use or to present the user with additional information when the mouse cursor hovers over the control.

✔ **Menus & Navigation:** Most of these scripts were created by Dynamic Drive. An essential part of most applications today is the capability to select features or to move to new locations. Menus and navigation features make it possible to turn a cumbersome page into one that's easily used. For example, you can find scripts to present menu selections in an accordion format. The CSS Based subcategory provides you with access to menus and navigational aids that rely on CSS to perform all or most tasks. The Multi-level Menus subcategory provides access to menus that allow you to make multiple levels of selections (menus and submenus).

✔ **Mouse & Cursor:** Most of these scripts were submitted by users. Each script changes the appearance of the mouse pointer or cursor in some way. Some of the more interesting scripts add colorful mouse trails to make it easier for someone using a mobile device to see the mouse cursor in bright light. Specialized cursors provide a cue to the user that the application mode has changed in some way.

✔ **Scrollers:** Most of these scripts were created by Dynamic Drive. A *scroller* is a box or other control used to display some bit of text or a graphic out of a larger sampling of text or graphics. For example, you might see the latest headlines with just one headline presented at a time in the scroller box. Every few seconds a new headline will scroll into view. Scrollers are useful for ads, headlines, or other sorts of changeable text where you want to present the user with a random sampling of information.

✔ **Text Animations:** Many of these scripts were created by Dynamic Drive. Each script seeks to provide a new manner in which you can display text onscreen. The goal of many of these animations is to emphasize the text in a specific manner so the user doesn't miss it. There's even a special effect that's based on the presentation of textual information in the movie *The Matrix* (see http://thematrix101.com/ for details).

✔ **User/System Preference:** Most of these scripts were created by Dynamic Drive. In all cases, the script changes how the browser and application work or the manner in which they present information onscreen. For example, you can find style-sheet switchers that let a user choose from multiple style-sheet options. There are also scripts that disable certain browser features (such as the use of right-click), or that detect host system functionality, such as the characteristics of the display. The whole idea is to make it possible to control the application environment, either automatically or through user selections.

✔ **Window and Frames:** Most of these scripts were created by Dynamic Drive. Both windows and frames act as containers for content. The manner in which you create and display a window or frame affects the user's perception of the content that appears within that window or frame. These scripts perform tasks such as displaying modeless windows or using animated effects to present information onscreen.

✔ **XML and RSS:** All of these scripts were created by Dynamic Drive. The basic purpose behind these scripts is to make it easier to display XML or Really Simple Syndication (RSS) information onscreen — generally within a small text box. The user then has the option of clicking a link (in most cases) to see additional information about the topic at hand.

✔ **Other:** Most of these scripts were created by Dynamic Drive. These scripts generally perform some useful task that doesn't fit within the other categories described in this list. For example, there's a special script for playing sound effects; you'll also find scripts that create interesting scrollbars. If you didn't see a script you need in one of the other categories, this is the place to look.

Locating the CSS for a Particular Feature

Many of the scripts provided on the Dynamic Drive site work with jQuery and jQuery UI. They're extensions of a sort that help you use these two APIs with greater efficiency. As a result, the tips and techniques described in Chapter 13 also apply to many of the Dynamic Drive scripts. The location of the jQuery and jQuery UI CSS doesn't change.

Some of the scripts provide custom CSS files that you must download and place on your system in order to use the script, as shown in Figure 14-1. These links can be hard to see at times. In this case, you're looking for the `anylinkcssmenu.css` link in Step 1.

Dynamic Drive tends not to provide a hosted link that you can use to access either the CSS or associated script. You can choose to modify the custom CSS directly, or provide changes to the CSS with internal or inline CSS modifications as described in the "Adding Modifications" section, later in this chapter. The important thing to remember is that you need the downloaded file to make the script work properly.

Make sure you look carefully at all of the materials for a particular Dynamic Drive script. In many cases, you see a `Customization` section like the one shown in Figure 14-2. This section provides insights on how you can customize the script to meet specific needs. In at least a few cases, you even see multiple examples of the effects that you can produce with the script by making a particular change. (You can see a better example of the customizations for the AnyLink CSS Menu v2.3 at `www.dynamicdrive.com/dynamicindex1/anylinkcss.htm`.)

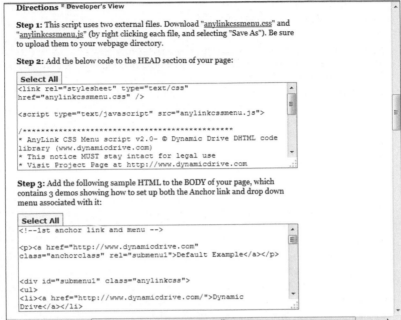

Directions · Developer's View

Step 1: This script uses two external files. Download "anylinkcssmenu.css" and "anylinkcssmenu.js" (by right clicking each file, and selecting "Save As"). Be sure to upload them to your webpage directory.

Step 2: Add the below code to the HEAD section of your page:

```
Select All
<link rel="stylesheet" type="text/css"
href="anylinkcssmenu.css" />

<script type="text/javascript" src="anylinkcssmenu.js">

/************************************************
* AnyLink CSS Menu script v2.0- © Dynamic Drive DHTML code
library (www.dynamicdrive.com)
* This notice MUST stay intact for legal use
* Visit Project Page at http://www.dynamicdrive.com
```

Step 3: Add the following sample HTML to the BODY of your page, which contains 3 demos showing how to set up both the Anchor link and drop down menu associated with it:

```
Select All
<!--1st anchor link and menu -->

<p><a href="http://www.dynamicdrive.com"
class="anchorclass" rel="submenu1">Default Example</a></p>

<div id="submenu1" class="anylinkcss">
<ul>
<li><a href="http://www.dynamicdrive.com/">Dynamic
Drive</a></li>
```

Figure 14-1: Download any CSS files required to use the script.

Customization

This script is very easy to customize and is flexible. The code of Step 3 shows the basic code for an Anchor link and its associated menu:

```
<p><a href="http://www.dynamicdrive.com" class="anchorclass"
rel="submenu1">Anchor Link</a></p>

<div id="submenu1" class="anylinkcss">
<ul>
<li><a href="http://www.dynamicdrive.com/">Dynamic
Drive</a></li>
<li><a href="http://www.cssdrive.com">CSS Drive</a></li>
<li><a href="http://www.javascriptkit.com">JavaScript
Kit</a></li>
<li><a href="http://www.codingforums.com">Coding
Forums</a></li>
<li><a href="http://www.javascriptkit.com/jsref/">JavaScript
Reference</a></li>
</ul>
</div>
```

The Anchor link in this case is "Anchor Link, and the drop down menu, the entire DIV that follows it. You can place the DIV **anywhere** on your page you see fit, and not necessarily directly below the anchor link.

Figure 14-2: Make sure you read any customization materials provided with the script.

Adding Modifications

Most of the Dynamic Drive examples include a mix of CSS and JavaScript. In general, you change the CSS to obtain just the right appearance and add the JavaScript to modify the functionality in some way. Most developers use the example functionality as-is or with just minor changes, but the CSS is another matter. An example that presents a look similar to the one you want is a good place to start, but most people will want to customize the appearance of the output to match the specifics of their sites.

When working with Dynamic Drive examples that use jQuery or jQuery UI, make sure you check out the changes you can make in Chapter 13. These changes help you customize the output even further. The example in the sections that follow doesn't rely on jQuery or jQuery UI; it works exclusively with a Dynamic Drive example so you can see how to make the modifications for Dynamic Drive more clearly.

In this case, you're working with the LCD Clock example that appears at `www.dynamicdrive.com/dynamicindex6/lcdclock.htm`. This example is designed to work with Firefox 1 and above, Internet Explorer 5 and above, and Opera 7 and above. However, testing shows that it also works just fine with newer versions of Chrome. (You can find complete code for this example in the `\Chapter 14\LCDClock` folder of the downloadable code as `LCDClock.HTML`.)

Obtaining the example

Before you can work with the example, you need to create it on your system. The Dynamic Drive site shows how the LCD clock will look and provides you with the code, but it doesn't provide an actual example. In addition, you can modify the example in various ways to make it easier to work with. The following steps help you create the example so you can get started working with it.

1. **Create a new HTML 5 page using your favorite text editor or IDE and save it as LCDClock.HTML.**

2. **Change the** `<title>` **tag as shown here:**

   ```
   <title>Modifying an LCD Clock</title>
   ```

3. **Add an** `<h1>` **tag to the page body as shown here:**

   ```
   <h1>Modifying an LCD Clock</h1>
   ```

4. **Click Select All in the Step 1 portion of the Dynamic Drive page.**

   You see the CSS code for the example highlighted.

5. **Copy the highlighted text to the clipboard, and then paste it within the `<head>` section of the example page.**

   The editor adds to CSS code to the `<head>` section.

6. **Click Select All in the Step 2 portion of the Dynamic Drive page.**

   You see the JavaScript code for the example highlighted.

7. **Copy the highlighted text to the clipboard, and then paste it within the `<body>` section of the example page.**

   The editor adds the JavaScript code to the `<body>` section.

8. **Save the modified `LCDClock.HTML` and load it in your browser.**

   You see the simple output shown in Figure 14-3.

Figure 14-3:
The LCD clock will accurately display the current time for you.

Modifying an LCD Clock

`10  48`

Making the example more flexible

The example works, but it's definitely only an example — not something you'd use in a production environment. The example assumes that everything should appear within a single file. However, when working in a production environment, you may want to use the clock on each page that needs it, which means being able to access the code from a central location. The following steps help you convert the example into something you can use on multiple pages.

1. **Create a new CSS file, using your favorite text editor or IDE, and save it as `LCDClockSource.CSS`.**

2. **Cut the .styling style from LCDClock.HTML and paste it into `LCDClockSource.CSS`.**

   The editor moves the code as requested.

3. **Save `LCDClockSource.CSS`.**

4. **Remove the** `<style>` **tag and any remaining content from** `LCDClock.HTML`.

5. **Create a** `<link>` **tag in the** `<head>` **area of** `LCDClock.HTML` **as follows:**

```
<link
    rel="stylesheet"
    href="LCDClockSource.CSS" />
```

This link tag creates a connection between `LCDClock.HTML` and `LCDClockSource.CSS` so that the LCD clock can use the required styles.

6. **Create a new JavaScript file using your favorite text editor or IDE and save it as** LCDClockSource.JS.

7. **Cut all of the JavaScript code from the** `<body>` **section of LCDClock. HTML except for the** `window.onload=show` **statement and paste it into LCDClockSource.JS.**

The editor moves the code as requested.

8. **Modify the** `show()` **function name in LCDClockSource.JS to read** `showLCDClock()`.

A simple function name such as `show()` isn't very useful in a production environment because you might have multiple functions by that name. Using `showLCDClock()` reduces the chance of a duplicate function name.

9. **Modify the call to** `setTimeout("show()",1000)` **to read** `setTimeout ("showLCDClock()",1000)`.

This function call provides automatic updates of the time. If you find that the clock isn't updating automatically, check this piece of code to ensure you made the correct change.

10. **Save LCDClockSource.JS.**

11. **Modify the** `<script>` **tag that appears in the** `<body>` **of LCDClock. HTML so that it calls the correct function after the window loads, like this:**

```
<script>
<!--
    window.onload=showLCDClock();
//-->
</script>
```

12. **Add a** `<script>` **tag to the** `<head>` **of LCDClock.HTML as follows:**

```
<script
    src="LCDClockSource.JS">
</script>
```

13. Save the modified LCDClock.HTML and load it in your browser.

You see the simple output shown in Figure 14-3.

The modified example works precisely the same as before. However, it now uses external files to perform tasks with less effort. Whenever you want to use the LCD clock on any page, you begin by adding the required <link> and <script> tags to the <head> of the file, like this:

```
<script
    src="LCDClockSource.JS">
</script>
<link
    rel="stylesheet"
    href="LCDClockSource.CSS" />
```

These two tags provide connectivity to the resources needed to make the LCD clock work. You then need to add a <span> and a <script> tag to the <body> of the page, like this:

```
<span id="digitalclock" class="styling"></span>

<script>
<!--
    window.onload=showLCDClock();
//-->
</script>
```

The <span> is used as a container for the clock. The <script> tells the browser to start the clock when the window loads.

Modifying the JavaScript

The clock currently displays hours and minutes, but not seconds. This section discusses what you need to do to modify the code in LCDClockSource.JS to provide a seconds output in the time display.

Modifying the JavaScript for any of the Dynamic Drive scripts is risky because it makes updating the scripts hard. Dynamic Drive does provide script updates occasionally, so make modifications with care. If you do perform an update, you'll need to add your changes back into the updated source code and test it fully.

In order to make the desired change, you need to modify the output code for this example. The output code consists of several if statement levels as shown here (reformatted to make the script easier to read and to also make it fit easily in the book).

```
if (standardbrowser)
{
   if (alternate==0)
      document.tick.tock.value=
         hours+" : "+minutes+" "+dn
   else
      document.tick.tock.value=
         hours+"   "+minutes+" "+dn
}
else
{
   if (alternate==0)
      clockobj.innerHTML=
         hours+"<font color='lime'> : </font>"+
         minutes+" "+"<sup style='font-size:1px'>"+
         dn+"</sup>"
   else
      clockobj.innerHTML=
         hours+"<font color='black'> : </font>"+
         minutes+" "+"<sup style='font-size:1px'>"+
         dn+"</sup>"
}
```

The first `if` statement tests whether the user has a standard browser — one that doesn't require any special formatting commands. When you view the example, you'll notice that the colon between the hours and minutes flashes on and off with each second. The `alternate` setting tests for this state and causes the code to alternate between two output settings (one with and one without the colon).

Adding the seconds to the output requires several steps. First, you must add a variable that contains the current number of seconds. You can add this code anywhere before the `if` statement, but it's best if you add it with the `hours` and `minutes` variables that already appear in the code, as shown here in bold.

```
var hours=Digital.getHours()
var minutes=Digital.getMinutes()
var seconds=Digital.getSeconds()
```

Second, you need to handle the situation where the seconds are a single digit. The example always uses a two-digit minutes and seconds output. You can add this `if` statement immediately after the `if` statement that handles the minutes, as shown here in bold.

```
if (minutes<=9)
  minutes="0"+minutes
if (seconds<=9)
  seconds="0"+seconds
```

Third, you need to modify the output code so that it displays the seconds. This means changing the `if` statements you saw earlier to include the seconds.

However, this example has two other problems that you need to fix. First, the AM/PM output is too small to see. It appears as a dash in Figure 14-3. Second, the code as written overrides the CSS so that you now need to make messy changes to the JavaScript in order to do something as simple as use a different color scheme. The changes that follow not only add the seconds, but also fix these two problems:

```
if (standardbrowser)
{
   if (alternate==0)
      document.tick.tock.value=
          hours+" : "+minutes+" : "+seconds+" "+dn
   else
      document.tick.tock.value=
          hours+"   "+minutes+"   "+seconds+" "+dn
}
else
{
   if (alternate==0)
      clockobj.innerHTML=
          hours+" : "+
          minutes+" : "+
          seconds+" "+"<sup style='font-size:50%'>"+
          dn+"</sup>"
   else
      clockobj.innerHTML=
          hours+
          "<span style='color:transparent'> : </span>"+
          minutes+
          "<span style='color:transparent'> : </span>"+
          seconds+" "+"<sup style='font-size:50%'>"+
          dn+"</sup>"
}
```

The main addition is the `seconds` variable you created earlier. With each tick of the clock, the display is updated so that you see the hours, minutes, and seconds.

The original code attempted to set the font color to match the background to hide the colon. Unfortunately, this approach works only when the background and the colon remain the same color. To make this example CSS-friendly, you still display the colon, but use transparent text to do it. Using transparent text lets the background show through so that the user doesn't actually see the colon.

Instead of setting a specific font size for the AM/PM output, the example follows the original author's intent by making the superscripted value half the size of the other text. No matter how you scale the text, the AM/PM output will scale with it. Save the LCDClockSource.JS file and reload the page. You'll see the seconds displayed as shown in Figure 14-4.

Figure 14-4:
The LCD clock display includes the seconds now.

Modifying an LCD Clock

`02 : 18 : 51 PM`

Modifying the CSS

The CSS for this example controls the appearance and size of the clock. Make sure you follow the techniques discussed in the previous "Modifying the JavaScript" section to fix some problems this example has that makes it CSS unfriendly before you read this section. Once you do have the script fixes in place, you can change the CSS as needed to make the clock appear any way you want. For example, try configuring the clock like this:

```
.styling
{
   background-color:Beige;
   color:DarkBlue;
   font: bold 22px Arial;
   padding: 4px;
   border: double;
}
```

You get a completely different look. Figure 14-5 shows what you can expect as output in this case. Notice that the colons disappear every other cycle, as anticipated, even though the background color has changed.

Figure 14-5:
Change
the CSS to
modify the
appearance
of the clock.

Modifying an LCD Clock

02　35　39 ^{PM}

Working with Menus

Dynamic Drive provides all sorts of different scripting examples (as described in the "Understanding the Script Categories" section, earlier in this chapter). However, one of the most commonly used features of any API is the menus. A developer needs to provide some means for people to get from one location to another on a site — to make it possible to review various resources that the site provides. With this in mind, the following sections discuss some of the things you can do using the Dynamic Drive menus found in the CSS-based Menu Scripts category (www.dynamicdrive.com/dynamicindex1/indexb.html). The techniques described in the following section will also work with scripts found in other categories, but the focus is on menus because everyone needs to create a menuing system for their sites at one point or another.

Defining a specialized menu

Split button menus offer one way to give your site a special look (as shown in Figure 14-6 later in this section). The split button tells viewers that the default menu selection is what they see at the moment, but that other selections are available. Simply clicking the split button takes the viewer to the default site. However, clicking the down arrow next to the button shows the other options and the viewer can easily select any of them as an alternative to a default.

This type of menu isn't limited to just directing people to other locations. It can also act as a kind of input field for a form. The button shows the default selection for that field. However, you can also choose one of the alternatives if they work better. The point is that split button menus provide a specialized approach to menu development.

The example in this section relies on the Split Menu Buttons v1.2 example shown at www.dynamicdrive.com/dynamicindex1/splitmenu buttons.htm. The following steps get you started using this specialized menu and offer suggestions on modifications you might want to make to it. (You can find complete code for this example in the `\Chapter 14\ SplitButton` folder of the downloadable code as `SplitButton.HTML`.)

1. **Download the splitmenubuttons.js file found in the Step 1 section of the Dynamic Drive page, and then place it in the folder you want to use for your test page.**

2. **Download the splitmenubuttons.css file found in the Step 1 section of the Dynamic Drive page, and then place it in the folder you want to use for your test page.**

3. **Create a new HTML 5 page using your favorite text editor or IDE, and then save it as** SplitButton.HTML.

4. **Change the** `<title>` **tag as shown here:**

   ```
   <title>An Example of Using a Split Button Menu</title>
   ```

5. **Click Select All in the Step 2 portion of the Dynamic Drive page.**

   You see the header code for the example highlighted.

6. **Copy the highlighted text to the clipboard, and then paste it within the** `<head>` **section of the example page.**

   The editor adds the code to the `<head>` section. If you look carefully at this code, you find a link to `splitmenubuttons.css` and a script reference to `splitmenubuttons.js`. This example also relies on jQuery, so you find a script reference to `jquery.min.js`.

   The code also includes a script for creating the split buttons that uses jQuery syntax. You won't need to modify this script as long as you follow a few simple rules in creating your menu. The steps that follow discuss these rules.

7. **Create links for each of the top menu entries in the** `<body>` **section of the page as follows:**

   ```
   <a href="SplitButton.HTML"
       class="splitmenubutton"
       data-showmenu="Home"
       data-splitmenu="false"
       data-menucolors="Brick,Brick">Home</a>
    <a href="Products.HTML"
       class="splitmenubutton"
       data-showmenu="Products"
       data-splitmenu="false"
       data-menucolors="Indigo,Red">Products</a>
   <a href="About.HTML"
       class="splitmenubutton"
       data-showmenu="About"
       data-menucolors="Indigo,Red">About</a>
   ```

Each of these entries is a top-level menu button for the page. When the user displays the page, it shows Home, Products, and About as three buttons. Each of the buttons will go to a specific location when clicked. However, you can substitute # for the `href` attribute if you don't want a button to do anything when clicked.

The `class` must appear as `splitmenubutton` in every case. You can find the CSS for this class in the `splitmenubuttons.css` file.

The `data-showmenu` attribute defines which submenu to use. You must define a name, even if you don't intend to use a submenu with a particular button. In this example, the Home button won't include any submenus.

The `data-splitmenu` attribute specifies whether a button should show the down arrow as part of the button or as a separate button. This example shows both cases. The default setting is true, which means the arrow appears as a separate button.

You use the `data-menucolors` attribute to specify the colors used for the default background color and the selected color. The default color is `DarkRed`, but most developers will want to override the defaults to obtain a specific look.

8. **Create a submenu for the Products menu, using the following code:**

```
<ul id="Products" class="splitdropdown">
   <li><a href="Products.HTML">Product 1</a></li>
   <li><a href="Products.HTML">Product 2</a></li>
   <li><a href="Products.HTML">Product 3</a></li>
   <li><a href="Products.HTML">Product 4</a></li>
   <li><a href="Products.HTML">Product 5</a></li>
</ul>
```

A submenu is simply an unordered list. Each of the list items contains an anchor that points to the location you want the viewer to go. The unordered list must have an `id` attribute value that matches the `data-showmenu` attribute value. In addition, the first level of unordered lists in a submenu must use the `splitdropdown` class.

9. **Create a submenu for the About menu, using the following code:**

```
<ul id="About" class="splitdropdown">
   <li><a href="About.HTML">Our History</a></li>
   <li class="separator">
      <a href="About.HTML">Privacy Statement</a>
   </li>
   <li><a href="#">Contact Us</a>
      <ul>
         <li><a href="About.HTML">By Telephone</a></li>
         <li><a href="About.HTML">By Mail</a></li>
```

```
        <li><a href="#">By E-mail</a>
            <ul>
                <li><a href="About.HTML">Webmaster</a></li>
                <li><a href="About.HTML">Support</a></li>
            </ul>
        </li>
    </ul>
  </li>
</ul>
```

This menu is a little more complex. If you want to create submenus of your submenus, simply place the corresponding unordered list within the list item as shown. The Contact Us submenu actually contains three levels of menu options.

Add the `class="separator"` attribute when you want to add a little extra space between menu items. Using this attribute makes it possible for users to see relations between menu items with greater ease.

10. Save the modified SplitButton.HTML and load it in your browser.

You see the simple output shown in Figure 14-6.

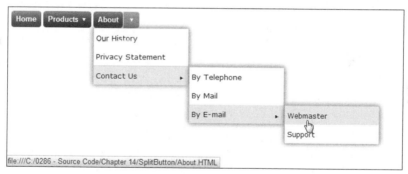

Figure 14-6:
A split button menu can provide a nice appearance on a page.

Notice, in Figure 14-6, that the Home button appears like any other button, but it lacks a down arrow because it doesn't have an associated menu. Clicking this button will take you to the home page.

As with any CSS-based menu, you can make a number of changes to the appearance of these menus. For example, it's possible to change the arrows to something other than the simple triangle shown. Of course, you need to know the values used to present various arrow types. You can see a list of typical Unicode arrows at `www.ssec.wisc.edu/~tomw/java/unicode.html#x2190`.

Developing menus with graphics

The split button setup described in the "Defining a specialized menu" section of the chapter uses two different styles for arrows:

✔ The `span.innerspan.downarrow::after` style (note the two colons) is for arrows that appear as separate buttons.

✔ The `.splitmenubutton span.innerspan.downarrow:after` style (note the single colon) is for arrows that appear as part of a single button.

You set the `content` attribute to the value of the Unicode arrow you want to use (or any other symbol for that matter). Here are examples of styles you can use with the example application.

```
<style type="text/css">
    span.innerspan.downarrow::after
    {
        content: '\21D3';
    }
    .splitmenubutton span.innerspan.downarrow:after
    {
        content: '\21B3';
    }
</style>
```

Reload the page after you make the changes. Figure 14-7 shows typical results. The Products button now uses a right-pointing down arrow — the About button uses a double downward arrow.

Figure 14-7:
The menu you create is completely flexible, so you can change features like the arrows.

You can also change the right-pointing arrow used for submenus. Simply change the `.rightarrow:after` style to whatever Unicode character you want to use. For example, if you want to use a white right-pointing triangle, then you'd change the content attribute to `'\25B9'`. If you want to use a larger triangle, then use `'\25B6'` or `'\25B7'` instead.

Creating specialized menu effects

The menu created in the previous two sections is nice, but there are still some fit-and-finish changes you can make. One that's especially important is to define the title attribute for each of the menu entries. For example, you might simply use `title="Go to the Home Page"` for the Home button. Adding the title attribute provides the viewer with a tooltip when hovering the mouse cursor (as shown in Figure 14-8) and also provides input for people using screen readers.

Figure 14-8:
Adding
tooltips
make the
menu even
easier
to use.

The menu doesn't provide a quick method for changing the text color or anything about the font used to display it. As with other examples in the book, you can use various kinds of CSS changes to affect the appearance of text in the menu. The buttons rely on the `.splitmenubutton` style to create the text appearance; the submenus rely on the `ul.splitdropdown li a` style. Try making these changes to the example styles and you'll see the interplay between the various split button menu elements.

```
.splitmenubutton
{
    color: Yellow;
}
ul.splitdropdown li a
{
    color: DarkOrchid;
    background: Lavender;
}
```

It's possible to modify the split button menu to meet any need you might have. The important thing to remember is to make as many changes as possible outside of the original files. Making changes to the files will cause you problems at some point because Dynamic Drive will likely make updates to the examples.

Part V
The Part of Tens

Enjoy an additional Part of Tens article about ten sites with unique designs at www.dummies.com/extras/css3.

In this part . . .

- ✔ Discover places you can go to find CSS libraries to make your work easier
- ✔ Find the CSS generator of your dreams
- ✔ Create amazing layouts that tantalize your viewers
- ✔ Obtain useful resources you can use as your CSS knowledge grows

Chapter 15

Ten Phenomenal Places to Find Libraries

. . . .

A number of chapters in this book discuss some of the more popular libraries that are available for use by developers. jQuery, jQuery UI, Dynamic Drive, and many others provide Application Programming Interfaces (APIs), which are libraries of programming routines, to use in creating your application. Because APIs provide a significant advantage over writing code by hand or using just the libraries that come with a particular programming product, their use is only going to increase.

This chapter presents ten libraries that you haven't seen in other areas of the book. What you find here is a listing of some of the better offerings for developers online. However, the chapter also serves to help you find good libraries on your own. By looking at how these libraries are put together and presented to the developer, you gain insights into what makes one library merely good and another library great.

Animating Page Elements with Animate.css

There are many ways to add animation to pages using CSS. The Animate. css library (`http://daneden.me/animate/`) provides access to a host of animation effects. Each of the effects is carefully categorized on the page, as shown in Figure 15-1. To see how a particular effect will appear, click its entry and then watch the "I fight for the user" block to see how the effect works.

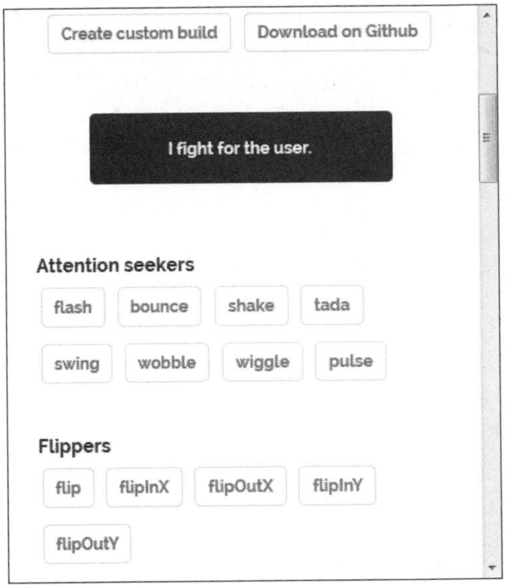

Figure 15-1:
Use
Animate.css
to add spe-
cial effects
to your
page.

The author tells you how to mix the library with jQuery, but you can use it with any other JavaScript library as well. You make the effects work by adding the `animated` class, followed by the name of the special effect you want to use, such as `class="animated flip"` when you want to use the flip effect.

Click Download on Github to obtain the entire library of animations at `https://github.com/daneden/animate.css`. This site also makes it possible to interact with other people who are using the library — and to obtain additional files, such as the README, associated with the library. The feature complete `animate.min.css` version of the library is significantly smaller than the full version that most developers will use when creating applications, so you may want to download this file for your production system.

Tell me about your favorite library

I'm always on the lookout for the next phenomenal library for my coding needs. If you find such a library and don't see it presented in the book, share the wealth with me by writing to `John@ JohnMuellerBooks.com`. I'd love to hear about the library and what makes it completely different from other offerings found in the book.

I often discuss reader input of this sort on my blog at `http://blog.johnmueller books.com/`. Just check out the entries for this book at `http://blog.john muellerbooks.com/categories/ 263/developing-with-css3-for- dummies.aspx`.

The library is really large and few developers will use all of the special effects, so you can also download a smaller version of the library. Simply click Create Custom Build and the associated wizard (shown in Figure 15-2) will help you create a custom version of the CSS library to use with your specific application. Check the animations you want to use and then click Build at the bottom of the page to complete the process. It's a good idea to get a reduced-size version of the animations for use with your site to enhance overall application performance.

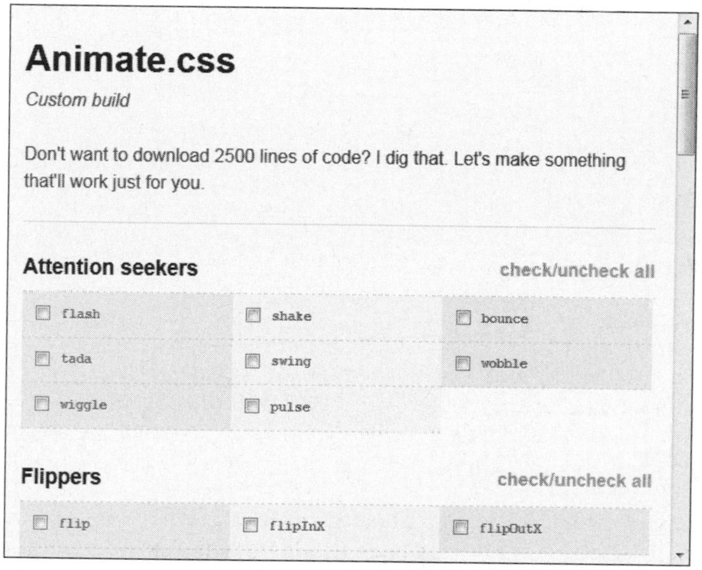

Figure 15-2:
The wizard makes it easy to get just the Animate.css features you want.

Animate.css

Custom build

Don't want to download 2500 lines of code? I dig that. Let's make something that'll work just for you.

Attention seekers   check/uncheck all

flash	shake	bounce
tada	swing	wobble
wiggle	pulse	

Flippers   check/uncheck all

| flip | flipInX | flipOutX |

Locating a Library Using CSSDB.co

A number of places online don't actually have libraries of their own, but they do host other people's libraries. An example of such a site for jQuery appears in Chapter 13 in the form of Unheap (www.unheap.com/). Knowing where to look for a library can be quite hard; search engines don't always provide the best results, so you need a site such as CSSDB.co (http://cssdb.co/) to get the libraries lined up in one location so you can review them.

Each of the entries on this site include the library name, a short description, some library statistics (the stars indicate the number of positive votes), and a link you can use to download the library as shown in Figure 15-3. The libraries are sorted in most popular order by default. However, you can also search for new libraries — a helpful feature when you're already familiar with the offerings on this site. In addition, you can submit your own library and join the group — making it far easier for other developers to find your code.

Figure 15-3:
Find the
library of
your dreams
using the
entries on
this hosted
site.

Combining CSS3 and JavaScript with JSter

Library hosting sites have a certain feel to them. Some sites are exclusive to a particular technology, while others cater to a variety of technologies, and still others combine technologies. The JSter site (`http://jster.net/tag/css3`) helps you locate combined CSS3 and JavaScript libraries to accomplish specific tasks.

This site offers a number of features as shown in Figure 15-4. You see the library name, a short description, and statistics such as the GitHub stars (rating), GitHub forks (number of versions), and JSter rating so you know more about the library's popularity. Each of the library entries also has tag links associated with it so that you can better categorize the library offering and find other libraries of the same type. Some libraries have special notes associated with them, such as whether the library author has made recent improvements.

Unlike many hosting sites of this sort, JSter also offers a blog that discusses libraries. In many cases, this means that you not only find the short description of a library, but also a longer write-up about it. It's also possible to get the latest news about issues concerning library developers and the general programming community, so even if you don't download any of the libraries, it would be worth the time to read the blog.

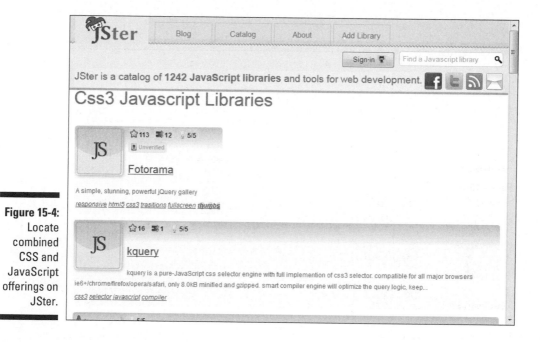

Figure 15-4:
Locate
combined
CSS and
JavaScript
offerings on
JSter.

Developing Background Animations with Animatable

Most animation libraries concentrate on foreground elements of a page. The Animatable library (`http://leaverou.github.io/animatable/`) focuses on backgrounds and borders instead. You can find all sorts of interesting special effects, such as a background that gives the appearance of moving. The default page setup displays the special effect when you hover the mouse cursor over a particular effect (as shown in Figure 15-5). However, you can also choose to display all of the effects at once.

To obtain details about each effect, click its associated box. A pop-up dialog box appears that contains additional information about the animation so you can reproduce it yourself.

The really interesting thing about these examples is that they're simple to implement. All you modify is the settings for a single CSS3 property to obtain the effect. The two values described for the target property are all you need to produce the effect.

Figure 15-5:
Background
and border
effects
can give
your page
special
emphasis.

Easing Your Way into a Transition with Easings

The introduction to this site tells you the main reason you'd want to use the animation it provides. Most real world events don't happen in linear fashion — the action speeds up or slows down at certain points during the transition. Easings (`http://easings.net/`) helps you create natural-looking transitions from one state to another. You have access to a number of easing effects, as shown in Figure 15-6.

To add a particular easing to your application, simply click the effect you want to use, such as easeInSine. The resulting page provides you with the JavaScript, Sassy Cascading Style Sheet (SCSS) (see `http://sass-lang.com/` for more information about SCSS), and CSS3 syntax for creating the effect. All you need to do is copy the code to your application.

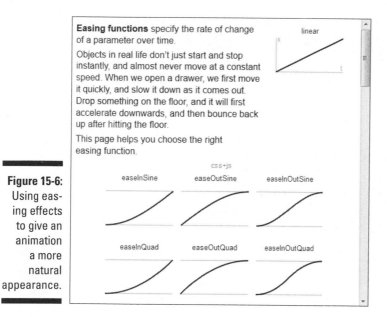

Figure 15-6:
Using easing effects to give an animation a more natural appearance.

Transitioning Elements Using Morf.js

There are many ways to animate items using easings. A transition can follow a natural or mathematical path, or it can provide a specialized effect that's entertaining, but clearly not natural. The Morf.js page (www.joelambert.co.uk/morf/) provides access to a number of specialized transitional effects. The effects are divided into native and custom categories as shown in Figure 15-7.

To see a particular effect, click its entry on the page. The square at the top of the page will demonstrate the effect for you. At the bottom of the page, you see a Generated Animated CSS field that contains the code required to reproduce the special effect. The code is pure CSS; all you need to do is copy it to your application.

This particular site seems to work best when using Chrome. Yes, you can get it to work with other browsers, but this is one situation where there's a distinct advantage in using one browser over another.

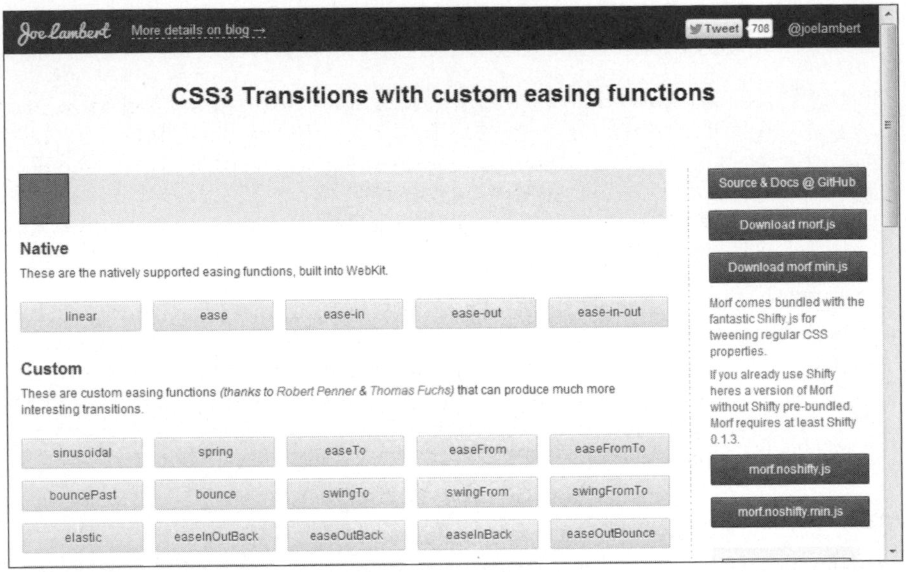

Figure 15-7: Specialized transition effects can add interest to a page.

Creating Full Interactive Applications with YUI

The Yahoo! User Interface (YUI) library (http://yuilibrary.com/) is a full-featured development — API akin to jQuery and jQuery UI combined in some respects, and richer than these libraries in others. This is a complex API designed to handle the needs of larger applications. In fact, you actually do need to go through the tutorials, examples, and user guides supplied at http://yuilibrary.com/yui/docs/ to really use this product. In short, this is the kind of library you use when you need to create a high-end, highly interactive application.

User interface support in YUI revolves around the concept of a skin. You add skinning support to your application and then extend it as needed to make use of various controls. The array of controls is rich, so you likely won't need to use any other library with this one. In addition, the library provides graded browser support for a wide range of browsers (see http://yui library.com/yui/environments/ for details).

You find a huge number of examples on the site (see http://yuilibrary. com/yui/docs/examples/) that demonstrate all sorts of tasks that developers normally perform. When learning to use this library, it's a good idea to look for an example that could perform the task you want to perform — and then extend it as needed to meet your needs.

As with any other programming technology aid, you need to consider the tradeoffs when using specific libraries. YUI is a great library for high-end development that requires the complex and flexible environment it provides. The reason many sites use products such as jQuery is that these libraries are simple and easy to debug. Always weigh the costs before you get too involved with a particular library.

Smart developers use an Integrated Development Environment (IDE) with a product such as YUI. The main reason to use an IDE is to reduce complexity and make it possible to work with the library without constantly referring to the documentation. A number of IDEs will work with YUI; however, most developers seem to prefer using Komodo Edit (see Chapter 16 for details) or JSEclipse (http://jseclipse.softpile.com/).

Displaying Tooltips Using HINT.css

Tooltips are an essential communication technique for your application. Users like to see something pop up when they hover the mouse over a field or other part of the page where they have a question. Using tooltips correctly makes your application much easier to use. Of course, the easiest way to create tooltips is to rely on the `title` attribute provided by HTML. However, the `title` attribute is extremely limited. Using HINT.css (http://kushagra gour.in/lab/hint/) makes it possible to create tooltips wherever you want on the page — and to format those tooltips so they're incredibly easy to see.

As with any CSS library, you have full control over how your tooltips appear when using HINT.css. You can display them in any position around the element and in any color. A tooltip can have sharp or rounded edges. In addition, you can control features such as the text size, font, and anything else you can imagine so that the tooltips are truly customized.

Ridding Yourself of Browser Differences with Normalize.css

Many of the chapters in this book have discussed differences in how browsers work with CSS3. Yes, most CSS3 features are standardized to the point that you can create some incredibly interesting applications, but there are just enough differences that it would be nice to get rid of them if possible. Using Normalize.css (`http://necolas.github.io/normalize.css/`) can help you overcome many of the issues you face when using CSS3 features such as transformations. This unique solution relies on a small CSS file to perform its work. The post at `http://nicolasgallagher.com/about-normalize-css/` tells you more about just what Normalize.css can do for you.

Ensuring Your Application Works with Mobile Devices Using Skeleton

Most users today want applications that work everywhere — and work about the same in every location and with every device. Of course, that's a really tall order, because various devices have differing browsers, operating systems, form factors, and all sorts of other differences. Even with browser-based applications, it's hard to create an application that works equally well on mobile and desktop devices. However, Skeleton (`www.getskeleton.com/`) can help you create applications that work at any size.

The technology behind Skeleton is CSS3-based, so you don't need to worry about whether a client can run scripts. In addition, the author has tested Skeleton on a number of platforms, so you have a better idea of whether it will work for you. The main requirement is that the client browser supports CSS3. The current implementation works on:

- Chrome (Mac/PC)
- Firefox 3.0 and above (Mac/PC)
- Safari
- Internet Explorer 7 and above
- iPhone (Retina)
- Droid (Charge/Original)
- iPad

Ten Phenomenal Places to Find Generators

C hapter 15 discusses libraries, which are collections of code you can use in your application. This chapter discusses *generators,* which are tools you can use to create, interact with, or test code. These tools include a wide range of specific types, including wizards, designers, Integrated Development Environments (IDEs), and a host of other items.

The following sections provide you with a quick overview of a number of truly amazing tools that help you generate code in some way. The idea is to create code that you can't readily obtain from a library. Perhaps you have a unique need or the code just doesn't lend itself to inclusion in a library.

It's important to review each tool carefully because each tool has special characteristics. I also try to categorize the tool and help you understand why you might need a tool of this type. Even if you don't think the tool will work for you (and everyone has unique needs), reading about these tools will make you better about finding tools that do meet your needs and provide the special features you require to do a great job of writing browser-based applications of your own.

Creating Animations Using Stylie

Getting an animation just right can be difficult. Each developer has different skills and ways of viewing tasks. Stylie (`http://jeremyckahn.github.io/stylie/`) is designed for developers who are more visually oriented. (See Figure 16-1.) You choose a starting and ending point for the animation, using the X and Y values. The R value determines the amount of rotation that the animated object performs. You can choose how long the animation occurs using the time values. In addition, the X, Y, and R values can each have an animation effect associated with them.

Tell me about your favorite tool

Most developers are tool addicts. We just can't help ourselves. A tool that looks even marginally useful is tried and tested to see if it saves time and effort, or at least does something interesting that we might need later. As with any developer, I'm always on the lookout for the next useful tool. Of course, I don't want a repeat of several other tools on the market — I want something unique. If you find such a tool and don't see it presented in the book,

share the wealth with me by writing to John@JohnMuellerBooks.com. I'd love to hear about the tool and what it does. Make sure you emphasize the tool's unique functionality. I often discuss reader input of this sort on my blog at http://blog.johnmuellerbooks.com/. Just check out the entries for this book at http://blog.johnmuellerbooks.com/categories/263/developing-with-css3-for-dummies.aspx.

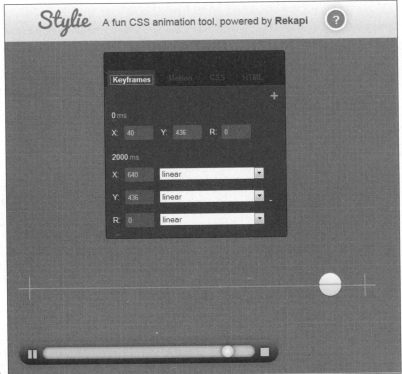

Figure 16-1:
Use Stylie
to visually
design ani-
mations for
your site.

Many animations move in more than one direction. Click the plus sign (+) to add another direction. This direction also has X, Y, and R values and you can set its duration and special effects as well. In short, you can use this interface to create incredibly complex animation effects that go in more than one direction.

The Motion tab defines characteristics of the animation, such as how many times you want the animation to execute (you can choose to make the execution an infinite loop) and how the object you're animating should interact with the animation path. This is also the tab you use to define the easing used to make the animated effect flow smoothly. A straight line animation is simple, but the easing becomes important when you start working with animations that move in more than one direction.

After you finish configuring your animation, you click the CSS tab, which contains the CSS you use to create the animated effect in your application. The CSS tab lets you choose a name for the animation class. You can also select which vendors to include as part of the CSS and the animation quality level. The HTML tab contains sample tags you need to complete the animation. This is where you'd need to make modifications to include the object you want to animate in place of the simple circle supplied by Stylie.

Designing CSS Styles Using CSSDesk

Most IDEs used to create HTML, CSS, and JavaScript files lack a designer interface, where you can immediately see the results of any code you create. Instead, you need to load the page to determine whether the coding changes you make actually create the effect you want. CSSDesk (http://cssdesk. com/) makes it possible to write code and immediately see the effect it has on the output (as shown in Figure 16-2).

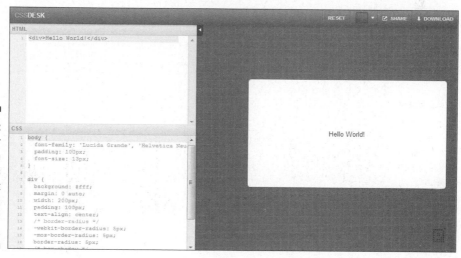

Figure 16-2: See your code changes take effect as you make them with CSSDesk.

The right pane shows the output as you make it. The default setup shows a simple Hello World example within a `<div>` element, but the editor works fine with any HTML code you provide. The HTML code appears in the upper left pane, while the CSS code appears in the lower left pane.

The main focus of this editor is creating the user interface for your application. However, you can modify the HTML pane to include `<head>` and `<body>` elements. Styles you create in the `<head>` section will appear in the output, just as if you had created them in a standard document. Some scripting functionality will work, other functionality won't. Inline scripts will generally work as anticipated, but don't expect anything even moderately complex to work as expected. For example, creating a button like this:

```
<input type="button"
        onclick="alert('Hello')"
        value="Say Hello" />
```

produces the expected output, but calling an external function may not. In short, the JavaScript support is limited, so you might not always see the anticipated result when working with external libraries such as jQuery.

Making Applications Run Faster with yepnope.js

Part of the problem with browser-based applications is that you request a single resource from a library and end up with the entire library loaded. The process is slow, cumbersome, error-prone, and simply inefficient. You can use `yepnope.js` (`http://yepnopejs.com/`) to help overcome these issues. When working with `yepnope.js`, you provide a condition that the product then tests, and then loads resources only as needed to support a specific condition. You can use this product with CSS3 or JavaScript files.

Fortunately, the `yepnope.js` tool goes further than simply loading resources based on conditions. For example, some applications will mindlessly call a script with the same input parameters multiple times when only one output is possible using a particular set of inputs. The multiple calls can prove especially time-consuming when calling another URL. You can use `yepnope.js` to keep events like this from occurring. The tool helps make the application code smarter so high-latency calls are avoided whenever possible.

Another problem with scripts is that they can continue to run, even when there's no hope that they'll ever complete. After a while, the user clicks the Back button or goes to a different site. You can add timeouts for scripts individually with yepnope.js so that it becomes possible to detect the time-outs and handle them as errors. With this capability in place, it's potentially possible to recover from scripts that continue running when they shouldn't.

The central focus of yepnope.js is the yepnope() function. It provides a syntax that looks like this:

```
yepnope([{
  test : /* A condition you want to test */,
  yep  : /* Tasks performed when true. */,
  nope : /* Tasks performed when false */,
  both : /* Tasks performed every time */,
  load : /* Resources loaded every time */,
  callback : /* A function to call during processing */,
  complete : /* A function to call after processing */
}, ... ]);
```

The basic idea is that you create a scenario where tasks are performed based on specific needs so that the application doesn't spend time performing unnecessary tasks (and wasting both time and resources as a result). Of course, yepnope.js provides more functionality than presented in this overview, but the short version is that this is a smart resource loader.

Generating Templates Using Initializr

There are many ways to create the templates you need to produce applications. If you're just starting out with HTML5, CSS3, and JavaScript development, the Initializr (www.initializr.com/) template generator may be precisely what you need. It helps you create three basic types of templates (as shown in Figure 16-3), based on the answers you provide to the wizard.

Of course, you may not know which of the templates to use. Click the Demo button under each of the template types to give them a try in your browser. The site will load a page that helps you understand how that particular template works.

Once you decide on a particular template, you click its button and the page expands to show the wizard inputs you need to provide (as shown in Figure 16-4). If you need help with the options, click the Docs button beneath the template button for the template you chose.

The final step is to click Download It!. The download will provide you with everything needed to create the template look you requested. You can then fill the template with content and upload it to your site.

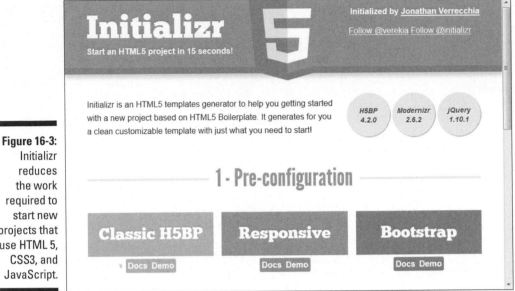

Figure 16-3: Initializr reduces the work required to start new projects that use HTML 5, CSS3, and JavaScript.

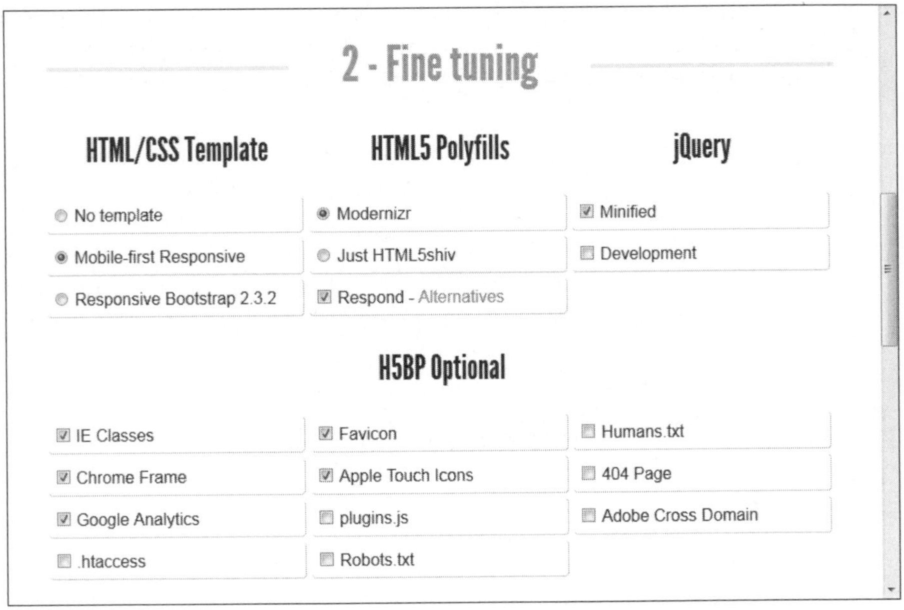

Figure 16-4: Provide any answers that the wizard requires to create the template you want.

Optimizing Applications to Work with Older Browsers with Modernizr

There are many different browsers and browser versions in use today. You can get some idea of just how many by looking at NetMarketShare (www. netmarketshare.com/browser-market-share.aspx?qprid= 2&qpcustomd=0). Many people refuse to give up their old browsers for any reason. For example, at the time of this writing, 6.13 percent of people are still using Internet Explorer 6. Catering to this group would mean not using a wealth of libraries, special effects, and newer coding techniques. In fact, it would be hard to create anything close to a modern application. This is where Modernizr (http://modernizr.com/) comes into play. You use Modernizr to optionally perform tasks and include application features based on the browser that the user has installed. As a consequence, users with newer browsers can enjoy the full functionality that your site has to offer, but you can also include users with older browsers (just not at the same functionality level, in many cases).

The creators of yepnope.js (described in the "Making Applications Run Faster with yepnope.js" section, earlier in this chapter) and Modernizr have worked to make their products highly compatible. You can use these two products together to create applications that are incredibly flexible, browser- and browser version-inclusive, and yet quite fast and resource-frugal.

Modernizr performs its task by using a number of techniques — not just the highly unreliable navigator.userAgent property — to detect a user's browser. It detects a wealth of browser features, and helps you avoid problems when a browser lacks a particular feature, using a yepnope.js paradigm. In fact, it checks for over 40 features that developers commonly use within their applications. You can read more about what Modernizr checks — and how it performs those checks — at http://modernizr.com/docs/.

Enhancing Selector Support Using Selectivizr

The CSS3 selector support in older browsers is nearly nonexistent. Of course, you have to have great selector support to make most special effects work properly. The answer to the problem is to use Selectivizr (http://selectivizr.com/) to overcome these issues. This tool is specifically designed to help with problems that crop up in Internet Explorer versions 6 through 8 — and it works with a number of libraries, including

- ✔ jQuery
- ✔ dojo
- ✔ prototype
- ✔ Yahoo!
- ✔ DOMAssistant
- ✔ MooTools
- ✔ NWMatcher

Even with this tool, you don't get complete selector support. Fortunately, the Selectivizr site provides a list of selectors and tells you which selector types it supports for a given library. With this knowledge, you can usually overcome any selector issues when working with older browsers.

Designing Unusual List Presentations with Liffect

Developers use lists for a number of tasks when creating a page. For example, lists play an important part in creating many menus. Another purpose for lists is to display content. You can display all of the content at once, or make the content special by presenting one item at a time. The purpose of Liffect (http://ademilter.com/lab/liffect/) is to make it possible to create special effects for lists.

This tool generates custom code for animating your content list. All you do is define the kind of animation you want, the time the animation requires to complete, the delay between items, and whether you want items selected randomly (as shown in Figure 16-5). At the bottom of the page are selections for the kind of browsers you want to support.

After you make your selections, click Generate. The utility outputs the HTML, CSS3, and JavaScript code required to create the animated sequence. Of course, you still have to provide the content by modifying the HTML code (or providing some automated method for generating it). Otherwise all you need to do is copy and paste the resulting code to your application.

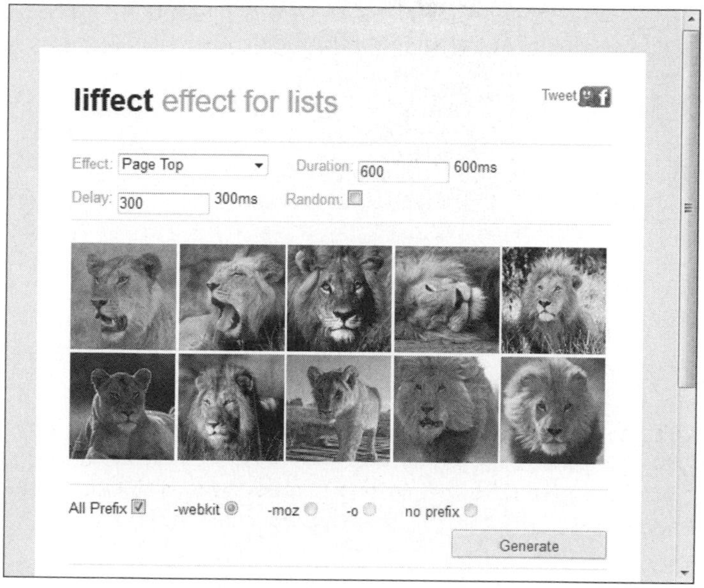

Figure 16-5:
Liffect
generates
CSS and
JavaScript
to display
list content
as an
animation.

Editing Code Using Komodo Edit

Yes, you can create any browser-based application you want by using a simple text editor. Any editor that outputs text without any formatting will work just fine. In fact, any method you have of producing pure text output will work. However, most developers opt for an environment that's friendlier and easier to use — often in the form of an IDE. Using an IDE provides you with helpful information, such as the properties available when you're working with CSS or the inputs required for a JavaScript call.

Komodo Edit (www.activestate.com/komodo-edit) provides good support for CSS3, HTML5, JavaScript and a host of other languages, including Perl, PHP, Python, Ruby and Tcl. The editor works on Windows, Macintosh, and Linux systems. The paid version of this product supports additional languages and a wealth of additional features, but the free version is perfectly usable for JavaScript coding. The biggest lack in the free version is a debugger, but you can easily use the debugger that comes with your browser to make up the difference.

Engineering Layer Effects Using LayerStyles

Creating the right appearance for a layer can be hard. A layer is composed of the outer shadow, border, and inner shadow of the elements (such as a <div>) that you create. LayerStyles (http://layerstyles.org/) makes it possible to visually design the layer effects that you create. You perform that task using a control panel (as shown in Figure 16-6).

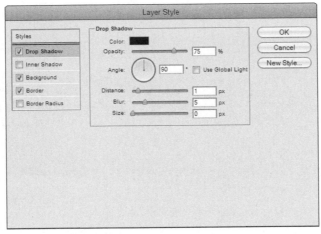

Figure 16-6: Create and manage layer effects to produce just the right appearance on a page.

The control panel helps you modify all of the characteristics of the layer effect, including the source of light. All of the effects appear on a square in the center of the page, which you can see by moving the control panel to a more convenient location (simply click the title bar and drag the control panel anywhere you want to see it on the page).

When you finish creating your layer effect, you can click the CSS tab that appears in the lower-left corner of the page. This act displays a window that shows the code required to create the layer effect you designed. Simply click Copy to copy the information to the Clipboard. You can then paste the code into your IDE for use in your application. The resulting CSS should work fine with Internet Explorer, Firefox, Chrome, and most other browsers that support CSS3.

Testing Your Font Stacks Using FFFFALLBACK

In Chapter 3 I discuss a common problem that developers have in working with fonts — the issue of font support on the client system. In that chapter, you see one solution to the problem, but the solution may not produce precisely the result you want in everyday operation. In some cases, you want to create a custom font stack so that your page appears precisely as you want it to appear to the end user. Another solution to this problem is to use FFFFALLBACK (`http://ffffallback.com/`) — a tool that makes it possible to try various font combinations on the target page.

The page contains instructions for using this tool. You simply drag the bookmarklet to the toolbar of your browser, where it becomes a clickable button. Go to the site you want to modify, and then click the FFFFALLBACK button. The tool analyzes the CSS on the page and creates a clone of the page. You'll also see a tool on the cloned page that you can use to test various fonts (as shown in Figure 16-7). To change the font, type the font name and press Enter in the field supplied.

Figure 16-7:
Define custom font stacks for your site to convey the message you want.

The fallback font you choose appears in an alternative color, below and to the right of the original font. To see just the fallback font, click Fallback. Likewise, to see just the original font, click Web Font.

This particular tool only works with webkit browsers such as Firefox, Chrome, and Safari. It doesn't work with other browsers, including Internet Explorer and Opera.

Chapter 17

Ten Quick Ways to Produce a Great Layout

. . . .

*T*his book discusses a lot of CSS-related techniques and tactics — but when you consider everything that CSS is used for today, it still comes down to a matter of layout. Creating a layout that helps the user navigate the site and actually see the content you're trying to present is essential. When you look online, you see that there are many kinds of layouts used to present information — some work better than others do.

The precise layout you create depends on just how fancy you want to get — and whether the content will be used on multiple devices (such as a combination of PCs and smartphones). However, most people will want either a fixed or a fluid (also called a *liquid*) layout. That's because most business sites online use one of these two layouts to good effect. The *layout type* defines the reaction of the page to client characteristics, such as the size of the screen, but doesn't determine issues such as the number of columns. Designers commonly group these layouts into two major and six minor layout types:

- ✔ Classic layouts:
    - **Absolute:** Each element is placed at a specific location on the page, no matter how much space is available.
    - **Fixed-width:** The content consumes a fixed amount of space on the page, no matter how much space is available.
- ✔ Modern layouts:
    - **Fluid (liquid):** Each element is assigned a percentage of the available space and content flows as needed.
    - **Elastic:** The size of the content and the availability of space determine the amount of space allocated for each element.
    - **Adaptive:** The size of the screen determines whether a fixed or fluid layout is used to display content.
    - **Responsive:** The content is allowed to flow to match the size of the screen without regard to placement of elements.

A designer needs to know all the details of the various layouts and then creates the CSS required to implement a particular layout determined by customer needs and content type. Most developers don't have time to ascertain all of these details and create a custom layout. This chapter helps you get past these details and create a layout quickly that simply looks good — that everyone feels matches the content format, consumer needs, and viewer expectations.

Learning the Layout Properties

No matter how you interact with CSS layouts, you'll eventually need to know what the properties are and how to interact with them. Even when you work with a generator, the generator will produce code that relies on those properties; if you don't know what the properties do, you won't be able to make required tweaks to the generated code. You can use a tutorial, such as the one on the W3Schools site (www.w3schools.com/css/), but an article often serves the purpose better.

The article entitled, "Master the New CSS Layout Properties" at www.net-magazine.com/tutorials/master-new-css-layout-properties provides precisely what you need in a short space. This article covers such diverse topics as vendor prefixes and the use of the various column properties. It gets you going quickly, even if you're using a generator to produce your code. If you find later on that you don't quite know every required property, you can always fall back on the W3Schools site (or an alternative that provides similar information).

Creating Basic Layouts Using CSS Layout Generator

The CSS Layout Generator (www.cssportal.com/layout-generator/) helps you create fixed or liquid layouts by filling out questions in a form as shown in Figure 17-1. You tell the wizard the version of HTML to use, what sort of layout you want, the specifics of the content area, and some aesthetics, such as the background color.

Once you're finished filling out the form, you click Create Layout. The wizard generates the layout you requested and displays it onscreen. Figure 17-2 shows a sample layout; yours may differ, depending on the settings you define.

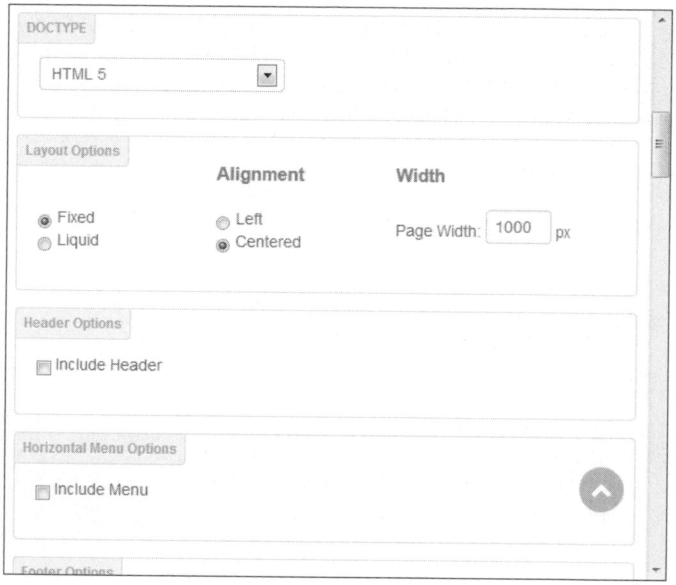

Figure 17-1:
Define the layout you want to create by answering a few simple questions.

Figure 17-2:
The wizard displays the result of the choices you make.

At this point, you need to determine whether the layout will work. Try resizing your browser to see how the layout will work with various device types. If you like the layout, then click Download Layout — otherwise you click the Back button on your browser and make additional changes. What you receive is a .ZIP file containing the HTML and CSS needed to create your layout. You can use these files as templates for customizing the content.

Getting Help Understanding CSS Layouts with Learn CSS Layout

This book provides everything most developers need to work through the vagaries of page layout and design using CSS. However, there are times when you're part of a larger team and may need to interact with designers and artists who really do love designing everything from scratch. In these situations, you sometimes need to bone up on your CSS layout terminology so that you can talk with these other groups intelligently. One of the better quick tutorials is Learn CSS Layout (`http://learnlayout.com/`). It provides you with the essentials you need to know without burdening you with all of the details.

There are several features that recommend this tutorial. For one thing, it comes in several languages, including English, German, French, Spanish, Portuguese, and several Oriental languages. You're also not stuck performing the tutorial one step at a time. Click Table of Contents and you see a listing of topics that tutorial covers, so you can skip to just the information you really need to know.

This particular tutorial is good at telling what's happening, why it needs to happen, and how to create an effect at a basic level. It doesn't provide business essentials or recommendations on when to use a particular technique. You won't find a list of best practices in this tutorial. The advantage of this tutorial is that it's both simple and fast — you get essential information fast.

Using a Reset to Overcome Errors

One of the worst scenarios you can encounter is when the amazing page you have labored over turns out to work only in a few browsers, and you have to listen to a host of users complain about the resulting site compatibility problems. Fortunately there are resets out there to help address this problem.

A *reset* is a special kind of style sheet that helps reduce or eliminate the differences between browsers. With a reset, even though you can't make your site's appearance on every browser look precisely the same, you can make the differences so small that no one will notice any errors. There are a number of good resets online. Here are a few you should review for potential inclusion in your project:

- **CSS:resetr:** `http://cssresetr.com/`
- **CSS Reset:** `www.css-reset.com/`

- ✔ **CSS Tools: Reset CSS:** `http://meyerweb.com/eric/tools/css/reset/index.html`

- ✔ **Eric Meyer's CSS Reset:** `http://meyerweb.com/eric/thoughts/2011/01/03/reset-revisited/`

- ✔ **HTML5 Reset Stylesheet:** `http://html5doctor.com/html-5-reset-stylesheet/`

- ✔ **normalize.css:** `http://necolas.github.io/normalize.css/`

- ✔ **Yahoo! Developer Reset:** `http://developer.yahoo.com/yui/reset/`

- ✔ **YUI Reset:** `http://yuilibrary.com/yui/docs/cssreset/`

 It's possible to roll your own reset. However, you need to make sure you understand the essentials of performing the task. You can find the instructions for developing your own reset at `http://net.tutsplus.com/tutorials/html-css-techniques/weekend-quick-tip-create-your-own-resetcss-file/`.

Creating Mobile-Friendly Layouts with the 960 Grid System

There are many different conventions in creating layouts. Developers are trying to standardize layouts to some extent because it's hard creating a layout that works everywhere without some standardization. The 960 Grid System (`http://960.gs/`) is an effort to standardize the layouts used for content. The advantages of this system include the ability to create incredibly complex mobile-friendly layouts. When you click the Big ol' DOWNLOAD button :) — well, that's what it's called —, you receive a .ZIP file containing the plug-ins and templates required to lay out your own 960 Grid System pages.

In addition to the software, the site shows you vendors who've used the 960 Grid System for their pages and these aren't small vendors either. The list of 960 Grid System adherents include Sony, Fedora, the Sacramento International Airport, and many others. Just looking at how others have used these layouts can prove helpful to a developer.

Finding Articles and Blog Posts Discussing Layouts

It's important to realize that other developers have had the same problem you're having now — finding just the right layout without spending hours doing it. In most cases, it pays to have someone else do the work for you. What this means is finding articles and blog posts that list resources you can use when you're in a hurry. The best policy is to create a folder in your browser to store a list of sites that provide these resources so you can turn to them immediately when you need them. Here are some places you can look for information on free layouts:

- **Mashable:** `http://mashable.com/2013/04/26/css-boiler-plates-frameworks/`

- **Noupe:** `www.noupe.com/css/css-layouts-40-tutorials-tips-demos-and-best-practices.html`

- **Smashing Magazine:** `http://coding.smashingmagazine.com/2007/01/12/free-css-layouts-and-templates/`

- **Web Designer Spot:** `www.webdesignerdepot.com/2012/04/15-great-html5-and-css3-generators/`

Obtaining Free Layouts Through Design Shack

There are many places online that will provide you with a free layout. In fact, it might be possible to write an entire book whose only purpose is to explore and evaluate these sites. The problem with most of these sites is that the layouts are either old (making them incompatible with modern devices) or the code is poorly explained. As a result, you spend a lot of time looking at a resource you really can't use.

Design Shack has put out an article that discusses and helps you evaluate 715 different layouts (`http://designshack.net/articles/css/715-awesomely-simple-and-free-css-layouts/`). The focus of these layouts is to create something simple that you can combine with other layouts or simply build upon as needed to make your site design work. Most importantly, the author takes time to discuss the design criteria used to choose the layouts, so you get a little essential education along with the layout you need to create that page the boss needed yesterday. Each of the entries contains a site name, description of the layout types on that site, and some examples of the layouts as shown in Figure 17-3.

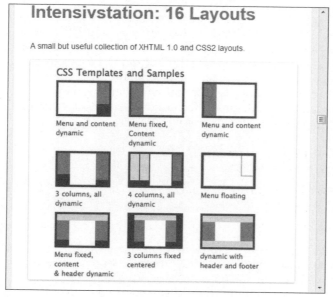

Figure 17-3:
Design Shack helps you locate simple layouts that are quite flexible.

To use a particular layout, click the link associated with it. You'll go to the site that sponsors the layout where you can interact with and download it for use in your project. The important thing to remember is that all of these sites focus on simplicity and flexible designs so that you don't have to perform a lot of rework. On the other hand, if you really are looking for a pre-made complex design of a certain type, this site won't help you.

Getting a Really Complex Design Through Free CSS Templates

Sometimes you really do need a complex setup and you need it today. You don't have time to go through any sort of a design process, but the resulting page has to look professional and convey the kind of message you want to present. Fortunately, Free CSS Templates (www.templatemo.com/) presents a wealth of professionally designed layouts that are ready for immediate use, as shown in Figure 17-4.

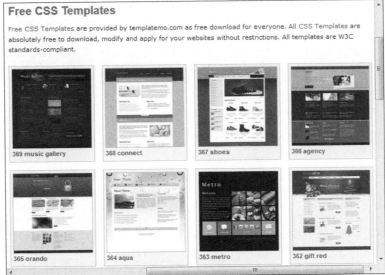

Free CSS Templates

Free CSS Templates are provided by templatemo.com as free download for everyone. All CSS Templates are absolutely free to download, modify and apply for your websites without restrictions. All templates are W3C standards-compliant.

369 music gallery   368 connect   367 shoes   366 agency

365 orando   364 aqua   363 metro   362 gift red

Figure 17-4:
Free CSS Templates specializes in more complex professional designs.

These designs are really beautiful and fully functional. To use a template, simply click on its entry. You're taken to another page where you see a button for a live demo. Click Live Demo and test out the design to determine whether it meets your needs. If you find that it does, click Download on the original page. What you receive is a .ZIP file containing the site you just tested. If the template you viewed online contains an About Us menu item and associated page, the template you download will contain the same resources. You also get all of the art displayed on the page. In short, all you really need to do is substitute the content you want to provide and your site is ready for use.

There's a hidden caveat using sites such as this one. The designs are indeed beautiful and you really don't have to do any design work. The problem you can encounter is that the designs tend to be inflexible unless you want to perform a lot of work to modify them. If you want to add another page, then you have to work through the code provided by Free CSS Templates to make the modification — and that can often take more time than if you had designed the page from scratch. The point is to make sure the template contains all the pages you want at the outset so the reworking is eliminated or at least reduced.

It's also important to realize these templates come with pre-defined content. You need to remove all that content before you start adding your own content. Fortunately, removing the old content isn't hard, but again, make sure you remove the content first and then add your content. Otherwise you might end up with an unfortunate mix that only serves to confuse the people using your site.

An alternative use for sites such as this one is as a teaching tool. You can get ideas from studying the templates and code, and then incorporate the parts you like into your own templates. By studying the code, you discover new techniques that you'll find useful when creating your own site. Learning by emulating what other professionals do is a time honored technique that the best developers use at some point in their careers.

Relying on a CSS Framework

A *CSS framework* provides a standardized set of concepts, practices, and tools for dealing with the problem of using CSS to create a great layout. The main reason to use a framework is to obtain a unique design without expending a lot of effort to do it. When you find that all of the free online tools, predefined layouts, and CSS generators simply don't meet your needs, you can use a CSS framework to reduce the work you have to perform.

There are many different frameworks online and only a few of them will meet your specific needs. The problem with most CSS frameworks is that they assume you're a designer and you have designer level tools. In some cases, it may actually be easier to call in a designer, rather than trudge through the requirements of using a CSS framework. However, the following CSS frameworks do provide a modicum of support for the developer and you may find one or two of them that meet your needs and prove simple enough to use without a huge investment in new software.

- ✔ **Blueprint:** www.blueprintcss.org/
- ✔ **BlueTrip:** http://bluetrip.org/
- ✔ **Bootstrap:** http://twitter.github.io/bootstrap/
- ✔ **Compass:** http://compass-style.org/
- ✔ **Elastic CSS:** http://elasticss.com/
- ✔ **Foundation:** http://foundation.zurb.com/
- ✔ **GroundworkCSS:** http://groundwork.sidereel.com/
- ✔ **Gumby:** http://gumbyframework.com/
- ✔ **Kube:** http://imperavi.com/kube/
- ✔ **Susy:** http://susy.oddbird.net/
- ✔ **Toast:** http://daneden.me/toast/
- ✔ **Unsemantic:** www.unsemantic.com/

Using Best Practices to Enhance Your Layouts

The use of best practices helps you avoid errors that other people have already made and resolved. That's what a best practice is all about — avoiding mistakes. In the case of CSS, a lot of people have made a host of mistakes over the years — resulting in sites that are nearly unusable. Consequently, the best way to improve your layouts is to discover what the best practices are — and then employ them on your own site.

The article, "30 CSS Best Practices for Beginners" by Glen Stansberry (`http://net.tutsplus.com/tutorials/html-css-techniques/30-css-best-practices-for-beginners/`) is an outstanding place to start. The author includes all sorts of useful tips and hints that anyone can use. For example, the author emphasizes the need to make your CSS readable so you can easily modify it later. Of course, that's probably the easiest of the best practices; the author also considers issues such as the use of frameworks and resets.

Index

● *O* ●

About the Author

John Paul Mueller is a freelance author and technical editor. He has writing in his blood, having produced 93 books and over 300 articles to date. The topics range from networking to artificial intelligence and from database management to heads-down programming. Some of his current books include a Windows 8 quick reference guide, an HTML5 and JavaScript programming book, and an Entity Framework 5 programming manual. His technical editing skills have helped more than 63 authors refine the content of their manuscripts. John has provided technical editing services to both *Data Based Advisor* and *Coast Compute* magazines. He's also contributed articles to magazines such as *Software Quality Connection, DevSource, InformIT, SQL Server Professional, Visual C++ Developer, Hard Core Visual Basic, asp.netPRO, Software Test and Performance,* and *Visual Basic Developer.* Be sure to read John's blog at http://blog.johnmuellerbooks.com/.

When John isn't working at the computer, you can find him outside in the garden, cutting wood, or generally enjoying nature. John also likes making wine and knitting. When not occupied with anything else, he makes glycerin soap and candles, which comes in handy for gift baskets. You can reach John on the Internet at John@JohnMuellerBooks.com. John is also setting up a website at www.johnmuellerbooks.com. Feel free to take a look and make suggestions on how he can improve it.

Dedication

This book is dedicated to a gem of a friend who once was lost and now is found, Debbie Patenaude.

Author's Acknowledgments

Thanks to my wife, Rebecca, for working with me to get this book completed. I really don't know what I would have done without her help in researching and compiling some of the information that appears in this book. She also did a fine job of proofreading my rough draft. Rebecca keeps the house running while I'm buried in work.

Russ Mullen deserves thanks for his technical edit of this book. He greatly added to the accuracy and depth of the material you see here. Russ is always providing me with great URLs for new products and ideas. However, it's the testing Russ does that helps most. He's the sanity check for my work. Russ also has different computer equipment from mine, so he's able to point out flaws that I might not otherwise notice.

Matt Wagner, my agent, deserves credit for helping me get the contract in the first place and taking care of all the details that most authors don't really consider. I always appreciate his assistance. It's good to know that someone wants to help.

A number of people read all or part of this book to help me refine the approach, test the coding examples, and generally provide input that all readers wish they could have. These unpaid volunteers helped in ways too numerous to mention here. I especially appreciate the efforts of Eva Beattie, Glenn Russell, Osvaldo Téllez Almirall, Muhammad Kharbush, Omar Garcia, and William Wonneberger, who provided general input, read the entire book, and selflessly devoted themselves to this project.

Finally, I would like to thank Steve Hayes, Christopher Morris, Barry Childs-Helton, and the rest of the editorial and production staff at Wiley for their assistance in bringing this book to print. It's always nice to work with such a great group of professionals.

Publisher's Acknowledgments

Executive Editor: Steve Hayes

Senior Project Editor: Christopher Morris

Senior Copy Editor: Barry Childs-Helton

Technical Editor: Russ Mullen

Editorial Assistant: Anne Sullivan

Sr. Editorial Assistant: Cherie Case

Cover Image: ©iStockphoto.com/Hakki Arslan

Project Coordinator: Sheree Montgomery

Layout and Graphics: Carrie A. Cesavice

Proofreader: Barbara Arany

Indexer: BIM Indexing & Proofreading Services

Apple & Mac

iPad For Dummies,
5th Edition
978-1-118-49823-1

iPhone 5 For Dummies,
6th Edition
978-1-118-35201-4

MacBook For Dummies,
4th Edition
978-1-118-20920-2

OS X Mountain Lion
For Dummies
978-1-118-39418-2

Blogging & Social Media

Facebook For Dummies,
4th Edition
978-1-118-09562-1

Mom Blogging
For Dummies
978-1-118-03843-7

Pinterest For Dummies
978-1-118-32800-2

WordPress For Dummies,
5th Edition
978-1-118-38318-6

Business

Commodities For Dummies,
2nd Edition
978-1-118-01687-9

Investing For Dummies,
6th Edition
978-0-470-90545-6

Personal Finance
For Dummies,
7th Edition
978-1-118-11785-9

QuickBooks 2013
For Dummies
978-1-118-35641-8

Small Business Marketing Kit
For Dummies,
3rd Edition
978-1-118-31183-7

Careers

Job Interviews
For Dummies,
4th Edition
978-1-118-11290-8

Job Searching with
Social Media
For Dummies
978-0-470-93072-4

Personal Branding
For Dummies
978-1-118-11792-7

Resumes For Dummies,
6th Edition
978-0-470-87361-8

Success as a Mediator
For Dummies
978-1-118-07862-4

Diet & Nutrition

Belly Fat Diet For Dummies
978-1-118-34585-6

Eating Clean For Dummies
978-1-118-00013-7

Nutrition For Dummies,
5th Edition
978-0-470-93231-5

Digital Photography

Digital Photography
For Dummies,
7th Edition
978-1-118-09203-3

Digital SLR Cameras &
Photography For Dummies,
4th Edition
978-1-118-14489-3

Photoshop Elements 11
For Dummies
978-1-118-40821-6

Gardening

Herb Gardening
For Dummies,
2nd Edition
978-0-470-61778-6

Vegetable Gardening
For Dummies,
2nd Edition
978-0-470-49870-5

Health

Anti-Inflammation Diet
For Dummies
978-1-118-02381-5

Diabetes For Dummies,
3rd Edition
978-0-470-27086-8

Living Paleo For Dummies
978-1-118-29405-5

Hobbies

Beekeeping
For Dummies
978-0-470-43065-1

eBay For Dummies,
7th Edition
978-1-118-09806-6

Raising Chickens
For Dummies
978-0-470-46544-8

Wine For Dummies,
5th Edition
978-1-118-28872-6

Writing Young Adult Fiction
For Dummies
978-0-470-94954-2

Language &
Foreign Language

500 Spanish Verbs
For Dummies
978-1-118-02382-2

English Grammar
For Dummies,
2nd Edition
978-0-470-54664-2

French All-in One
For Dummies
978-1-118-22815-9

German Essentials
For Dummies
978-1-118-18422-6

Italian For Dummies
2nd Edition
978-1-118-00465-4

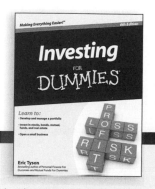 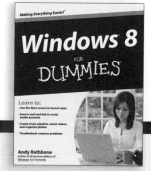  

Available in print and e-book formats.

Math & Science

Algebra I For Dummies,
2nd Edition
978-0-470-55964-2

Anatomy and Physiology
For Dummies,
2nd Edition
978-0-470-92326-9

Astronomy For Dummies,
3rd Edition
978-1-118-37697-3

Biology For Dummies,
2nd Edition
978-0-470-59875-7

Chemistry For Dummies,
2nd Edition
978-1-1180-0730-3

Pre-Algebra Essentials
For Dummies
978-0-470-61838-7

Microsoft Office

Excel 2013 For Dummies
978-1-118-51012-4

Office 2013 All-in-One
For Dummies
978-1-118-51636-2

PowerPoint 2013
For Dummies
978-1-118-50253-2

Word 2013 For Dummies
978-1-118-49123-2

Music

Blues Harmonica
For Dummies
978-1-118-25269-7

Guitar For Dummies,
3rd Edition
978-1-118-11554-1

iPod & iTunes
For Dummies,
10th Edition
978-1-118-50864-0

Programming

Android Application
Development For
Dummies, 2nd Edition
978-1-118-38710-8

iOS 6 Application
Development For Dummies
978-1-118-50880-0

Java For Dummies,
5th Edition
978-0-470-37173-2

Religion & Inspiration

The Bible For Dummies
978-0-7645-5296-0

Buddhism For Dummies,
2nd Edition
978-1-118-02379-2

Catholicism For Dummies,
2nd Edition
978-1-118-07778-8

Self-Help & Relationships

Bipolar Disorder
For Dummies,
2nd Edition
978-1-118-33882-7

Meditation For Dummies,
3rd Edition
978-1-118-29144-3

Seniors

Computers For Seniors
For Dummies,
3rd Edition
978-1-118-11553-4

iPad For Seniors
For Dummies,
5th Edition
978-1-118-49708-1

Social Security
For Dummies
978-1-118-20573-0

Smartphones & Tablets

Android Phones
For Dummies
978-1-118-16952-0

Kindle Fire HD
For Dummies
978-1-118-42223-6

NOOK HD For Dummies,
Portable Edition
978-1-118-39498-4

Surface For Dummies
978-1-118-49634-3

Test Prep

ACT For Dummies,
5th Edition
978-1-118-01259-8

ASVAB For Dummies,
3rd Edition
978-0-470-63760-9

GRE For Dummies,
7th Edition
978-0-470-88921-3

Officer Candidate Tests,
For Dummies
978-0-470-59876-4

Physician's Assistant Exam
For Dummies
978-1-118-11556-5

Series 7 Exam
For Dummies
978-0-470-09932-2

Windows 8

Windows 8 For Dummies
978-1-118-13461-0

Windows 8 For Dummies,
Book + DVD Bundle
978-1-118-27167-4

Windows 8 All-in-One
For Dummies
978-1-118-11920-4

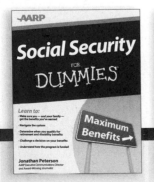 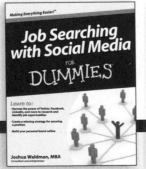  

Available in print and e-book formats.